THE KING JAMES VERSION
OF THE ENGLISH BIBLE

THE KING JAMES VERSION
OF THE ENGLISH BIBLE

An Account of the Development and Sources of the English
Bible of 1611 with Special Reference to the Hebrew Tradition

By

DAVID DAICHES

ARCHON BOOKS
1968

LIBRARY OF CONGRESS CATALOG CARD NUMBER: 68-16338
PRINTED IN THE UNITED STATES OF AMERICA

PREFATORY NOTE

THIS study does not attempt to provide a complete solution to the textual problems of the "King James" or "Authorized" Version of the Bible. My task has been, first, to write the history of English Bible translation from 1523 to 1611 as accurately and succinctly as was possible and, second, while confining my textual investigations to the rendering of the Book of Isaiah, to throw some light on the sources, equipment, and methods of the translators. I have throughout been more concerned with the Old Testament than with the New, discussing problems connected with the translation of the latter in considerably less detail. The somewhat lengthy excursus into the development of Hebrew scholarship in Europe was no part of the original plan of the work, but I was gradually led into it in endeavoring to trace the origin of the Hebrew scholarship of the translators. In general, this work is presented as prolegomena to a study of the English Bible of 1611, and it is hoped that others will find these preparatory studies useful in clearing the ground for further research as well as perhaps possessing some interest in their own right.

The usual contractions have been employed in referring to standard works of reference. In the final chapter, A.V., GenB, BB, GB, and C are used, respectively, for the Authorized (1611) Version, Geneva Bible, Bishops' Bible, Great Bible, and Coverdale's Bible. The references are to first editions unless otherwise stated. The text of the Hebrew Bible, the Targum, and the Vulgate (in the collation, chap. iv) is in each case that of the Antwerp Polyglot. The Septuagint text is that of Antwerp compared with Alfred Rahlfs's edition (*Septuaginta id est Vetus Testamentum Graece iuxta LXX interpretes* [Stuttgart, 1933]). The text of Kimchi's commentary is that of the Rabbinical Bible (Warsaw, 1866), compared with sixteenth-century editions and with L. Finkelstein's edition of Kimchi on Isaiah (New York, 1925).

TABLE OF CONTENTS

CHAPTER I

IN THE summer of 1523 William Tyndale, then probably in his early or middle thirties, presented himself before Cuthbert Tunstall, bishop of London, with a translation of a speech of Isocrates as proof of his scholarship and a request that he might be taken into the bishop's service so that he might translate the Bible into English.

But god which knoweth what is within hypocrites, sawe that I was begyled, ād that that councell was not the nexte way vnto my purpose. And therefore he gate me no favoure in my lordes sight. Wheruppō my lorde answered me, his hovse was full, he had mo thē he coude well finde, and advised me to seke in London wher he sayd I coude not lacke a service.[1]

So he abode in London almost a year, noting the abuses of the time, and eventually he came to the conclusion "not only that there was no rowme in my lorde of Londons palace to translate the new testament, but also that there was no place to do it in all englonde, as experience doth now openly declare." He retired, therefore, to the Continent, where he spent the rest of his life in English Bible translation.

Tyndale's desire to translate the Bible was not the product of literary ambition or a casual thought prompted by a wish to do something interesting and profitable. His aim was identical with that of the earlier translators, of Wyclif and Hereford and Purvey—he wished to have the one origi-

---

[1] *The fyrst boke of Moses called Genesis.* "Emprented at Malborow in the lande of Hesse by me Hans Luft, the yere of our Lorde MCCCCCXXX the xvii dayes of Januarij." W. T. to the Reader. (See below, pp. 8–9.)

nal source of Christianity laid open to the ordinary reader. Foxe tells how, in discussion with a "learned man" who was praising the pope's law above God's, "Maister Tyndall . . . . answered hym, I defie the Pope and all his lawes, and sayde, if God spare my lyfe ere many yeares, I wyl cause a boye that dryveth ye plough, shall knowe more of the scripture then thou doest."[2] This was the old Lollard ideal, more vigorously affirmed than ever before. It is true that Tyndale and those who thought like him maintained a violence of opinion on other matters—in their attitude to the pope, for example, and to the ecclesiastical hierarchy generally—which had not characterized at least the first generation of Lollards.[3] But his attitude to the Bible was essentially the Lollard attitude, and his conflict with orthodoxy involved the same principles as the conflict of Wyclif and his followers with the orthodox opinion of their time, except that Tyndale had given even greater offense by the publication of his general theological views—sometimes violent and fanatical in the extreme—in such works as *The Obedience of a Christen Man* (1528)[4] and *The Practyse of*

[2] *Acts and Monuments* (ed. 1563), p. 514. Cf. also the words of Erasmus, which Tyndale was probably consciously echoing (see below, p. 77).

[3] Attitudes to vernacular Bible-reading before Tyndale are fully discussed by M. Deanesly, *The Lollard Bible* (Cambridge, 1920).

[4] James Gairdner's analysis of this work (*Lollardy and the Reformation in England* [London, 1908], I, 371 ff.) and of Tyndale's ideas generally puts the case against Tyndale as a social and theological thinker at its strongest. Though it is true that " 'The Obedience' for the first time stated clearly the two great principles of the English Reformation—the supreme authority of scripture in the Church and the supreme authority of the king in the state" (*Dictionary of National Biography* [hereafter cited as *DNB*], XIX, 1353), there is no doubt that his polemical work is marred by much fantastic extravagance. See, e.g., the quotation given by Gairdner (I, 378) concerning Tyndale's view of the prohibited degrees of marriage.

Prelates (1530) and in his heretical glosses to his New Testament.

By the time Tyndale wrote there were other forces at work which gave impetus to the attack on the practices and traditions of the church and to the demand that all questions should be referred to the Bible as the final court of appeal and the only really competent authority. And in other respects the invention of printing, the rise of humanism, and the "Renaissance" movement generally,[5] had already wrought a considerable change in European thought and culture. Tyndale did not address the same world that Wyclif had endeavored to persuade.

On leaving London in 1524, Tyndale went first to Hamburg, "having some ayde and prouision, by Gods prouidence ministred unto hym by Humphrey Mummouth,"[6] a London merchant who afterward got into trouble for the help he had given Tyndale. There he completed his translation of the New Testament.[7] The copy was in the hands of a Cologne printer before December, 1525,[8] and printing had

[5] This matter is discussed in chap. ii.

[6] Foxe, *op. cit.* (ed. 1583), p. 1078.

[7] Tyndale may have first issued separately the books of Matthew and Mark. There are references which suggest this in *The Life of John Frith*, by Foxe, prefixed to Frith's writings in Foxe's edition of *The Whole Workes of W. Tyndall, John Frith and Doctor Burnes* (London: John Day, 1573), and in a letter written by Robert Ridley, chaplain to the Bishop of London, to Henry Gold, chaplain to the Archbishop of Canterbury, in 1527 (see A. W. Pollard, *Records of the English Bible* [hereafter cited as *Records*], pp. 110–11, 122 f.). But no traces of such issues are extant.

[8] *Records* (p. 108) prints an extract from a letter to Henry VIII written at Bordeaux by Edward Lee, afterward archbishop of York, dated December 2 (1525). The extract begins: "Please it your highnesse morover to vnderstond, that I ame certainlie enformed as I passed in this contree, that an englishman your subiect at the sollicitacion and instaunce of Luther, with whome he is, hathe translated the

proceeded as far as the signature K—eighty pages of an edition of three hundred copies in quarto—when, owing to the
interference of Johann Dobneck,[9] or, in the Latinized ver-

---

newe testament in to Englishe, and within four dayes entendethe to arrive with the
same emprinted in England." The reference to Tyndale's association with Luther
cannot be taken to prove that Tyndale actually worked with Luther, or even that
he met him, because Lee was not in a position to know the facts about the origin of
the translation. There are, however, other contemporary authorities who lead us
to believe that between Tyndale's first arrival in Hamburg about May, 1524, and
his second visit there in April, 1525, he was with Luther in Wittenberg. These are
cited by Demaus, *Life of Tindale* (new ed. revised by Lovett, 1886), pp. 98–99, who
concludes that Tyndale was in Wittenberg. We know that in September he was in
Cologne with Roy seeing his translation through the press.

[9] *Records* (pp. 99 ff.) quotes from the "Commentaria Ioannis Cochlaei de Actis et
scripti Martini Lutheri Saxonis chronographice ex ordine ab anno Domini 1517
usque ad annum 1546 inclusiue, fideliter conscripta. *Apud S. Victorem prope Mo-
guntiam, ex officina Francisci Behem typographi.* 1549, pp. 132–135," where Cochlaeus
gives the last and fullest of his three accounts of his share in the business.
The relevant portion is as follows: "Hinc Typographis Coloniensibus notior
ac familiarior factus, audiuit eos aliquando inter pocula fiducialiter iactitare,
Velint Nolint Rex & Cardinalis Angliæ, totam Angliam breui fore Lutheranam.
Audiuit item, duos ibi latitare Anglos, eruditos linguarumque peritos et diser-
tos, quos tamen uidere aut alloqui nunquam potuit. Vocatis itaque in hos-
pitium suum quibusdam Typographis, postea quam mero incaluissent, unus eorum
in secretiori colloquio reuelauit illi arcanum, quo ad Lutheri partes trahenda esset
Anglia. Nempe uersari sub prælo Tria Milia Exemplarium Noui Testamenti Lu-
therani, in Anglicanam linguam translati, ac processum esse iam usque ad literam
Alphabeti K. in ordine Quaternionum. Impensas abunde suppeti a Mercatoribus
Anglicis, qui opus excusum clam inuecturi per totam Angliam latenter dispergere
uellent, antequam Rex aut Cardinalis rescire aut prohibere possit. Cochlaeus intra
se metu & admiratione uarie affectus, foris mirabundus mœrorem dissimulabat.
Altero autem die, periculi magnitudinem tristis secum expendens, cogitabat, quo
nam pacto possit commode pessimis illis conatibus obsistere. Abijt igitur clam ad
Hermannum Rinck, Patricium Coloniensem, ac Militem Auratum, qui & Cæsari &
Regi Angliæ familiaris erat & Consiliarius, eique rem omnem, ut acceperat uini
beneficio, indicauit. Ille, ut certius omnia constarent, alium misit exploratum in
eam domum, ubi opus excudebatur iuxta indicium Cochlæi. Cunque ab illo ac-
ceppiset rem ita habere, & ingentem Papyri copiam ibi existere: adijt Senatum,

sion of his name which he preferred, Cochlaeus, a strong anti-Lutheran, Tyndale and his secretary, William Roy, had to depart suddenly from Cologne and seek refuge in Worms. The portion of the translation already printed Tyndale saved only by managing to take it with him in his flight. A single copy of eight of the ten quires of the Cologne New Testament survives in the Grenville Library of the British Museum. In Worms, Tyndale prepared two editions of his translation: one in quarto with marginal glosses and one in octavo without glosses. As no copies of the Worms quarto survive, we cannot tell whether it embodied the sheets printed at Cologne or whether reprinting was undertaken from the beginning. The octavo was printed by Peter Schoeffer, son of the pioneer printer of Mainz of that name, and must have come into England at the beginning of 1526. It survives in a copy (perfect except for the lack of the title-page) at the Baptist College, Bristol, and there is an imperfect copy in the library of St. Paul's Cathedral. The extant portion of the Cologne printing (thirty-one leaves, to the end of sheet H, ending with the words "Friend, how camest thou in hither, and" [Matt. 22:12]) contains marginal notes, some of them strongly antiecclesiastical. These glosses derive to a large extent from Luther, whose influence in Tyndale's translation of the text is also considerable.

The king had been warned by Edward Lee's letter to expect copies of Tyndale's translation to come into the country, but this knowledge did not prevent copies from

atque effecit, ut Typographis interdiceretur, ne ultra progrederentur in eo opere. Duo Apostatae Angli, arreptis secum Quaternionibus impressis, aufugerunt, nauigio per Rhenum ascendentes Vuormaciam, ubi plebs pleno furore Lutherizabat, ut ibi per alium Typographum cœptum perficerent opus."

being smuggled in in large numbers. In October, 1526, Bishop Tunstall issued a prohibition to the archdeacons of his diocese "for calling in of the newe Testamentes translated into Englyshe."[10] Tunstall preached against the translation at Paul's Cross, professing, according to Roy, to have found three thousand errors in it,[11] and after the sermon copies of the book were burned. Earlier still (February 11, 1526) it had been denounced by Fisher, bishop of Rochester. Every attempt was made by the ecclesiastical authorities to prevent its circulation. Tunstall, if we are to trust Halle's *Chronicle*, sent an agent to buy up all available copies, so that they could be destroyed. But the only result of this was that it put money into Tyndale's pocket which went toward the expenses of a new edition.

There can, however, be little doubt that the translation circulated widely.[12] The coming of the printing press had

---

[10] Foxe, *Acts and Monuments* (ed. 1563), p. 449. Foxe has the text of the prohibition, which is reprinted in *Records*, pp. 131 ff.

[11] *Rede Me and Be Nott Wrothe*, ed. Arber ("English Reprints" [1871]), p. 46:

> "In sothe the Bisshoppe of London/
> With the Cardinallis authorite.
> Which at Paulis crosse ernestly/
> Denounced it to be heresy/
> That the gospell shuld come to lyght.
> Callynge theym heretikes execrable/
> Whiche caused the gospell venerable/
> To come vnto laye mens syght.
> He declared there in his furiousnes
> That he founde erroures more and les/
> Above thre thousande in the translacion.
> Howe be it when all cam to pas/
> I dare saye unable he was/
> Of one erroure to make probacion."

[12] There seem to have been at least three reprints before Tyndale's revision of 1534 (see *Records*, p. 7; M. E. Kronenberg, *Notes on English Printing in the Low*

made the suppression of forbidden books quite a different matter from what it had been in the days of manuscripts. The ecclesiastical authorities had no machinery to enable them to suppress a whole edition of a printed work. We know from the confession of Robert Necton[13] that in 1527 English New Testaments were being bought and sold freely "for vii or viii grotes a pece," and we gather from the constant activities of the authorities that the suppression of Tyndale's Testament was an achievement they could not accomplish. Toward the end of 1528 Wolsey wrote to Hermann Rinck (the "Patricium Coloniensem" mentioned by Cochlaeus), commissioning him to arrest Tyndale and Roy and to buy up their books, but neither they nor their accomplices had been seen at Frankfurt since Easter, and their whereabouts were unknown to Rinck. Rinck, however, believed that he had bought up all copies except two. It had been intended to send them packed in bales of linen to Scotland and England.[14] On May 14, 1530, Richard Nix, bishop of Norwich, wrote to the Archbishop of Canterbury asking that the king should make it quite clear that he was opposed to the "Arronious bokes in engleshe," as many people thought that the king was inclined to favor such books, and this encouraged them to obtain and read them.[15] On May 25 the king consulted his council and the bishops and after long debatyng, it was alleged that the translacion[s] of Tyndall and Joy [sic] were not truely translated, and also that in theim were prologues and prefaces which sounded to heresie, and

---

Countries [London: Bibliographical Society, 1928], pp. 149–50; Joye's Apologye . . . . To Satisfye . . . . W. Tindale, ed. Arber ["English Scholars' Library" (London, 1882)]).

[13] Printed in Records, p. 155, from Strype's Ecclesiastical Memorials.

[14] L. P. Hen. VIII, Vol. IV, Part II, 4810, p. 2083.   [15] Records, p. 159.

rayled against the bishopes vncharitably, wherefore all such bokes were prohibited and commaundement geven by the kyng to the bishoppes, that thei callyng to theim the best learned men of the vniuersities should cause a new translacion to be made, so that the people should not be ignoraunte in the law of god: And notwithstandyng this commaundement the bishopes did nothing at all to set furth a new translacion, which caused the people to stody Tindalles translacion. . . . .[16]

In June, 1530, there was issued a royal proclamation "for dampning of erronious bokes and heresies, and prohibitinge the hauinge of holy scripture, translated into the vulgar tonges of englisshe, frenche, or duche."[17]

Meanwhile Tyndale proceeded with his work abroad. As we know from his Epilogue to the Worms octavo, he had not regarded his translation as definitive. "Count it as a thynge not havynge his full shape, but as it were borne afore hys tyme, even as a thing begunne rather than fynnesshed." But before revising his New Testament he proceeded to do some work on the Old Testament as well as to take up again his polemical writing. With his controversial theological writings—*The Parable of the Wicked Mammon* and *The Obedience of a Christen Man*—we are not here concerned, except to note that they give some indication of his study of the Pentateuch and of Hebrew.[18] Tyndale's translation of the Pentateuch was printed in 1530–31. Genesis alone has the colophon: "Emprented at Malborow

---

[16] *Records*, pp. 162–63, from Halle's *Chronicle, The Union of the Two Noble Houses, etc.* (London: Grafton, 1548), fol. 192.

[17] *Records*, pp. 163–69. For other measures taken in England against Tyndale's New Testament see R. Demaus, *Life of Tindale* (London, 1886), pp. 151–64. For some interesting references to English action abroad see Kronenberg, *op. cit.*, pp. 148–49.

[18] Demaus, *op. cit.*, p. 209.

in the lande of Hesse by me Hans Luft, the yere of oure Lorde MCCCCCXXX the xvii dayes of Januarij."[19] The dating was probably Old Style, corresponding to New Style 1531. The five books of the Pentateuch seem to have been printed separately and intended for separate issue.[20] A second edition of the Pentateuch appeared without date or imprint perhaps later in the same year,[21] perhaps as late as 1534. The printer was probably Martin Emperor of Antwerp.[22] In the first edition Genesis and Numbers are in black letter; Exodus, Leviticus, and Deuteronomy in roman type.

The identity of the printer who styled himself Hans Luft of Marburg has been at last definitely established by Miss M. E. Kronenberg, who shows that the Pentateuch, like other works with the Hans Luft of Marburg colophon, was printed by Johannes Hoochstraten of Antwerp.[23] The fol-

---

[19] See above, p. 1, n. 1.

[20] There is in the Bodleian (Mar. 364) a separate copy of Genesis, bound with Tyndale's translation of Erasmus' "An Exhortation to the diligent studye of Scripture "and his, Tyndale's,"Exposition into the seuenth chaptre of the first epistle to the Corinthians." There is no copy of Tyndale's complete Pentateuch in the Bodleian, but from a comparison of the Bodleian Genesis with the facsimiles of pages of Genesis from Tyndale's Pentateuch in Mombert's edition (*William Tindale's Five Books of Moses . . . . a Verbatim Reprint . . . .*, ed. J. I. Mombert [London, 1884]) it is obvious that it is the same as the Genesis found in the Pentateuch. It is from the Bodleian Genesis that I have quoted on p. 1. In the Bodleian copy of *A Short-Title Catalogue of Books Printed in England, Scotland and Ireland and of English Books Printed Abroad, 1475–1640*, compiled by A. W. Pollard and G. R. Redgrave (London, 1926) [hereafter cited as *STC*] this book is described as an incomplete copy of the Pentateuch. The different books may, however, have been issued separately. The variations in type suggest this.

[21] *Records*, p. 10.   [22] *Ibid.*

[23] "De geheimzinnige drukkers Adam Anonymus te Bazel en Hans Luft te Marburg ontmaskerd," *Het Boek*, VIII (The Hague, 1919), 241–80, and the same author's *Notes on English Printing in the Low Countries*, pp. 154–58.

lowing year (probably) Tyndale issued his translation of
the Book of Jonah, which, having neither date nor colophon, it is impossible to date accurately or to assign with
complete certainty to any given printer, though we can be
fairly sure that it was printed at Antwerp.[24] The translation of Jonah is preceded by a long introduction

teachinge to vnderstōde him and the right vse also of all the scrip-
ture/ and why it was written/ and what is therin to be sought/
and shewenge wherewith the scripture is locked vpp that he
which readeth it/ can not vnderstōde it/ though he studie therin
neuer so moch: and agayne with what keyes it is so opened/ that
the reader can be stopped out with no sotilte or false doctrine of
man/ from the true sense and vnderstondynge therof.[25]

In August, 1534, before Tyndale's own revision of his
New Testament was ready, George Joye issued, from the
press of the widow of Christoffel van Endhoven, a version
which was substantially Tyndale's with some alterations
which Joye deemed an improvement. This unauthorized
and unsatisfactory revision naturally annoyed Tyndale and
started a controversy between the two which is the source
of much of our information on the matter.[26] Tyndale's own
revision of his New Testament was printed at Antwerp in
1534 by Martin Emperor. Marginal notes were added, and

[24] Cf. the facsimile reproduction by Francis Fry (London, 1863), Introd., pp.
9–10.

[25] Title-page, from Fry's facsimile.

[26] Tyndale's case against Joye is put in the extra Preface to his revised New Testament (Antwerp, 1534). Joye's *Apology* . . . . *To Satisfye* . . . . *W. Tindale* replied
to Tyndale at length. Joye had defended himself more briefly against Tyndale's
charges in a preface to his second edition (Antwerp, January 9, 1535). This is conciliatory in tone, but the reconciliation soon broke down. Tyndale seems to have
been in the right (cf. Demaus, *op. cit.*, p. 373), and the tone of Joye's *Apologye* made
a further reconciliation impossible.

the text revised. This edition is the first to include a translation of "The Epistles taken out of the olde testament, which are red in the Church after the vse of Salsburye vpon certen dayes of the yere." The translation of these "epistles" is of particular interest in our investigation of the development of the authorized version of the Book of Isaiah, as they consist mostly of passages from the Prophets, of which eleven are from Isaiah. As we shall see later, these passages have not the same direct relation to the Authorized Version as the rest of Tyndale's translation, but they are important as being the first English translation of parts of the prophetical books made from other sources than the Vulgate alone. Two further revisions of the New Testament, the second of which alone contains the epistles from the Old Testament, appeared in 1535, the year of Tyndale's arrest. The first of these editions exhibits peculiarities of spelling that have given rise to some equally peculiar theories but which are probably merely due to the Flemish compositors. This was probably printed by Hans van Ruremond at Antwerp.[27] The second, probably the last revised by Tyndale himself, was printed by G. H. (Godfrid van der Haghen) at Antwerp, or more probably printed at the press of Martin Emperor for van der Haghen.[28]

In 1536 further editions of Tyndale's New Testament appeared. These are a folio edition probably printed in London;[29] the three quarto editions distinguished by the varia-

[27] *Records*, p. 9; *STC*, No. 2828. Miss Kronenberg (*Notes on English Printing in the Low Countries*, pp. 150–51) has shown that the book was actually printed by Hans van Ruremond's *widow*.

[28] *Historical Catalogue of the Printed Editions of Holy Scripture in the Library of the British and Foreign Bible Society*, by the Rev. T. H. Barlow and H. F. Moule (London, 1903–12), I, 5 [hereafter cited as *Hist. Cat.*]. *STC*, No. 2830.

[29] *STC*, No. 2831.

tions[30] in a woodcut of St. Paul, prefixed to the eleven epistles, printed probably at Antwerp; and three—or perhaps four—octavo editions which, while agreeing closely, differ throughout in many small points.[31]

Already in December, 1534, there were signs of change in the attitude of the authorities to Bible translation in England. On the nineteenth of that month the synod of the province of Canterbury petitioned the king to suppress books of suspected doctrine ("libri suspecte doctrine") and to decree "quod sacra Scriptura in vulgarem linguam Anglicanam, per quosdam probos et doctos viros per dictum illustrissimum regem nominandos transferatur, et populo pro eorum eruditione deliberetur et tradatur."[32] Like Sir Thomas More, Convocation no longer considered Bible translation per se as heretical and realized that the only effective way of combating translations which they thought to be dangerous was to produce an authorized translation free from heretical glosses and individual interpretations. Further, the political situation had changed a great deal since Tyndale was repulsed by the Bishop of London in 1523. Cromwell had succeeded Wolsey, the king had become supreme head of the church, and the unity of Christendom with its hierarchy and traditions had for the first time since its establishment been seriously challenged, and that by the action of an autocratic monarch consulting only his personal convenience. The old order was changing with a suddenness that surprised the whole nation and for a reason

---

[30] The "mole," the "engraver's mark," and the "blank stone." The printer has not been identified (see Kronenberg, *Notes on English Printing in the Low Countries*, pp. 151-52).

[31] *Hist. Cat.*, I, 11 ff.   [32] *Records*, p. 176.

which the most ardent reformers could not conscientiously approve, however much they might believe that the end justified the means.

But amid all the changes in the theory and practice of church government and Christian doctrine for which Henry VIII was responsible, the cause of the English Bible progressed steadily. It may be that "the King's open repudiation of the authority of the Pope left him inferentially pledged to the paramount authority of Scripture"[33] or, more likely, that once the traditions of Catholic Christianity had been interfered with the traditional attitude of the church on any matter became of less importance; but, for whatever reason, we find official opinion coming rapidly to favor an authorized English version of the Bible almost immediately after Tyndale's New Testament had made the question of Bible translation a vital issue once more. The influence of the "New Learning," too, was becoming more and more widespread and has a very clear relation to the new attitude to English Bible translation; a discussion of this and kindred aspects of the subject we are leaving to the following chapter.

In June, 1530, the king had issued a proclamation condemning Tyndale's translation and "prohibitinge the hauinge of holy scripture translated into the vulgar tonges." The same proclamation, however, went on to say:

And farthermore, for as moche as it is come to the herynge of our saide soueraigne lorde the kynge, that report is made by diuers and many of his subiectes, that as it were to all men not onely expedyent, but also necessarye, to haue in the englisshe tonge bothe the newe testament and the olde: and that his high-

---

[33] H. W. Hoare, *The Evolution of the English Bible* (London, 1902), p. 165.

nes, his noble men, and prelates were bounden to suffre them so to haue it: His highnes hath therfore semblably there vpon consulted with the sayd primates and vertuous, discrete, and well lerned personages in diuinite forsayde, and by them all it is thought, that it is not necessary, the sayde scripture to be in the englisshe tonge, and in the handes of the commen people: but that the distribution of the sayd scripture, and the permyttyng or denyenge therof, dependeth onely vpon the discretion of the superiours, as they shall thynke it conuenyent. And that hauing respecte to the malignite of this present tyme, with the inclination of people to erronious opinions, the translation of the newe testament and the olde in to the vulgare tonge of englysshe, shulde rather be the occasion of contynuance or increace of errours amonge the sayd people, than any benefyte or commodite towarde the weale of their soules. And that it shall nowe be more conuenient that the same people haue the holy scripture expouned to them, by preachers in their sermons, accordynge as it hath ben of olde tyme accustomed before this tyme. All be it if it shall here after appere to the kynges highnes, that his saide people do vtterly abandon and forsake all peruerse, erronious, and sedicious opinyons, with the newe testament and the olde, corruptly translated in to the englisshe tonge nowe beinge in print: And that the same bokes and all other bokes of heresy, as well in the frenche tonge as in the duche tonge, be clerely extermynate and exiled out of this realme of Englande for euer: his highnes entendeth to prouyde, that the holy scripture shalbe by great lerned and catholyke persones, translated in to the englisshe tonge, if it shall then seme to his grace conuenient so to be.[34]

[34] *Records*, pp. 167–68. Cf. Sir Thomas More: "Nowe yf yt so be that yt wold happely be thought not a thyng metely to be aduentured, to set all on a flushe at onys, & dash rashly out holy scrypture in euery lewde felowys tethe, yet thynketh me there mighte suche a moderacion be taken therin, as neyther good vertuous lay folk shold lacke yt, nor rude and rashe braynes abuse yt. For it might be with dylygence well and truly translated by som good catholyke and well lerned man, or by dyuerse dyuydynge the laboure amonge theym, and after conferryng theyr seuerall partys together eche with other" (*Records*, p. 84 from Dial. fol. XCVIIr). More wished the bishops to have the power to grant or withhold a license for the

So in 1530 we find the king, while strongly condemning extant vernacular translation, affirming his intention to provide for an authorized translation when the time was ripe. At the end of 1534 the upper house of Convocation of the province of Canterbury petitioned the king for an English translation. In 1535 there was printed, probably at Zurich,[35] "The Byble: that is the holy Scrypture of the Olde and New Testament, faythfully translated in to Englyshe,"[36] with a dedication to the king. This dedication is signed by Miles Coverdale, who is thus responsible for the *editio princeps* of the English Bible. There is little doubt that had Tyndale lived he would have produced a version of the whole Bible. But the production of the first English Bible to be printed was reserved for a man of much less scholarship and less burning intensity of purpose.

---

reading even of an authorized version. The bishop of the diocese may "after hys dyscrecyon and wysedome delyver to suche as he perceyueth honest sad and vertuous, with a good monicyon & fatherly counsayl to vse yt reuerently wyth humble hart and lowly mynd, rather sekyng therin occasyon of deuocyon than of dyspycyon" (*ibid.*, p. 85). We may note that More was justified in objecting to Tyndale's heretical glosses, which were no part of the text of the Bible and were calculated to give the ignorant reader a quite wrong conception of the meaning of the text. It was because More believed Tyndale's translation to be inaccurate, misleading, and heretical that he attacked it, not because he objected to Bible translation per se. He objected particularly to Tyndale's individual rendering of traditional ecclesiastical terms, such as his translating "priests" by "seniors," "church" by "congregation," and "charity" by "love." Tyndale's defense on this point is at least logical and consistent, but his ironical glosses are less defensible, as they are calculated to mislead the simple. The relevant passages from More's *Dialogue* are printed by Pollard in *Records*, Nos. II, III, XIV.

[35] *STC*, No. 2063; *Hist. Cat.*, I, 6; *Records*, pp. 12–13.

[36] This is the second title-page, which replaced the original one bearing the explanatory "oute of Douche and Latyn" after the word "translated" (see below, p. 19).

Miles Coverdale was born in 1488 and seems to have become acquainted with Thomas Cromwell some years before 1530. We find him writing to Cromwell "from the Augustines, this May day" probably not later than 1527:[37]

Now I begin to taste of Holy Scriptures; now, honor be to God I am set to the most sweet smell of holy letters, with the godly savour of holy and ancient doctors, unto whose knowledge I cannot attain without diversity of books, as is not unknown to your most excellent wisdom. Nothing in the world I desire but books, as concerning my learning. They once had, I do not doubt but Almighty God shall perform that in me, which He of His most plentiful favor and grace hath begun.[38]

Soon after this it seems that Coverdale became engaged in heretical activities, left the Austin friars to whose order he had been admitted in 1514, and assumed the habit of a secular priest. He graduated bachelor of canon law at Cambridge in 1531 probably after having spent some time abroad, where he remained until 1535. Foxe states that in 1529 Coverdale met Tyndale at Hamburg and helped him with his translation of the Pentateuch, but there is no confirmation of this, and it seems unlikely from internal evidence.

Coverdale's dedication to the king is remarkable for its fulsomeness and for the assumptions underlying it:

.... Agayne, consyderynge youre Imperiall maiestye not onely to be my naturall soueraigne liege Lorde & chefe heade of the church of Englonde, but also the true defender and maynteyner of Gods lawes, I thought it my dutye, and to belonge vnto my al-

---

[37] The year is not given in the letter, and it is difficult to determine it accurately. Gairdner (*op. cit.*, II, 248–55) discusses the matter at length and concludes (p. 254) that "it seems . . . . as if 1527 were the latest possible date."

[38] *Ibid.*, p. 249; L.P. Hen. VIII, V, 106.

legiaunce, whan I had translated this Bible, not onely to dedicate this translacyon vnto youre highnesse, but wholy to commytte it vnto the same: to the intent that yf any thynge therin be translated amysse (for in many thynges we fayle, euen whan we thynke to be sure) it may stonde in youre graces handes, to correcte it, to amende it, to improue it, yee and cleane to reiecte it, yf youre godly wysdome shall thynke it necessary. And as I do with all humblenes submitte myne vnderstondynge, and my poore translacyon vnto the spirite of trueth in your grace, so make I this protestacyon (hauyng God to recorde in my conscience) that I haue nether wrested nor altered so moch as one worde for the mayntenaunce of any maner of secte: but haue with a cleare conscience purely and faythfully translated this out of fyue sundry interpreters, hauyng onely the manyfest trueth of scripture before myne eyes: Trustynge in the goodnes of God, that it shalbe vnto his worshippe: quietnes and tranquilite vnto your highnes: a perfecte stablyshment of all Gods ordynaunces within youre graces domynion: a general comforte to all Christen hertes, and a continuall thankfulnesse both of olde and yonge vnto god, and to youre grace, for beynge oure Moses, and for bringynge vs out of this olde Egypte from the cruell handes of our spirituall Pharao.[39]

Coverdale here assumes not only that his translation would be acceptable to the king but that the king is personally interested in the question of Bible translation to a degree that would lead him to correct this new version, "to amende it, to improue it, yee and cleane to reiecte it, yf youre godly wysdome shall thynke it necessary." The implication is that the king would without question welcome a translation of the Bible into English, though he would be gravely concerned about the accuracy of the text of any given translation. Coverdale was aware of the change of atmosphere, and in his dedication he tries at once to take

[39] Coverdale's Bible, Dedication.

advantage of it and to flatter the king by attributing it to his policy and wisdom.

Coverdale's Bible forestalled the bishops in their plan for an authorized version. But there is some evidence that the bishops had not been entirely idle in the matter. Strype tells how in 1535 Cranmer made plans for an English translation of the New Testament:

It was not long-after this time, that the archbishop, whose mind ran very much upon bringing in the free use of the holy Scripture in English among the people, put on vigorously a translation of it. And, that it might not come to be prohibited, as it had been, upon pretence of the ignorance or unfaithfulness of the translators, he proceeded in this method. First, he began with the translation of the New Testament; taking an old English translation thereof, which he divided into nine or ten parts, causing each part to be written out large in a paper book, and then to be sent to the best learned bishops, and others; to the intent they should make a perfect correction thereof. And when they had done he required them to send back their parts, so corrected, unto him at Lambeth, by a day limited for that purpose: and the same course, no question, he took with the Old Testament.[40]

And there follows the anecdote about Bishop Stokesly, who would not do his share because he objected to Bible translation as leading to heresy, and who was wittily rebuked by Mr. Thomas Lawney. Strype based his information on a manuscript of Ralph Morice, Cranmer's secretary, and there can therefore be no doubt of its genuineness. Morice's version is as follows:

My lorde Cranmer, mynding to have the New Testament thoroughlie corrected, devided the same into ix or x partes, and caused it to be written at large in paper bokes and sent unto the

[40] Strype, *Memorials of Cranmer* (ed. 1848), p. 70.

best lernyd bishopps, and other lernyd men, to th' intent they
sholde make a perfect correction therof, and when thei hadd done
to sende them unto hym at Lambeth by a day lymyted for that
purpose. It chanced that the Actes of the Apostelles were sent to
bisshopp Stokisley to oversee and correcte, than bisshopp of
London. . . . .[41]

There is a letter, quoted by Gairdner,[42] sent by Stephen
Gardiner to Cromwell, which contains the following sentence: "Nevertheless I have as great cause as any man to
desire rest and quiet for the health of my body; whereunto I
thought to have intended, and to abstain from books and
writing, having finished the translation of St. Luke and St.
John, wherein I have spent a great labor." This is further
evidence that the bishops were taking some steps toward
the accomplishment of an authorized version of the English
Bible. But when Coverdale's Bible appeared in 1535, no
authorized translation had yet been given to the public.

Coverdale's Bible was printed in folio probably by
Christopher Froschover at Zurich.[43] The earliest title-page
has "faithfully and truly translated out of Douche and
Latyn in to Englishe" but this was later replaced by a new
title printed in English black letter, bearing simply "faythfully translated in to Englyshe." A second folio edition was

[41] Printed in J. G. Nichols' *Narratives of the Reformation* ("Camden Society"
[London, 1857]), p. 277, from MS Harl. 422, fol. 87. C. Anderson (*Annals of the
English Bible* [London, 1845], I, 453) says: "Cranmer took an existing translation—
Tyndale's of course, for as yet there was no other," and this seems reasonable, especially as Morice used the word "corrected," which would imply that the translation used was one recognized to be faulty. Gairdner's attack on Anderson's statement (II, 270) is perverse and unjustified: his contention that the version sent was
probably a Wyclifite version is ridiculous.

[42] *Op. cit.*, pp. 267–68. See also *Records*, pp. 196–97.

[43] *DNB, s.v.* "Coverdale"; *Records*, pp. 12–13.

printed in 1537 by James Nycholson in Southwark, and a
third in quarto by the same printer in the same year.[44] Two
octavo editions of Coverdale's version of the New Testament were published probably in London by James Nycholson in 1537.[45] The 1537 folio is described as "newly ouersene & corrected," and the quarto as "newly ouersene and
correcte," the phrase in neither case having very much
justification. None of these editions was ever formally prohibited, Coverdale having Cromwell's influence behind
him. And the translation itself was much more conciliatory
than Tyndale's: there were no offensive glosses and Coverdale did not consistently refrain from using the traditional
ecclesiastical terms, using for the same word in the original
now one term and now another, as he explains in his Prologue. The 1537 quarto bears the significant legend "Set
foorth with the Kynges moost gracious licence," and is thus
the first English Bible to be issued under official sanction.
(And it must be remembered that the king, being by now
"supreme head" of the church as well as the state, his
"licence" implied a twofold authorization.) In one sense,
then, the first authorized version of the English Bible was
the 1537 quarto edition of Coverdale's translation.[46]

Coverdale, as we shall see in a later chapter, did not
translate from the original Hebrew and Greek. He himself
refers to "fyve sundry interpreters," and though he does
not specify them we can be fairly sure that they were the
Zurich Swiss-German Bible of 1524–29 (by Zwingli and Leo
Juda), Luther's German Bible, Pagninus' Latin Bible of

---

[44] STC, Nos. 2064, 2065; Hist. Cat., I, 13, 14.   [45] Hist. Cat., I, 12, 13.

[46] Gairdner (op. cit., II, 276) argues that Cromwell supported Coverdale's Bible for political reasons.

1528, the Vulgate, and Tyndale's New Testament and Pentateuch. Thus Coverdale's Bible was essentially a make-shift: it was to serve until time and increased scholarship could produce a more definitive work.

Coverdale's purpose in translating is clearly set forward in the Prologue, "Myles Coverdale Vnto the Christen reader":

Considerynge how excellent knowlege and lernynge an inter-preter of scripture oughte to haue in the tongues, and ponderyng also myne owne insufficiency therin, and how weake I am to perfourme the office of translatoure, I was the more lothe to medle with this worke. Notwithstondynge whan I consydered how greate pytie it was that we shulde wante it so longe, and called to my remembraunce the aduersite of them, which were not onely of rype knowlege, but wolde also with all theyr hertes haue per-fourmed that they beganne, yf they had not had impediment: [the reference is, of course, to Tyndale] considerynge (I saye) that by reason of theyr aduersyte it coulde not so soone haue bene broughte to an ende, as oure most prosperous nacyon wolde fayne haue had it: these and other reasonable causes consydered,. I was the more bolde to take it in hande. . . . . But to saye the trueth before God, it was nether my laboure nor desyre, to haue this worke put in my hande: neuertheles it greued me that other nacyons shulde be more plenteously prouyded for with the scrip-ture in theyr mother tongue, then we: therfore whan I was in-stantly requyred, though I coulde not do so well as I wolde, I thought it yet my dewtye to do my best, and that with a good wyll.

Coverdale, unlike Tyndale, had no zeal to translate of his own accord: his work was commissioned (probably by Cromwell): he was "instantly requyred" and did his best out of duty. Further on in the Prologue he says:

. . . . For the which cause (accordyng as I was desyred) I toke the more vpon me to set forth this speciall translacyon, not as a

checker, not as a reprouer, or despyser of other mens translacyons
(for amonge many as yet I haue founde none without occasyon of
greate thankesgeuynge vnto god) but lowly and faythfully haue I
folowed myne interpreters, and that vnder correccyon. And
though I haue fayled eny where (as there is noman but he mysseth
in some thynge) loue shall constyrre all to the best without eny
peruerse iudgment. . . . . He that can do better then another,
shulde not set him at naught that vnderstondeth lesse: Yee he
that hath the more vnderstondyng, ought to remembre that the
same gyfte is not his but Gods, and that God hath geuen it him
to teach & enfourme the ignoraunt. Yf thou hast knowlege
therfore to iudge where eny faute is made, I doute not but thou
wilt helpe to amende it, yf loue be ioyned with thy knowlege.
Howbeit wherin so euer I can perceaue by my selfe, or by the
informacyon of other, that I haue fayled (as it is no wonder) I
shall now by the helpe of God ouerloke it better and amende it.

Coverdale had not long to wait before others arose "to
teach and enfourme the ignoraunt." In the same year as the
two London editions of Coverdale's Bible appeared there
was printed, probably at Antwerp, for R. Grafton and E.
Whitchurch of London, "The Byble, which is all the holy
Scripture: In whych are contayned the Olde and Newe
Testament truly and purely translated into Englysh by
Thomas Matthew." And this, too, was "set forth with the
Kinges most gracyous lycence." The following summary[47]
of a series of three letters sent from Cranmer to Cromwell
shows clearly how this new Bible stood with reference to
official opinion in England.

Cranmer to Cromwell:

You will receive by the bearer a bible in English both of a new
translation and of a new print, dedicated to the King. Likes it

---

[47] Taken from L.P. Hen. VIII, XII, Part II (1537), 434, 512. The letters are
printed by Pollard in *Records*, pp. 214–17.

better than any other translation, and wishes Cromwell to obtain a licence that it may be read freely till the bishops can set forth a better, which he thinks will not be till after Doomsday. God will one day requite Cromwell's pains in setting forth His word. FORDE, 4 Aug., (1537).

Cranmer to Cromwell:

Thanks Cromwell for having exhibited the Bible to the King and got his Grace's permission that it shall be bought and read within the realm. Cromwell has done him more pleasure in this than if he had given him 1,000 *l.* Doubts not the results will redound to his honour. He may reckon Cranmer his bondman for the same, and, he will be bold to say, my lord of Worcester also. FORDE, 13 Aug.

The third letter, dated August 28, [1537], is only relevant in its first three sentences, which run:

My very singuler and especiall good Lorde in my most hartie wise I comend me to your Lordeship. Theis shalbe to give to you most hartie thanks that any harte can thinke, and that in the name of theym all which favoreth goddes wourde, for your Diligence at this tyme in procuring the Kinges highnes to set forth the said goddes wourd and his gospell by his graces auctoritie. For the whiche acte not only the Kinges maiestie, but also you shall have a perpetuall Lawde and memorye of all theym that be now or hereafter shalbe goddes faithfull people and the favorers of his wourde.[48]

And finally we may give summaries of two letters sent by Richard Grafton, the printer, to Cromwell. The first is dated August 28, 1537:

As requested sends six bibles. . . . . Begs him to take them as a gift for his pains in moving the King to license such a work. As my lord of Canterbury said, the tidings thereof did him more good than the gift of 10,000 *l.;* yet there are men who believe not that

[48] *Records,* pp. 216–17.

the King licensed it. Begs him, therefore, to license it under the privy seal. Is sure the lords of Canterbury, Worcester, and Salisbury will thank him for what he has done, and that God will reward him.[49]

The second letter is not dated but must have been written soon after August 28:[50]

Richard Grafton to Cromwell:

According to your lordship's commission, by your servant, I have sent you certain bibles and beg you to accept them as well done. Where I wrote to your Lordship for a privy seal as a defence against the enemies of this bible, and you thought it unnecessary; this work has cost us 500 *l*. and I have printed and booked 1,500 copies, but now others are printing the same work in a lesser letter, intending to sell their little books cheaper than I can sell my great, and so prevent my selling any. Will by this be undone, and so will his creditors who have assisted him. Those who are printing this new copy from his will falsify the text; for they do it not for God's glory but covetousness. Dutchmen dwelling here who can neither write nor speak good English are printing it, and to save 20 *l*. or 40 *l*. to a learned man to oversee it, will issue it full of errors. Desires the King's privilege that none shall print them till these be sold, which shall not be this three year, and will "consider" Cromwell's favour, and doubtless so will my lord of Canterbury and other friends. . . . . Desires that, as this goes abroad with the King's licence and is the pure Word of God, Cromwell will command every curate to have one. Every abbey should have six set in different places for the convent and resorters to read. Would have none but the papistical sort compelled to have them, and then there would be enough in my lord of London's diocese "to spend away a great part of them." A very small commission to my lords of Canterbury, Salisbury and Worcester would cause it to be done in their dioceses. It would terminate the schism that is in the realm, some calling themselves of the Old and some of the

---

[49] L.P. Hen. VIII, XII, 2, 593.   [50] L.P. (end of August?).

New; for now we should all follow one God, one book, and one learning. . . . .[51]

We can see from these letters what lay behind the simple sentence "set forth with the Kinges most gracyous lycence." Cranmer was anxious that the bishops should implement their promise to produce an authorized version, at least nominally, so he persuaded Cromwell (who in any case would not have needed much persuasion) to induce the king to give official sanction to "a bible in English both of a new translation and of a new print." We see too from Grafton's second letter to Cromwell that the popularity of this Bible had made the danger of pirated editions imminent, and Grafton was anxious to have his monopoly safeguarded until he had cleared his profits. At the end of this letter we find in Grafton's scheme that every curate should have a Bible and every abbey should have six, etc., an indication of the lengths to which he thought Cromwell could reasonably be expected to go in popularizing the English Bible. Cromwell himself had led the way with the injunction he issued to the clergy in August, 1536, requiring the incumbent of every parish to procure, before the following feast of St. Peter ad Vincula, a complete Bible in Latin and one in English.[52] But this injunction was never carried into effect, as we know from its omission from the copy of the injunctions in Cranmer's register.[53]

But what was this version that Cranmer sponsored so

---

[51] L.P. Hen. VIII, Appen. 35. Strype's *Cranmer* has the whole letter (Appen. 20).

[52] Wilkins, *Concilia*, III, 815.

[53] Gairdner, *op. cit.*, II, 277. The English Bible could only have been Coverdale's, as no other complete English version existed in 1536. Cromwell did carry his point in September, 1538.

enthusiastically? It was a composite version, made up of Tyndale's translation of the Pentateuch and his hitherto unpublished translation of the Old Testament from Joshua to II Chronicles, Coverdale's translation of the rest of the Old Testament including the Apocrypha, and Tyndale's New Testament (the 1535 "I. H." edition). Further, Thomas Matthew does not seem to have been a real person at all.[54] The Bible was edited and arranged by John Rogers, the proto-martyr of the Marian persecution, who had been an associate of Tyndale in his last years, and who probably received from Tyndale his incomplete translation of the Old Testament. Rogers seems to have busied himself with this Bible throughout 1536. His choice of the maximum amount of Tyndale's work was fortunate, for it was "Matthew's Bible" that provided the basis for the series of revisions that culminated in the Authorized Version. He might indeed have included Tyndale's Jonah instead of Coverdale's and made use of the epistles from the Old Testament that Tyndale printed with the 1534 revision of his New Testament; but his rejection of these is a small matter compared with his inclusion of so much of Tyndale's work. Tyndale's translation was the product of a scholarship, and a familiarity with Greek and Hebrew, which Coverdale did not possess, and Rogers did well to prefer his work to Coverdale's.

The text of "Matthew's Bible" from Joshua to II Chronicles is not acknowledged to be by Tyndale, but we can be fairly sure that it is his. We find it stated in Halle's *Chronicle* that Tyndale "translated the New Testament into Englishe and fyrst put it in prynt, and likewise he translated the v. bookes of Moses, Josua, Judicum, Ruth, the bookes of the

---

[54] *Records*, pp. 228 *et passim*.

Kynges and the bookes of Paralipomenon, Nehemias or the fyrst of Esdras, the Prophet Ionas, and no more of the holy scripture."[55] We know for certain that Halle is right about the five books of Moses, and there is no reason why he should be wrong about the rest. Certainly the text of the Old Testament from Joshua to II Chronicles in "Matthew's Bible" differs greatly from that of Coverdale, and we can be fairly certain that Rogers, who associated closely with Tyndale during the last few months of his life and seems to have been what we should today call his literary executor, received Tyndale's unpublished work from him just before his death and embodied it in the Bible he brought out in 1537. There is, however, no trace of Tyndale's translation of Nehemiah.

It is not difficult to account for the mystification indulged in by those who brought out "Matthew's Bible."

Almost childish as the device of attributing a translation of the Bible made up of the work of Tyndale and Coverdale to a fictitious or man-of-straw Thomas Matthew now appears, it served to save the face of the king and the bishops by the pretence that this was a new version, and so one which might be considered to have been made in compliance with the petition sent to the king by the Upper House of Convocation in December 1534.[56]

But it is difficult to understand why Cranmer was not content to take Coverdale's version which, as the legend on the 1537 edition testifies, was licensed by the king. And Coverdale's translation, though not so accurate, and moreover derivative throughout, did not offend by using noneccle-siastical terms as Tyndale's did, nor did it have violent marginal notes or strongly Protestant prologues. Cranmer,

[55] *Records*, pp. 195–96.   [56] *Ibid.*, p. 15.

in his letter to Cromwell, a summary of which we have quoted, stressed the fact that "Matthew's" was a new Bible, calling it "a Bible in Englishe, both of a new translacion and of new prynte"; but this was not the case at all, as the translation was partly Tyndale's and partly Coverdale's.[57] And Cranmer's remark that "as for the translation, so farre as I have redde therof I like it better than any other translation hertofore made" may have applied to the hitherto unpublished translation of Joshua to Chronicles by Tyndale, but applied to the Bible as a whole it was nonsense. Obviously the king, or Cromwell, or Cranmer, or all three, were anxious that a Bible should be brought out which could plausibly be called "new" but did not particularly care whose the text actually was. "No doubt," remarks Pollard, "in 1537 the King had moved a long way in the direction of Protestantism for the moment—but considering his character the whole transaction bore a remarkable resemblance to playing with gunpowder."[58] Certainly the almost casual way in which "Matthew's Bible" received official sanction is extraordinary when we consider how Tyndale's Bible had been opposed by the same people who now welcomed a text which was to a large extent identical with it; and it is no less remarkable that Coverdale should have been encouraged while Tyndale was still active and that in 1537 his version should have received a royal license.

In 1538, as well as further revisions of Tyndale's New

----

[57] Rogers seems to have himself translated the brief Prayer of Manasses (included in "Matthew's Bible" for the first time in a printed English Bible), basing his translation on the text of the French Bible of Olivetan.

[58] *Records*, p. 16.

Testament, one of which prints also the Latin of Erasmus,[59] there appeared two quarto editions of Coverdale's translation of the New Testament from the Vulgate, along with the Vulgate text, another edition appearing in octavo in the same year.[60] Coverdale's version of the New Testament "wyth a true concordaunce in the margent & many necessary annotacions declarynge sondry harde places cōteyned in the text" was twice printed by itself in Antwerp, also in 1538.[61] The first of the quarto editions of Coverdale's diglot Testament was full of misprints and errors,[62] and Coverdale repudiated the translation, arranging for a corrected edition to be brought out in Paris, where he then was, supervising the printing of the Great Bible. This corrected edition is the Paris octavo, printed in November, 1538, under his own supervision. The second quarto edition of Coverdale's diglot Testament mentioned above was brought out by Nycolson in London while Coverdale was preparing his own revision in Paris: in most copies the title-page bears the name of

[59] *Hist. Cat.*, I, 17; *STC*, No. 2815.   [60] *Hist. Cat.*, I, 18–19.

[61] *Hist. Cat.*, I, 19–20; *STC*, Nos. 2836, 2837. There were three other editions of the English New Testament published probably in 1538, two in octavo and one in sixteens (*STC*, Nos. 2838–40). The octavo editions were probably printed by Nycolson. I have not examined the text of these editions, but *STC* notes them as "Coverdale's revision" (presumably of Tyndale) and *B.M. Cat.* as "translated by Miles Coverdale." All the extant copies are imperfect, none having the title-page.

[62] *Records*, p. 243. Letter of Richard Grafton to Cromwell: ".... And also founde the booke so folyshly done, ye and so corrupt, that yt did not only greue him that the prynter had so defamed him and his learnyng by addynge his name to so fonde a thinge, but also that the commen people was depryued of the true and syncere sence of godes true worde, and also that soche an occasyon was mynystred to the enemyes of Godes worde, that rather seke occasyons to rayle and sclaunder, then to be edefyed. And therfore at his moost honest and lawfull request (although I had ynough to do besyde) I haue prynted the same agayne, translated and corrected by Master Couerdale him selfe."

Johan Hollybushe instead of Miles Coverdale,[63] Nycolson evidently bringing out this edition without authority from Coverdale and wishing to disguise the fact that it was Coverdale's translation. The same year saw the publication of yet another edition of the New Testament,[64] this time "newly translated into Englysshe by Thomas Matthew." This is Tyndale's translation edited by John Rogers. The edition of Tyndale's New Testament with the Latin of Erasmus, as well as the three editions of Coverdale's diglot, announce on the title-page that they are printed with the king's license.

In 1539 there was printed in London by John Byddell for Thomas Barthlet "the most sacred Bible which is the holy scripture, conteyning the old and new testament, translated into English, and newly recognised with great diligence after most faythful exemplars, by Rychard Taverner." Taverner's Bible is not in the direct line of succession from Tyndale to the Authorized Version, as it is a reissue and revision of "Matthew's Bible" by an independent scholar, and did not form the basis of any subsequent revision. Two editions of Taverner's New Testament—one in quarto and one in octavo—were printed by T. Petyt for Barthlet in the same year.

Taverner's Bible was a private enterprise of which Cromwell took no notice. He had already turned his attention to the production of a version which should supersede both Coverdale's and "Matthew's." This task he intrusted to Coverdale, who had already professed himself willing to "overlook and amend" his earlier translation if and when it

[63] *Hist. Cat.*, I, 18; *STC*, No. 2818. See *Records*, pp. 136 n., 206.
[64] *STC*, No. 2841.

should be thought necessary. This new revision was printed in Paris "pource que les impressions y sont plus belles qu'en autre lieu, et pour le grand nombre des Imprimeurs, et la grande abondance de papier qui y est, les liures y sont plustost expediez qu'en nul autre pays."[65] The printers were the famous Paris firm of François Regnault, who printed Coverdale's corrected diglot Testament in 1538 and had been accustomed to printing service-books for the English market for over forty years.[66] Coverdale and Richard Grafton, the printer of "Matthew's Bible," went over to Paris to supervise the printing, and we find them writing to Cromwell in August, 1538,[67] informing him that the work is progressing, and in September interceding on behalf of Regnault that he might still have the right to print English books—a right that had just been threatened by a royal proclamation forbidding English books printed abroad to be brought into the country and forbidding any person to print English books except after examination by some of the Privy Council or other persons appointed or to use the words *cum privilegio regali* without adding *ad imprimendum solum*.[68] This proclamation caused Grafton and Coverdale considerable alarm, as we gather also from another letter from Grafton to Cromwell, written on the first of December:

[65] From a letter written by Castillon, the French ambassador in England, to the Constable of France, December 31, 1538 (*Records*, p. 250 [from Brit. Mus. MS Add. 33514, fol. 9]).

[66] *Records*, p. 239, letter from Coverdale and Grafton to Cromwell: ". . . . Where as of long tyme he [Regnault] hath bene an occupier in to England more then xl. yere, he hath allwayes provyded soche bookes for England, as they moost occupied, so that he hath a great nombre, at this present in his handes, As prymers in Englishe, Missales with other soche like. . . . ."

[67] *Ibid.*, pp. 237–40.   [68] *Ibid.*, pp. 18, 240–42.

. . . . And the day before this present came there a post named Nycolas which brought your lordshipes letters to my lorde of harfforde, with thewhich was bounde a certen inhibicion for pryntynge of bookes, and for addynge of these wordes Cum priuilegio. Then assone as my lorde of harfforde had receaued yt, he sent ymedyatlye for Mr. Couerdale and me, readynge thesame thynge vnto vs, in thewhich is expressed, that we shuld adde these wordes (ad imprimendum solum) which wordes we neuer heard of before. Nether do we take it that those wordes shuld be added in the pryntynge of the scripture (if yt be truly translated) for then shuld yt be a great occasyon to the enemyes to saye that yt is not the kynges acte or mynde to set yt forth, but only lycence the prynters to sell soche as is put forth. Wherfore moost humbly we beseke your lordship to take no dyspleasor for that we haue done, for rather then any soche thynge shuld happen, we wolde do yt agayne, but I trust the thynge yt selfe is so well done, that it shall not only please your lordship, but also the Kynges highnes and all the godly in the realme. And where as your lordship hath added in thesayd inhibicions that your lordship and all the Kynges most honorable councell wylleth no booke from henceforth to be put in prynt, but that fyrst yt be alowed at the least by one bysshop. We moost humbly beseke your lordship to apoynt certen therto, that they maye be as readye to reade them, as other good men be to put them forth. For yt is now vij yere, sence the bysshopes promysed to translate and set forth the byble, and as yet they haue no leasor, I praye god they maye haue.[69]

As far as the phrase "cum privilegio ad imprimendum solum" is concerned, this letter was unavailing, for the Bible duly appeared with that phrase on the title-page.

Much worse trouble than the "certen inhibicion for pryntynge of bookes" was in store for Grafton and Coverdale.

[69] *Ibid.*, pp. 244–45. No episcopal supervision took place in the case of the first edition of the Great Bible, nor any of the Great Bibles except the fourth and sixth (*ibid.*, *ad. loc.;* see also *ibid.*, p. 23).

The relations between Francis V and Henry were becoming strained, and at the end of the year the ambassador in England wrote home, suggesting the seizure of the English Bibles in Paris.[70] Coverdale, writing to Cromwell on December 13, 1538, "about thexposycon of darke place of the byble" concludes by referring to the threatened confiscation and expresses his intention of sending as many as are printed to Cromwell by the Bishop of Hereford, beseeching him "to be the defender & keper thereof: To the intent that yf these men proceade in their cruelnesse agaynst us & confiscate the rest, yet this at the leest maye be safe by the meanes of your lordshippe." On December 17, four days after this letter was written, the Inquisitors descended on Regnault's printing office; Grafton and Coverdale had to flee, and Regnault himself was arrested.[71] All the Bibles on the premises were seized, to be conveyed to the custody of the University of Paris. At the end of December Cromwell asked the ambassador to help to get the Bibles back and to get permission from the king and the Constable of France to print the Bible in Paris, mentioning that they cost him six hundred marks ("qui sont troys mil six cens liures tournoys").[72] Foxe's narrative is not at all reliable, but we gather from it that "4 great dry fattes" of the Bibles were recovered, the rest being burned "to the great and impor-

[70] We gather from the postscript of a letter written by the imperial ambassador in England to the emperor Charles V on January 9, 1539, that the suggestion that the Inquisition should be allowed to seize the Bibles came from the French ambassador (*Records*, pp. 251–53).

[71] *Records*, p. 246, prints the citation of François Regnault for printing the Bible at Paris, December 17, 1538.

[72] See the letter of Castillon to the Constable of France, December 31, 1538 (*Records*, pp. 249–51).

tunate losse of those that bare the charge of them."[73] We gather from Foxe that

the French authorities, while holding the bulk of the stock as an asset in their negotiations with Cromwell, made a pretence of burning it, and that of the copies set aside to be burnt, Grafton rescued a certain number, possibly sixty or eighty, as it would need a large vat to hold more than a score of them. Add the copies deposited with Bonner [Bishop of London and English ambassador at Paris] before the raid, and there may have been a hundred or so available for issue, enough for distribution, but not a quantity which could be put on the market. When, therefore, on the arrival of type and printers from France, the missing sheets were printed and the first edition finished, a new one, answering to the first page for page, so that sheets would be interchangeable, was put in hand, at the expense this time, not of Cromwell, but of a member of the Haberdashers' Company, Anthony Marler.[74]

We need not here go into the details recorded—very inaccurately—by Foxe, or conjecture concerning the further activities of Grafton in Paris; suffice it to note that, whether the rest of the confiscated stock was rescued or not, the Great Bible was ready for publication before the end of 1539—that is, before the end of March, 1540, in our present reckoning—and the first edition duly appeared in April, printed by Richard Grafton and Edward Whitchurch.[75]

[73] *Acts and Monuments* (ed. 1583), p. 1191.

[74] *Records*, pp. 20–21, 260.

[75] The colophon reads: "The ende of the New Testament;/ and of the whole Byble, Fynisshed in Apryll,/ Anno M.CCCCC.XXXIX. A dño factũ est istud." Pollard comments (*Records*, p. 19): "It seems probable that in the colophon just quoted there was at least a touch of bravado. Doubtless the completion in any form of the edition in April 1539 was indeed 'the Lord's doing,' and doubtless its editors desired that it should appear marvellous in the eyes of their enemies. But it is far from certain that the existence of the colophon denotes the existence of sufficient copies for an edition to have been issued anywhere near the date named."

This Bible—"The Byble in Englyshe, that is to saye the content of all the holy scrypture, bothe of ye olde and newe testament, truly translated after the veryte of the Hebrue and Greke textes, by ye dylygent studye of dyuerse excellent learned men, expert in theforsayde tongues"—was a large and handsome folio volume, popularly known as the "Great Bible." The Great Bible was thus a revision of "Matthew's Bible," made by Coverdale at the instance of Cromwell. The nature of the revision and the sources used will be discussed below.

The second edition of the Great Bible followed within a few weeks of the first, a third in the following July, and four others before the end of 1541. In May, 1541, a royal proclamation was issued "for the Byble of the largest and greatest volume to be had in every churche."[76] This proclamation refers to earlier injunctions, which had been issued by Cromwell, that in every parish church there should be "one boke of the whole Bible of the largest volume in Englyshe" set up "in summe conuenyent place."[77] Provisions are made against the misuse of public Bible-reading:

.... the Kynges royall maiestye intended, that his louynge subiectes shulde haue and vse the commoditie of the readyng of the sayd Bybles, for the purpose aboue rehersed, humbly, mekely,

[76] Wilkins, *Concilia*, III, 856.

[77] As early as August, 1536, there had been similar injunctions issued to the clergy by Cromwell (see above, p. 25). These, however, had remained a dead letter. The injunctions referred to in the proclamation of 1541 were probably issued at the end of 1538, although they are dated 1536 in Wilkins. A reference to the "whole Bible of the largest volume in Englyshe" must have meant the Great Bible and therefore could not have been made until it was at least in preparation. Also the reference in the proclamation to the injunctions having ordered the provision of Bibles "by a certain day now expired" suggests that the time had only recently expired. As a year was the limit given, the end of 1538 fits in very well.

reuerently and obediently; and not that any of them shulde reade the sayde Bybles, wyth lowde and hyghe voyces, in tyme of the celebracion of the holye Masse and other dyuyne seruyces vsed in the churche, nor that any hys lay subiectes redynge the same, shulde presume to take vpon them, any common dysputacyon, argumente or exposicyon of the mysteries therein conteyned, but that euery suche laye man shulde humbly, mekely and reuerentlye reade the same, for his owne instruction, edificacion, and amendement of hys lyfe, accordynge to goddes holy worde therin mencioned.

This sentence explains a great deal of the orthodox opposition to Bible-reading.

The proclamation goes on to express surprise that the previous injunction had not been universally obeyed and continues:

And myndynge the execucion of his sayde former, moost godly and gracyous Iniunctions: doeth straytlye charge and commaunde that the Curates and paryshioners of euerye towne and paryshe within thys hys realme of Englande, not hauynge already Bybles prouyded wythin theyr paryshe churches, shall on thys syde the feaste of Alsayntes next commynge, bye and prouyde Bybles of the largest and greatest volume, and cause the same to be set and fyxed in euery of the sayde paryshe churches, there to be vsed as is aforesayd: accordynge to the sayde former Iniunctions; vpon payne that the Curate and inhabitauntes of the paryshes and townes, shal lose and forfayte to the Kynges maiestye for euery moneth that they shall lacke and want the sayde Bybles, after the same feast of Alsayntes fourty shyllynges. . . . . And fynally, the kynges royall maiestie doeth declare and sygnifye to all and syngular his louynge subiectes, that to thentent they maye haue the sayde Bybles of the greatest volume at equall and reasonable pryces, His hyghnes by the aduyse of hys counsayle hath ordeyned and taxed: that the sellers therof, shall not take for any of the sayde Bybles vnbounde, aboue the pryce of ten shyllynges. And for euery of the sayde Bybles well and sufficientlye bounde,

trymmed and clasped, not aboue twelue shyllynges, vpon payne,
the seller to lose for euerye Byble solde contrary to this his hyghnes
proclamacion fourty shyllynges. . . . .[78]

The price fixed was certainly low, and the publishers
must have suffered from this attempt to suit the price to the
pockets of the public. Documents relating to the commer-
cial side of the publication of the Great Bible, which need
not delay us here, will be found in Pollard's *Records*.[79]

The title-page of the Great Bible is significant. At the
top, immediately above the small rectangle of print which
proclaims the title, sits the king handing a Bible each to
two respectful figures standing at either side of his throne.
Below, flanking the rectangle of print, Cranmer and Cromwell are handing Bibles to the people. At the bottom, a full
third of the page is taken up with a concord of people ex-
claiming "Vivat Rex." The king came first. Royal supremacy over the church had been established, and the reversal
of the historic policy of the ecclesiastical authorities in the
matter of Bible translation was due not so much to changing
views and beliefs about the place of the Bible in the Christian religion—though these existed, and the king exploited
them—as to the personal policy of the "supreme head of the
Church in England." The final victory of the cause cham-

[78] *Records*, pp. 263–64; Wilkins, *Concilia*, III, 856. I take the text from *Records*
rather than from Wilkins, as the latter is obviously inaccurate in many details
("intendeth" for "intended" in the first sentence quoted on p. 35 is a glaring
example), besides changing the spelling and punctuation of the original. *Records*
prints "from the original edition in the British Museum" and Pollard's transcripts
are always more trustworthy than those of Wilkins, especially when the original
text is in English.

[79] Pp. 260 f. See also *ibid.*, p. 22, and the article by H. R. Plomer, "Anthony
Marler and the Great Bible," *Library*, I (3d ser., 1910), 200-206.

pioned by Wyclif and Tyndale was not the result of their views prevailing among a majority in the country—it would have taken much longer if victory had to wait until then—but arose from the king's desire to license English Bibles for personal and political reasons.

Strype, drawing on a manuscript of Foxe, gives the following account of the reception of the Bible by the public:

It was wonderful to see with what joy this book of God was received, not only among the learned sort, and those that were noted for lovers of the reformation, but generally all England over, among all the vulgar and common people; and with what greediness God's word was read, and what resort to places where the reading of it was. Every body that could, bought the book, or busily read it, or got others to read it to them, if they could not themselves; and divers more elderly people learned to read on purpose. And even little boys flocked among the rest to hear portions of the holy Scripture read. One William Maldon, happening in the company of John Fox, in the beginning of the reign of Queen Elizabeth, and Fox being very inquisitive after those that suffered for religion in the former reigns, asked him, if he knew any that were persecuted for the Gospel of Jesus Christ, that he might add it to his book of martyrs; he told him he knew one that was whipped by his own father in King Henry's reign for it. . . . . When the King had allowed the Bible to be set forth to be read in all churches, immediately several poor men in the town of Chelmsford in Essex, where his father lived and he was born, bought the New Testament, and on Sundays sat reading it in the lower end of the Church: many would flock about it to hear their reading; and he among the rest, being then but fifteen years old, came every Sunday to hear the glad and sweet tidings of the Gospel. But his father observing it, once angrily fetched him away, and would have him to say the Latin mattins with him: which grieved him much. And as he returned at other times to hear the Scripture read, his father would fetch him away. This put him upon the thoughts of learning to read English, that so he might read the New Testament himself: which when he had by diligence effected, he and his father's apprentice bought the New Testament, joining their stocks together; and, to conceal it, laid it under the bed-straw, and read it at convenient times. One night, his father being asleep, he and his mother chanced to discourse concerning the crucifix, and kneeling down to it . . . . ; this he told his mother was plain idolatry, and against the commandment of God, where he saith, *Thou shalt not make any graven image, nor bow down to it, to worship it.* . . . . The sum of this evening's conference she presently repeats to her husband: which he is impatient to hear, and boiling in fury against his son, for denying worship to be due to the cross, arose forthwith, and goes up to his son's chamber, and, like a mad zealot, taking him by the hair of his head with both his hands, pulled him out of the bed, and whipped him unmercifully.[80]

This story of Foxe's, whether it be true or not, illustrates clearly the two attitudes to the Bible at the time. The reformers, who included many of the younger men, welcomed it as a source of texts which they could use against the abuses of the church and any practices which they deemed to be undesirable because not based on scripture; the more orthodox and conservative viewed the English Bible with suspicion and especially resented the arguments drawn from scripture against traditional practices. It is hardly possible that there was at this time such general zeal for the reading of the English Bible as Foxe and Strype describe. The majority of the people must have viewed this official *volte-face* with suspicion, and it is significant that official steps were taken to encourage Bible-reading.[81]

[80] *Memorials of Cranmer* (ed. 1812), I, 91–92. The manuscript of Maldon's narrative, written for Foxe's *Acts and Monuments*, is printed in *Records*, pp. 268 ff., from Brit. Mus. Harl. MS 590, fol. 77.

[81] See, as well as the documents already referred to, the draft for a proclamation "towching the reading of the Byble" printed in *Records*, pp. 265–66, from Cotton MS Cleopatra E. v. 327. Grafton, when he appeared before the Privy Council

The second edition of the Great Bible, that of April, 1540, as well as the later issues, have Archbishop Cranmer's prologue, and these are thus frequently called "Cranmer's Bible." The edition of April has on the title-page the important announcement: "This is the Bible appoynted to the vse of the churches"; the fourth and sixth editions have a more qualified statement:

The Byble in Englyshe of the largest and greatest volume, auctorised and apoynted by the commaundement of oure moost redoubted prynce and soueraygne Lorde, Kynge Henry the VIII, supreme head of this his church and realme of Englande: to be frequented and vsed in euery church w'in this his sayd realme, accordynge to the tenoure of hys former Iniunctions geuen in that behalfe. . . . . Ouersene and perused at the comaundement of the kynges highnes by the ryght reuerende fathers in God, Cuthbert, bysshop of Duresme, and Nicholas bisshop of Rochester.

This last must have been in accordance with the proclamation of 1538, to which Grafton referred in his letter to Cromwell in December of that year.[82] The supervision seems to have been merely nominal.

That the bishops were not altogether satisfied with the version presented by the Great Bible is evident from the discussions that went on in the Convocation of the province of Canterbury in January and February, 1542. The archbishop denounced the English Bible "quod in Testamento tam Veteri quam Novo in lingua Anglicana habentur multa,

---

charged with printing William Gray's scurrilous verses, was charged also with the printing of "Matthew's Bible" and "examined of the Great Bible, and what notes he was purposed to make" (*Acts and Monuments* [ed. 1583], II, 119). Yet both these Bibles had the royal license, which cannot therefore have meant that the Bibles were generally approved.

[82] Above, p. 32.

quae reformatione indigent." In the third session, on February 3, after a discussion on the matter

reverendissimus rogavit singulos, utrum sine scandalo et errore ac offensione manifesta Christi fidelium magnam Bibliam in Anglico sermone tralatam vellent retinere. Visum est majori parti eorundem dictam Bibliam non posse retineri, nisi prius debite castigetur et examinetur juxta eam Bibliam, quae communiter in ecclesia Anglicana legitur [i.e., the Vulgate] . . . . tempus ad exhibenda notata et errata in Veteri Testamento protraxit.

In the fifth session

post colloquium inter episcopos habitum de modo et forma procedendi in et circa examen sacri voluminis, prolocutor intrans praesentavit librum, continentem notata per eos ex Veteri Testamento in diversis paginis, quae comisit rever. et patrum acri judicio examinanda. In coetu selecto pro examinandis Bibliis, Novum Testamentum tradebatur episcopis Dunelm. Winton. Hereford, Roffen. et Westmon. cum doctoribus Wotton, Day, Coren, Wilson, Leighton, May et aliis e domo inferioris convocationis: Vetus Testamentum archiepisc. Ebor. episcopo Elien. cum Redman, Taylor, Haynes, Robertson, Cocks, etc. viris in Hebraica, Graeca, Latina et Anglicana peritis.

Finally, we gather from the proceedings of February 17 that the chief fault found with the Great Bible was its abandonment of the Latin ecclesiastical terms (coming from Tyndale through "Matthew's Bible"):

Prolocutore autem intrante, antequam discessissent membra ejus, episcopus Winton. publice legebat verba Latina in sacro volumine contenta, quae voluit pro eorum germano at nativo intellectu et rei majestate, quod poterit vel in sua natura retineri, vel quam accommodatissime fieri possit in Anglicum sermonem verti.[83]

[83] Wilkins, *Concilia*, III, 860–61. Wilkins appends a list (from Fuller's *Church History* [ed. 1655], p. 236) of the Latin terms read out by the Bishop of Winchester.

But in spite of these detailed preparations for a revision on more conservative lines, nothing came of the scheme.[84] It was not until Archbishop Parker, perhaps at the instigation of the Bishop of Ely, revived the project of a revision to be done mainly by the bishops that the work was taken in hand. The first edition of the Bishops' Bible did not appear until 1568, and by that time events had moved.

Nothing further in the way of English Bible translation was produced in the reign of Henry VIII. The position that had been reached by the publication and authorization of the Great Bible was illogical and arbitrary, but it was the furthest step forward the cause of English Bible translation had yet progressed, and it was from this point that any further advance was to start. It was some time before any such advance took place. During the rest of the reign of Henry VIII the freedom for English Bible-reading that had been won by 1540 became increasingly restricted. Not only was audible Bible-reading by individuals in public severely

---

[84] The king sent a message to Convocation, asking them to proceed no further in the matter, as he proposed to refer the translation of the Bible to the two universities (Gairdner, *op. cit.*, II, 298). Gairdner (pp. 294–303) puts the case against both "Matthew's Bible" and the Great Bible, and their authorization, at its most extreme, asserting that "the combined work of Tyndale and Coverdale was actually forced upon the clergy in spite of all remonstrances." In his attempt to do justice to the conservative point of view, Gairdner is unfair to the translators throughout his whole section on "The Story of the English Bible," assuming that the conservative point of view, because "time-honoured" (p. 294), represented moderation and intelligence against the unreasonable attitude of the reformers. He takes no account of those on the side of the "new" ideas who were both reasonable and disinterested in their demands, and exaggerates the strength of feeling against the English Bible, which among the masses of the people was probably not very clearly defined one way or the other.

punished, as in the case of John Porter, recorded by Foxe,[85] but in 1543 an act of Parliament prohibited all Tyndale's translations and ordered that no women, except noble or gentle women, or artificers, apprentices, journeymen, servingmen, husbandmen, or laborers, should read to themselves or to others, publicly or privately, any part of the Bible under pain of imprisonment. In 1546 a further prohibition of Tyndale's books, among others, was issued in a royal proclamation; Coverdale's New Testament was among the prohibited books. Only the Great Bible, there-

[85] *Acts and Monuments* (ed. 1583), II, 1206-7. Foxe's account of the reaction against English Bible-reading is interesting if not strictly accurate: "After this, the bishops bringing their purpose to passe, brought the Lord Cromwell out of fauour, and shortly to his death: and not long after, great complaint was made to the king of the translation of the Bible, and of yᵉ preface of the same, and then was the sale of the Bible commaunded to be stayed, the B. promising to amend & correct it, but neuer performing the same: Then Grafton was called, & first charged with the printing of Mathewes Bible, but he being fearefull of trouble, made excuses for himselfe in all things. Then was he examined of the great Bible, and what notes he was purposed to make. To the which he aunswered, that he knewe none. For his purpose was to haue retayned learned men to haue made the notes, but when he perceyued the kynges maiestie, and his Clergie not willing to haue any, he proceded no further. But for al these excuses, Grafton was sent to the Fleet, and there remayned vi wekes, and before he came out, was bound in CCC.*l* that he should neither sell, nor imprint, or cause to be imprinted any moe Bibles, vntill the king & clergy should agree vpon a translation. And thus was the Bible from that tyme stayed, during the raigne of Kyng Henry the VIII" (*ibid.*, pp. 1191-92). The last sentence is, of course, inaccurate. The king never publicly reversed his policy in favor of Bible translation once it had been determined, though the regulations governing the use of the Bible were considerably tightened up in the latter part of his reign. After the fall of Cromwell conservative opinion carried more weight in the affairs of the English church. But the fact that the king himself had publicly approved of English Bible translation, and made his will in the matter known in no uncertain way, prevented the conservatives from even attempting any general condemnation of Bible translation. The bishops condemned the translation in use only in order to show the necessity for a new translation.

fore, remained permitted, and the reading of that was hedged about with restrictions. The first edition of the Great Bible had indeed been authorized with more circumstance than the mere royal license granted to the Coverdale Bible of 1537 and to "Matthew's Bible" of the same year; but the legend on the title-page read significantly, "appoynted to the vse of the churches"—not the indiscriminate use of private individuals. The authorities were still inclined to be suspicious of private Bible study by individuals. The proclamation of 1541 had enjoined the people to read the Bible "humbly, meekly, reuerently and obediently," which was a rather vague way of hinting that the citation of texts for reforming purposes would not be tolerated. The reading and interpretation of the Bible aloud by individuals in churches was also potentially dangerous, and in 1542 we find Bishop Bonner issuing "an admonition and advertisement . . . . to all readers of the Bible in the English tongue":

To the intent, that a good and wholesom thing, godly and virtuously for honest intents and purposes set forth for many, be not hindered or maligned at, for the abuse, default, and evil behaviour of a few, who for lack of discretion and good advisement commonly without respect of time or other due circumstances proceed rashly and unadvisedly therein, and by reason thereof rather hinder than set forward the thing, that is good of itself; it shall therefore be very expedient, that whosoever repaireth hither to read this book, or any such like in any other place, he prepare himself chiefly and principally with all devotion, humility, and quietnes, to be edified and made the better therby, adjoining thereto his perfect and most bounden duty of obedience to the king's majesty, our most gracious and dread sovereign lord, and supreme head, especially in accomplishing his grace's most honourable injunctions and commandments, given and made in that behalf: and right expedient, yea necessary it shall be also, that leaving behind him vain glory, hypocrisy, and all other carnal and corrupt affections, he bring with him descretion, honest intent, charity, reverence, and quiet behaviour to and for the edification of his own soul, without the hindrance, let, or disturbance of any other his christian brother; evermore foreseeing, that no number of people be especially congregate therefore to make a multitude, and that no exposition be made thereupon otherwise than is declared in the book itself; and that especially regard be had, no reading thereof be used, allowed, and with noise in the time of any divine service or sermon, and that in the same be used any disputation, contention, or any other misdemeanour; or finally, that any man justly may regard himself to be offended thereby or take occasion to grudge or malign thereat.[86]

Such precautions were very necessary, for the zeal of some knew no bounds and sometimes caused unpleasant public disturbances. But that such caution should be displayed in allowing the English Bible to the people shows at once what a novel step it was and how enthusiastic at least a certain section of the people was to read and declaim the Scriptures. That enthusiasm itself shows that Bible-reading was something still new and unusual. A generation to whom Bible-reading is an occupation that has been permitted for over three and a half centuries is not likely to be riotous in its enthusiasm.to read the familiar book. At least, we can see no signs of such a tendency.

By 1547, when Henry VIII died (January 28), the reaction against English Bible-reading had become fairly pronounced; Cromwell was no longer alive to champion its cause, and many people were beginning to be disturbed by the unruly attitude of some of the more fanatical reformers.

[86] Wilkins, *Concilia*, III, 863–64.

The Bible was not a fit subject for alehouse brawling. But with the accession of Edward VI the English Bible was again encouraged. The young king himself had asked the Bible to be brought and carried before him at his coronation.[87] During the short reign of Edward VI the printing of the English Bible went on steadily. Reprints of all the versions up to and including the Great Bible were numerous,[88] and injunctions were issued in 1547 requiring that a copy of the Great Bible should be procured by "ecclesiastical persons" and set up within each parish church, together with a copy of the " 'Paraphrasis' of Erasmus also in English upon the Gospels." The injunction further provided that no man ("authorized and licensed thereto") should be discouraged from the reading of the Scriptures either in English or in Latin but that the clergy should rather "conform and exhort every person to read the same, as the very lively word of God, and the special food of man's soul that all Christian persons are bound to embrace, believe and follow, if they look to be saved."[89] In 1548 Bucer and Fagius were "honourably invited into England by repeated letters of the Lord

---

[87] Camden's *Remains* (ed. 1604), p. 229; Strype's *Ecclesiastical Memorials*, II, 35 (from Bale).

[88] *STC* shows sixteen editions of English Bibles between 1549 and 1553, of which seven are "Matthew's" version (two being revised by E. Becke), five are the Great Bible, two are Coverdale's Bible, one is Tyndale's Pentateuch, and one is "the thyrde parte of the byble" (Psalms—Song of Solomon) in the text of Becke's revision of Matthew. There were also ten editions of Tyndale's New Testament (one printed probably in Antwerp) between 1548 and 1553 as well as editions of the New Testament in Coverdale's and the Great Bible version.

[89] Edward Cardwell, *Documentary Annals of the Reformed Church of England* (2d ed.; Oxford, 1844), p. 9; Wilkins, *Concilia*, IV, 4. Wilkins reads "comfort and exhort," with the first edition of Cardwell. Cardwell's second edition reads "conform and exhort."

Protector and Archbishop Cranmer,"[90] the first becoming professor of divinity and the second professor of Hebrew at Cambridge. Cranmer suggested that they should undertake a revision of the English Bible. "As it had been a great while his pious and most earnest desire, that the whole Bible should come abroad in the greatest exactness, and true agreement with the original text: so he laid this work upon these two learned men."[91] Illness, however, prevented them from carrying out this task, after Fagius, who was to do the Old Testament, had already made a start with the Book of Isaiah and Bucer had begun the Gospel of John. Fagius died soon afterward, before he could take up his duties as professor of Hebrew at Cambridge. The only new Bible translation which was done in Edward VI's reign was the rendering of Matthew and part of Mark by Sir John Cheke. This was an entirely individual translation, made from the Greek: it was neither much influenced by, nor had it any influence on, other English versions, remaining unpublished until the middle of the nineteenth century.[92]

Before we proceed to discuss later versions of the Bible, a word must be said about the activity of George Joye, to whose unauthorized revision of Tyndale's New Testament we have already referred.[93] As early as 1531 Joye had brought out at Strasbourg an independent English version of the Book of Isaiah. Only two copies of this are extant, one of which is in the Bodleian and is imperfect, and the other in Cambridge University Library. In 1532, Joye, then

[90] Strype's *Cranmer* (ed. 1812), p. 281.   [91] *Ibid.*

[92] Sir John Cheke's translation was edited by J. Goodwin (Cambridge, 1843).

[93] Above, p. 10.

at Bergen op Zoom, sent two specimen pages of a translation of Genesis to Henry VIII and Anne Boleyn, to try and get a license to translate the whole Bible. In this he was unsuccessful. Joye removed to Antwerp in 1534, and there published his translation of Jeremiah and Lamentations with "the Songe of Moses . . . . added in the ende to magnifye our Lorde for the fall of our Pharao, the Bisshop of Rome." In the same year he published his translation of the Psalms with Martin Emperor at Antwerp. The only extant copy of this is in the Cambridge University Library. An earlier translation of the Psalms, made from the Latin text of Bucer ("Aretinus Felinus"), had appeared in 1530 printed by Francis Foxe. This differs considerably from Joye's version of 1534. In 1539 there appeared "A Paraphrasis vpon all the Psalmes of Dauid, made by Johannes Campensis, reader of the Hebrue lecture in the vniuersitie of Louane, and translated out of Latin into Englysshe" printed by Thomas Gybson. There were also several reprints of the Book of Psalms in the version of the Great Bible. The numerous metrical versions of the Psalms and other parts of the Bible which appeared throughout the sixteenth century do not come within the scope of our inquiry.

The printing of vernacular Bibles in England came to an abrupt stop with the accession to the throne of Mary. But, although the setting-up of Bibles in churches was no longer allowed and those already set up were burned, there was no general proscription of English Bible-reading or any attempt made to prevent individuals from possessing and reading the English Bible in their own homes. No translation of the Bible was mentioned in the proclamation issued against heretical books.[94] No official use of the English Bible was allowed, and no printers were allowed to print English versions; but no more drastic steps seem to have been taken. The official attitude, though now Catholic and orthodox, was not the same as that of the orthodox to the Lollards had been in the previous century. Probably Mary had enough trouble without concerning herself too much with the possession of English Bibles by individuals. But, whether this policy arose from caution or from conscience, it was certainly much less vigorous in its attitude to individual Bible-reading than orthodox policy had been in the past, however severe it was in other matters.

The Marian persecution drove many English Protestants abroad, and in a short time a colony of English Protestant exiles was established at Geneva. It was here that the next step forward in English Bible translation was taken. The first product of the work done at Geneva was a translation of the New Testament by William Whittingham, printed at Geneva by Conrad Badius in 1557. The Preface tells us that this translation was done chiefly for "the simple lambes, which partely are already in the folde of Christ, and so

---

[94] The works of Coverdale and Tyndale were forbidden, but no specific reference is made to the Bible. The "proclamation for restraining books and writings against the Pope" issued in 1555 mentioned "any book or books, writings or works made or set forth by, or in the name of Oecolampadius, Zwinglius, John Calvin, Pomerane, John a Lasco, Bullinger, Bucer, Melancthon, Bernardinus Ochinus, Erasmus Sarcerius, Peter Martyr, Hugh Latimer, Robert Barnes, otherwise called Friar Barnes, John Bale, otherwise called Friar Bale, Justus Jonas, John Hooper, Miles Coverdale, William Tyndall, Tho. Cranmer, late archbishop of Canterbury, William Turner, Theodore Basil, otherwise called Tho. Beacon, John Frith, Roy, and the book commonly called Hale's Chronicle, or any of them in the Latin tongue, Dutch tongue, English tongue, Italian tongue, or French tongue . . . ." (Cardwell, *op. cit.*, I, 198–99).

heare willingly their Shepeherds voyce, and partly wandering astray by ignorance, tary the tyme tyll the Shepherde
fynde them and bring them vnto his flocke." The text, as
the Preface goes on to tell us,

was diligently reuised by the moste approued Greke examples,
and conference of translations in other tonges as the learned may
easely iudge, both by the faithful rendering of the sentence, and
also by the proprietie of the wordes, and perspicuitie of the
phrase. Forthermore that the Reader might be by all meanes prof-
fited, I haue deuided the text into verses and sections, according
to the best editions in other langages and also, as to this day the
ancient Greke copies mencion, it was wont to be vsed. And because the Hebrewe and Greke phrases, which are strange to rendre
in other tongues, and also short, shulde not be so harde, I haue
sometyme interpreted them without any whit diminishing the
grace of the sense, as our langage doth vse them, and sometyme
haue put to that worde, which lacking made the sentence obscure, but haue set it in such letters as may easely be discerned
from the commun text.[95]

Whittingham's translation was scholarly and intelligent,
and his method in many ways similar to that of the Authorized Version translators. The book contained ample
marginal notes, "that both the learned and others might be
holpen: for to my knollage I haue omitted nothing vnex-
pounded, wherby he that is anything exercised in the
Scriptures of God, might iustely complayn of hardeness."
Whittingham's use of italics to translate words not actually
in the original but "which lacking made the sentence obscure"—a practice first adopted by Beza in his New Testament of 1556—was copied by later English versions and by
the Authorized Version, and his division of the chapter into

[95] *The New Testament . . . . at Geneva, Printed by Conrad Badius*, Preface.

verses taken from Etienne's Greek-Latin New Testament (1551) was also adopted by later English translations.

The Bible which appeared at Geneva, printed by Rowland Hall, in 1560, was the final fruits of the work of the Geneva exiles. The translation was made by Whittingham together with Anthony Gilby and Thomas Sampson, and probably others whose names we do not know. Elizabeth had succeeded to the throne in November, 1558, and the company of English Protestants at Geneva had thereupon broken up, many returning home; but "Whittyngham with one or two more, being resolved to go through with the work, did tarry at Geneva an year and an half after Qu. Elizabeth came to the Crown."[96] The "one or two more" were probably Gilby and Sampson.[97] Among those who helped to defray the cost of producing the Geneva Bible was John Bodley, father of Thomas Bodley. John Bodley afterward received from Elizabeth the sole patent to print the Geneva Bible, of which he does not seem to have availed himself.

The New Testament version in the Geneva Bible of 1560 is by no means identical with that published by Whittingham in 1557 but shows much evidence of careful and scholarly revision. The Geneva Bible as a whole is easily the most accurate and scholarly English translation of the Bible before the Authorized Version; the translators were obviously better equipped than any who preceded them and than the translators of the Bishops' Bible, though that was a later version. We shall attempt to prove this, with refer-

[96] Wood's *Ath. Oxon.* (ed. 1691), I, 154.

[97] Anderson, *Annals of the English Bible* (London, 1854), II, 320–21.

ence at least to the Book of Isaiah, when we come to deal
with the purely textual side of English Bible translation.

The Preface to the Geneva Bible gives a detailed statement regarding the aims and methods of the translators.
After referring at some length to "the manifolde and con-
tinual benefites which almightie God bestoweth vpon vs,"
the translators continue:

> To the intent therefore that we may not be vnmyndeful of these
> great mercies, but seke by all meanes (according to our duetie) to
> be thankeful for the same, it behoueth vs so to walke in his feare
> and loue, that all the daies of our life we may procure the glorie
> of his holy name. Now forasmuche as this thing chefely is at-
> teyned by the knollage and practising of the worde of God
> (which is the light to our paths, the keye of the kingdome of
> heauen, our comfort in affliction, our shielde and sworde against
> Satan, the schoole of all wisdome, the glasse wherein we beholde
> Gods face, the testimonie of his fauour, and the only foode and
> nourishment of our soules) we thoght that we colde bestowe our
> labours & studie in nothing which colde be more acceptable to
> God and comfortable to his Churche then in the translating of the
> holy Scriptures into our natiue tongue: the which thing albeit
> that diuers heretofore haue indeuored to atchieue yet considering
> the infancie of those tymes and imperfect knollage of the tongues,
> in respect of this ripe age and cleare light which God hath now
> reueiled, the translations required greatly to be perused and re-
> formed.

Here we have the Protestant view of the importance of
the Bible put at its most vigorous. Concerning their treatment of the text, the translators say:

> Now as we haue chiefely obserued the sense, and laboured
> alwaies to restore it to all integritie, so haue we moste reuerently
> kept the proprietie of the wordes, considering that the Apostles
> who spake and wrote to the Gentiles in the Greke tongue, rather

constrayned them to the liuely phrase of the Ebrewe, then en-
treprised farre by mollifying their langage to speake as the
Gentils did. And for this and other causes we haue in many places
reserued the Ebrewe phrases, notwithstanding that thei may
seeme somewhat hard in their eares that are not wel practised and
also delite in the swete sounding phrases of the holy Scriptures.

The Geneva Bible was printed in roman type, and in both
the Old and the New Testament the chapters were divided
into verses. The division into verses, though it makes for
ease of reference, is in many ways an undesirable feature,
interfering with the continuity of the sense and the run of
the paragraph. As one writer has put it, "The fact that this
was the first Bible to introduce the misleading and injurious
practice [of verse division] is the most serious charge that
can be brought against the masterpiece of Whittingham and
his associates."[98]

The popularity of the Geneva version was assured from
the moment of the publication of the first edition. As well
as being more accurate than former versions, it was issued
in a handy size, in quarto, while most previous English
Bibles had been large and heavy folios. Between 1560 and
1640 ninety-six editions of the complete Geneva Bible were
issued, of which fifty-five appeared before 1600 and eight
after the appearance of the Authorized Version in 1611.
There were also many issues of parts of the Bible in the
Geneva version.

Soon after the accession of Elizabeth the injunction that
the Great Bible was to be set up in the churches was repeated, copying almost verbatim the injunction issued under Edward VI in 1547. The relevant paragraph reads:

[98] Richard Lovett, *The Printed English Bible 1525–1885* (London, 1909), p. 123.

They [the clergy] shall provide within three months next after this visitation, at the charges of the parish, one book of the whole Bible of the largest volume in English; and within one twelve months next after the said visitation, the paraphrases of Erasmus also in English upon the gospel, and the same set up in some convenient place within the said church. . . . . And they shall discourage no man from reading any part of the Bible, either in Latin or in English, but shall rather exhort every person to read the same with great humility and reverence, as the very lively word of God, and the especial food of man's soul, which all Christian persons are bound to embrace, believe and follow, if they look to be saved; thereby they may the better know their duties to God, to their sovereign lady the queen, and their neighbours; ever gently and charitably exhorting them, and in her majesty's name straightly charging and commanding them, that in the reading thereof, no man to reason or contend, but quietly to hear the reader.[99]

It is interesting to note that while the injunction of 1547 had read "they shall discourage no man (authorised and licensed thereto) from the reading any part of the bible," the qualifying phrase was omitted in 1559. The idea that individuals had to be licensed before reading the Bible in English seems by this time to have disappeared for good from the minds of the majority of Englishmen.

Three editions of the Great Bible were printed between 1561 and 1566; the 1566 edition, printed at Rouen by Cardin Hamillon "at the coste and charges of Richard Carmarden," bore on the title-page the phrase "According to the translation apoynted by the Queenes Maiesties Iniunctions to be read in all churches with in her Maiesties Realm," as well as the formula "cum priuilegio" at the foot of the page. But the injunction in favor of the Great Bible did not mean that there was any official opposition to the Geneva

[99] Wilkins, *Concilia*, pp. 182–83.

version, of which, as we have seen, numerous editions continued to be printed throughout the reign. The Calvinist flavor of the Geneva marginal notes cannot, however, have been very pleasing to Archbishop Parker[100] or to the church generally after the Elizabethan settlement. Parker must have realized that the Geneva Bible was far superior as a translation to the Great Bible, and thoughts of a revision of the authorized version, as the Great Bible then was, were natural.

On January 19, 1561, Richard Cox, bishop of Ely, wrote a letter "to the most honorable Sir William Cecill knight Secretary to the Quenes maiestie" which included the following paragraph:

A nother thing ther is worthy to be consydered, the translation of the bible to be committed to mete men and to be vewed ouer and amended. I called apon it in bothe my masters tymes sed frustra. Yet god be praised, ye haue men hable to do it thoroughly. Thus muche I signifie to you because god hath apoynted you a speciall instrumente to the furtheraunce of his heavenly truthe, vnder so gratiouse a soverayn, who I trust doth not mislyke the apologie.[101]

[100] In his letter to Queen Elizabeth accompanying the presentation copy of the Bishops' Bible, Parker referred to the Geneva Bible as containing "diverse preiudicall notis which might have ben well spared" (*Records*, p. 295). See also *ibid.*, pp. 39-40: ". . . . It is highly significant that during Parker's life no edition of the Geneva Bible was printed in England. . . . . He died on May 17, 1575, and the first Geneva New Testament printed in London is dated in this year without specifying the month; we have, however, documentary evidence that Parker was dead before its publication, and there are excellent reasons for placing this in the latter half of the year. It is impossible therefore to avoid the conclusion that to the very end of his life Parker used his control over the Stationers' Company to prevent the Geneva version being printed in England, and also to secûre for Jugge the monopoly of printing the Bishops' Bible."

[101] *Records*, p. 287.

We hear nothing more of the new version until 1566, when Archbishop Parker wrote to Cecil, saying that he had "destributed the bible in partes to dyuerse men," and would like him, "yf ye could spare so moche leysur eyther in mornyng or evenyng" to take a small part in the work by looking over "one epistle of S. Paul or Peter, or Jamys."[102] Strype gives a summary of other correspondence on the subject by bishops engaged in the work.[103] Finally, on September 22, 1568, Parker wrote to Cecil to announce the completion of the work:

. . . . Sir, after much toyle of the Printer and sum Labors taken of sum parties for the setting owte and Recognising of the Englishe bible, we be nowe come to a conclusion for the substance of the booke. Sum ornamentes of the same be yet lacking, prayeng your Honor to beare in pacience till yt be fully reedy. I do meane by gods grace, yf my health will serve me better than yt is at this tyme, to present the Quenes highnes with the first, as sone as I can here her Maiestie to be come to Hampton Courte which we here will be within eight or nyne dayes.[104]

On October 5, 1568, Parker sent Cecil a copy of the new version to present to the queen, inclosing a letter to accompany the Bible:

. . . . pleaseth yt your highnes to accept in good parte, the endevor and diligence, of sum of vs your chapleins, my brethren the Bisshoppes, with other certaine Learned men, in this newe edicion of the bible, I trust by comparisone of divers translacions put forth in your realme will apeare as well the workemanshippe of the printer, as the Circumspeccion of all such as have traveiled in the recognicion. Amonge divers observacions which have bin regarded in this recognition one was, not to make yt varye much

---

[102] *Ibid.*, p. 288.

[103] *Life and Acts of Matthew Parker* (Oxford, 1821), I, 415–17.

[104] *Records*, pp. 291–92.

from that translacion which was comonlye vsed by Publike order, except wher eyther the verytie of the hebrue & greke moved alteracion, or wher the text was by sum negligence mutilated from the originall. So that I trust your Loving subiectes shall se good cause in your Maiesties dayes to thanke god, and to reioyce, to see this his treasor of his holy worde, so set oute, as may be proved . . . . to be faithfully handeled in the vulgar tonge, besechinge your highnes, that yt may have your gracious favor, License and proteccion to be com[un]icated abrode, aswell for that in many Churches they want their bookes, and have longe tyme loked for this: as for that in certaine places be publikely vsed sum translations which have not byn Labored in your Realme having inspersed diverse preiudicall notis which might have ben also well spared.[105]

Parker sent to Cecil at the same time a list of the translators and a note of the "observations respected of the translators," so that we have considerable external evidence for determining the methods of this version.

The Bishops' Bible, as the version came to be called, was first printed in 1568 by Richard Jugge in a handsome folio volume. Twenty-two editions were printed between 1568 and 1602, when the last edition appeared. Between 1602 and 1611 the Geneva Bible enjoyed unchallenged supremacy. A comparison of the number of editions of the Geneva Bible issued with those of the Bishops' Bible will show at once how far behind the latter version lagged in popularity.[106] That the Bishops' Bible should have failed to oust

---

[105] *Ibid.*, p. 294.

[106] It is, however, rash to judge the popularity of each Bible by such a standard alone. "How far this superiority [of the Geneva Bible] was the result of demand, how far it was produced by a control of the supply, is a question which, difficult as it is to answer, deserves more attention than it has received. It is clear, on the one hand, that during Parker's life the circulacion of the Geneva version was artificially

its predecessor is not surprising. The version was a combination of the work of different revisers, subject to little general discipline and no real general editorship. Thus it is very patchy; some parts are much better done than others. So this further step forward in the preparation of an authorized version still left room for further advance. Throughout the rest of the century the Bishops' Bible fought a losing battle with the Geneva version, and this fact soon made obvious the necessity of still another revision. Subsequent editions of the Bishops' Bible show a certain amount of revision, but not sufficient to change the character of the translation.

The next English version to appear was out of the main current of English Bible translation. This was the Roman Catholic translation, of which the New Testament appeared at Rheims in 1582 and the Old Testament at Douai in 1609–10. The moving spirit in the preparation of this version was Cardinal Allen, president of the English College at Rheims—the college had removed from Douai to Rheims in 1578 on account of the expulsion order against English residents issued by the magistrates in that year[107]—and a distinguished Bible scholar. Allen, in a letter to Dr. Vende-

---

barred, and nothing was done to popularise its rival. It is clear, I think, also, that from the death of Parker to the appointment of Whitgift, the positions were reversed, and that in these years the Geneva version, which was not only favoured, but pushed, by the aid of Walsingham and his friends . . . . was put on the market in such quantities as to give it a real hold on the English people" (*ibid.*, pp. 44–45). But this hardly explains the popularity of the Geneva Bible between 1602 and 1611.

[107] *The First and Second Diaries of the English College at Douai, Edited by the Fathers of the Congregation of the London Oratory, with an Historical Introduction by T. F. Knox* . . . . (London, 1878), Introd., pp. li–liii.

ville, regius professor of canon law at Douai, dated September 15, 1578, explained how the Catholic preachers were at a disadvantage compared with the Protestant, who were familiar with the English Bible and did not therefore require to translate extempore from the Vulgate when preaching to a popular audience. The Catholic preacher was liable to stumble in his English renderings, which would make a bad impression on his hearers:

. . . . In quo genere vel imperiti alioquin haeretici multis doctoribus catholicis saepe praestant, quod hi in academiis et scholis educati non habent ferre Scripturae textum nec allegant nisi latinum, quem cum pro concione indocta coguntur mox in vulgarem linguam vertere, quia statim alicujus versionis vulgaris verba non sunt aut non accurunt, saepe parum accomodate et non sine ingrata haesitatione transferunt; ubi adversarii ad unguem tenent ex haeretica aliqua versione omnia Scripturae loca quae pro ipsis facere videantur, et quadam composita fraude ac mutatione sacrorum verborum efficiunt tendem ut nihil loqui videantur nisi ex Bibliis. Cui malo utrinque mederi possit, si et nos haberemus aliquam catholicam versionem Bibliorum; omnes enim anglicae versiones sunt corruptissimae. Quales in Belgio vestro habeatis nescio; certe nos si sua Sanctitas faciendum judicabit, id etiam agemus ut fideliter, pure et genuine secundum approbatam ecclesiae editionem Biblia vertantur; cum ad hanc rem viros jam habeamus aptissimos. Licet enim optandum esset fortasse ut nunquam in barbaras linguas Scripturae verterentur, tamen cum tanta sint hodie vel ex haeresi vel aliunde curiositas hominum etiam non malorum et saepe etiam propter confutationem adversariorum legendi necessitas, satius est ut fidelem et catholicam habeant translationem, quam aut cum periculo aut ad perditionem quorundam locorum lectione commodis quibusdam annotationibus occurri possit.[108]

---

[108] *The Letters and Memorials of William Cardinal Allen* (1532–1594), *Edited by the Fathers of the Congregation of the English Catholics of the London Oratory, with an Historical Introduction by Francis Knox* (London, 1882), pp. 64–65.

This letter throws a very clear light on the motives that prompted the English Catholic version. Although it were perhaps better that no translation into "barbaras linguas" were made, yet the disadvantages the Catholic cause suffered by not having an English version while the Protestants had, were sufficient to overrule the traditional objections to vernacular versions.

Although Cardinal Allen (cardinal from 1587) seems to have been the main force behind the Rheims translation, most of the work was done by Gregory Martin, who had been a fellow of St. John's College, Oxford, and was a considerable scholar.[109] He spent some time at the English College at Douai after his conversion to Catholicism and eventually settled at Rheims as a lecturer in divinity. A marginal note in the second *Douai Diary* reads as follows:

Octobris 16 vel circiter D. licent. Martinus Bibliorum versionem in Anglicum sermonem auspicatus est; ut sic tandem haereticorum corruptionibus, quibus jamdiu misere toti fere populo patriae nostrae imposuerunt, saluberrime obviaretur: et ut opus istud, ut speratur longe utile, citius prodeat, ipse *ver*tendo quotidie duo capita absolvit; ut autem emendatius, eadem ipsa capita praeses noster D. Alanus et Mr n. D. Bristous diligenter perlegunt, atque etiam, si *quidquid alicubi dig*num videatur, pro sua sapientia fideliter corrigunt.[110]

The Rheims New Testament was printed by John Fogny in 1582, the title-page reading:

The Newe Testament of Iesvs Christ, translated faithfvlly into English, out of the authentical Latin, according to the best cor-

[109] J. G. Carleton, *The Part of Rheims in the Making of the English Bible* (Oxford, 1902), p. 18. Martin seems to have had some knowledge of Hebrew as well as Greek. There are references to his lecturing in Hebrew in the *Douai Diaries, passim.*

[110] *Douai Diaries*, ed. Knox, p. 154. The italicized words have been clipped from the manuscript and are conjecturally supplied by Knox.

rected copies of the same, diligently conferred with the Greeke and other editions in diuers languages: With Argvments of books and chapters, Annotations, and other necessarie helpes, for the better vnderstanding of the text, and specially for the discouerie of the Corrvptions of diuers late translations, and for cleering the Controversies in religion, of these daies. . . .

The Preface treats "of these three points: of the translation of Holy Scriptures into the vulgar tongues, and namely [especially] into English; of the causes why this New Testament is translated according to the auncient vulgar Latin text: & of the maner of translating the same." The heads of the argument, as given in the margin, are as follows:

Translation of the Scriptures into the vulgar tongues, not absolutely necessarie or profitable, but according to the time.

Many causes why this new Testament is translated according to the auncient vulgar Latin text. It is most auncient. Corrected by S. Hierom. Commended by S. Augustine. Vsed and expounded by the fathers. Only authenticated by the holy Council of Trent. Most grave, least partial. Precise in following the Greek. Preferred by Beza himself. All the rest misliked of the Sectaries themselves, eche reprehending another. It is truer than the vulgar Greek text itself.

Certain wordes not English nor yet familiar in the English tongue. Amen. Alleluia. Parascene. Pasche, Azymes.

Why we say *our Lord*, not *the Lord* (but in certaine cases). See the Annotations 1. Tim. 6 . . . .

Catholike termes proceding from the very text of Scripture.

Certain hard speaches and phrases.

The Protestants presumptuous boldnes and libertie in translating.

And there are others dealing with purely textual matters.

These marginal heads give a very fair idea of the point of view of the translators and the subjects they thought necessary to discuss in their prefaces. Their attitude is elaborated in the Preface to the Douai Old Testament.

The Rheims New Testament, though not in the direct line of English biblical versions, nor yet one of the texts recommended to the translators of the Authorized Version, had yet a considerable influence on the phraseology of the Authorized Version of the New Testament.[111] The Douai Old Testament has less to recommend it and had very little if any influence on the Authorized Version. Both the Rheims and the Douai Bibles contain controversial marginal notes.

The Rheims Preface had begun with a reference to "the old Testament lying by vs for lacke of good meanes to publish the whole in such sort as a worke of so great charge and importance requireth." It was not until 1609 that the first volume of the Old Testament was brought out, at Douai.[112] The second volume, from Psalms to Esdras, appeared in the following year.

The Douai Old Testament bore the title "The Holie Bible faithfvlly translated into English ovt, of the avthentical Latin. Diligently conferred with the Hebrew, Greeke, and other Editions in diuers languages." Like the Rheims New Testament, it was a translation from the Vulgate, and the Preface again explains why the translators thought fit to translate from the Vulgate rather than the original Hebrew text. They repeat the medieval charge that "both the Hebrew and Greke Editions are fouly corrupted by Iewes." To explain the differences between the secondary version

---

[111] See Carleton's detailed analysis, *op. cit.*, and Westcott, *History of the English Bible* (3d ed., revised by W. Aldis Wright, 1905), p. 106.

[112] The English were invited back to Douai within eight months of their expulsion (*Douai Diaries*, Introd., liv), but the college did not return until 1593.

and the original in such a fashion could hardly have been a convincing argument even in the sixteenth century.[113]

An edition of the Rheims New Testament was brought out together with the Bishops' version in parallel columns by W. Fulke in 1589, with a second edition in 1601, the object being to show the faults in the translation and to confute "all such annotations that conteine manifest impietie." The Rheims Testament was reprinted at Antwerp in 1600 and in 1621 and at Rouen in 1633. The second edition of the Douai Old Testament did not appear until 1635 at Rouen.

Meanwhile the standard English translation was still nominally the Bishops' Bible. But it had not secured the popularity due to an authorized version. Jugge had, through Parker's influence, secured the monopoly of printing it,[114] and this does not seem to have helped to increase the circulation. There is little doubt that Parker did not go out of his way to encourage the circulation of the Bishops' Bible among private readers. In 1577 the complete monopoly of English Bible printing was granted to Christopher Parker.[115]

The position at the beginning of the seventeenth century

[113] Cartwright, in his *Answere to the Preface of the Rhemish Translation* (1602), called vigorous attention to the curious attitude of the Catholic translators on this point—"the defacing and dis-authorizing of the Scriptures, as it were taking from them their girdle or garter of honour, by a false surmise of corruption in them, in the languages wherein they were first written" (H. Cotton, *Rhemes and Douay* [Oxford, 1855], p. 21).

[114] See above, p. 55, n. 100. Jugge later compromised with the other London printers and retained the sole right to print the Bible in quarto and the New Testament in sixteens.

[115] The history of the printing of the Bible at this time is discussed fully by Pollard in his Introduction to *Records*, pp. 40–45. Cf. also the documents relating to English Bible printing in *ibid.*, pp. 313–29.

was that, while the Bishops' Bible was used in churches as the official version, the translation most used by the people at home was the Geneva. This was obviously an unsatisfactory state of affairs. It was not, however, until the Hampton Court Conference of 1604 that proposals for a new revision began to be acted upon.[116] The suggestion came from the leader of the Puritan deputation, Dr. John Rainolds (Reynolds), president of Corpus Christi College, Oxford, and dean of Lincoln. The fullest contemporary account of the proceedings at the Hampton Court Conference is given by William Barlow, dean of Chester, in his book, *The Svmme and Svbstance of the Conference, Which, It Pleased His Excellent Maiestie To Haue with the Lords, Bishops, and Other of His Clergie . . . . in His Maiesties Priuy-Chamber, at Hampton Court. January 14. 1603.*[117] Dr. Rainolds, after making some general complaints which were resented by the Bishop of London and by the Dean of St. Paul's,

moued his Maiesty, that there might be a new *translation* of the *Bible*, because, those which were allowed in the raignes of *Henry* the eight, and *Edward* the sixt, were corrupt and not aunswerable

[116] There is extant an undated draft (Brit. Mus. Add. MS 34729, fol. 77) for an act of Parliament for a new version of the Bible, belonging to the latter part of the reign of Elizabeth. It is headed, "An act for the reducing of diversities of Bibles now extant in the English tongue to one settled vulgar translated from the originall." The question of a further revision was raised many times between the first publication of the Bishops' Bible and 1604. E.g., we find the following statement in Hugh Broughton's *Epistle to the Learned Nobilitie of England Touching the Translation of the Bible* (Middleburg, 1597): "Wherefore they must lay their hande vpon their mouth, that say, the Queene will not haue the translation bettered. Her maiesties footemen knowe that shee sent an othergates worde to Sir *Francis Walsingham* euen to consider of furthering the matter: and Bishop Elmer [Aylmer, bishop of London] the best Ebrician of all the Bishops, was very earnest with my selfe to take the matter in hande . . . ." (p. 16).

[117] I.e., 1604 New Style.

to the truth of the Originall. . . . . To which motion, there was, at the present, no gainsaying, the obiections being triuiall and old, and already, in print, often answered; only, my Lord of *London* wel added, that if euery mans humor should be followed, there would be no ende of translating. . . . . Whereopon his Highnesse wished, that some especiall pains should be taken in that behalf for one vniforme translation (professing that he could neuer, yet, see a Bible well translated in Englisshe; but the worst of all, his Maiestie thought the *Geneua* to be) and this to be done by the best learned in both the Vniuersities, after them to be reuiewed by the Bishops, and the chiefe learned of the Church; from them to be presented to the *Priuy Councell;* and lastly to bee ratified by his *Royall authority;* and so this whole Church to be bound vnto it, and none other: Marry, withal, he gaue this caueat (vpon a word cast out by my Lord of London) that no marginall notes should be added, hauing found in them, which are annexed to the *Geneua* translation (which he saw in a Bible giuen him by an English Lady) some notes very partiall, vntrue, seditious, and sauouring, too much, of dangerous, and trayterous conceipts. . . . . And so concludeth this point, as all the rest, with a graue and iudicious aduise.[118]

The proposal once taken up by the king, it was not long before active steps were taken toward the preparation of the new revision. On June 30 of the same year Bishop Bancroft wrote:

His Majesty being made acquainted with the choice of all them to be employed in the translating of the Bible, in such sort as Mr Lively [professor of Hebrew at Cambridge] can inform you, doth greatly approve of the said choice. And for as much as his Highness is very desirous that the same so religious a work should admit of no delay, he has commanded me to signify unto you in

---

[118] *The Summe and Substance of the Conference* . . . . pp. 45–47. We can hardly take the report of the king's speech given by Barlow as accurate. James must have been familiar with the Geneva Bible from his youth, and would not require "an English lady" to draw his attention to it.

his name that his pleasure is, you should with all possible speed meet together in your University and begin the same.[119]

On July 31 we find Bishop Bancroft circulating among the other bishops a letter from the king to the effect that he (the king) had "appointed certain learned men, to the number of four and fifty, for the translating of the Bible" for whose maintenance the bishops were to help to provide by taking note whenever there was a vacancy of "any prebend or parsonage, being rated in our book of taxations, the prebend to twenty pound at the least and the parsonage to the like sum and upwards," and refraining from filling it until the king had recommended "for the same some such of the learned men, as we shall think fit to be preferred unto it." The king's letter continues:

Furthermore we require you, to move all our bishops to inform themselves of all such learned men within their several dioceses, as having especial skill in the Hebrew and Greek tongues, have taken pains, in their private studies of the scriptures, for the clearing of any obscurities either in the Hebrew or in the Greek, or touching any difficulties or mistakings in the former English translation, which we have now commanded to be thoroughly viewed and amended, and thereupon to write unto them, earnestly charging them, and signifying our pleasure therein, that they send such their observations either to Mr Lively, our Hebrew reader in Cambridge, or to Dr Harding, our Hebrew reader in Oxford, or to Dr Andrews, dean of Westminster, to be imparted to the rest of their several companies; so that our said intended translation may have the help and furtherance of all our principal learned men within this our kingdom.[120]

[119] Anderson, *op. cit.*, I, 372.

[120] *Records*, pp. 331–33. Bancroft was in charge, as the see of Canterbury was vacant.

On the same day Bancroft wrote to the bishops, drawing their attention to the clause in the king's letter referring to the filling of vacancies and asking them also to contribute to the costs of the translation. To this appeal there does not seem to have been any response.

There is extant a list of the translators as well as a list of the rules to be observed in the translation. These will both be discussed in some detail when we come to consider the text of this version[121] in our final chapter. The translators are grouped into six companies: one from "Westminster," to translate the Pentateuch and the rest of the Old Testament from Joshua to II Kings; one from Cambridge, to translate from I Chronicles to Ecclesiastes; one from Oxford, to translate the major prophets, Lamentations, and the twelve minor prophets; one from Cambridge, to translate the Prayer of Manasses and the rest of the Apocrypha; one from Oxford, to translate the Four Gospels, the Acts of the Apostles, and the Apocalypse; and one from Westminster, to translate the rest of the New Testament. The number of translators mentioned by the king was fifty-four, but we have the names of only forty-seven. The choice was catholic and intelligent on the whole, including most of the ablest men available, whether High Church or Puritan. Militant Puritans, however, such as Hugh Broughton, were excluded.

The methods of the translators we shall discuss later, but we may mention here that Dr. John Boys, who was one of those intrusted with the translation of the Apocrypha, is

---

[121] Popularly known, of course, as the "King James" or the "authorized" Version.

said by his biographer, Dr. Anthony Walker, to have worked in the following manner:

> All the time he was about his own part, his commons were given him at St John's; where he abode all the week, till Saturday night; and then went home to discharge his cure [at Boxworth]: returning thence on Monday morning. When he had finished his own part, at the earnest request of him to whom it was assigned, he undertook a second; and then he was in commons in another college. . . . .
>
> Four years were spent in this first service; at the end whereof the whole work being finished, and three copies of the whole Bible sent from Cambridge, Oxford and Westminster to London; a new choice was to be made of six[122] in all, two out of every company, to review the whole worke; and extract one [copy] out of all three, to be committed to the presse.
>
> For the dispatch of which business Mr Downes and Mr Bois were sent for to London. Where meeting (though Mr Downes would not go till he was either fetcht or threatned with a pursivant) their four fellow labourers, they went dayly to Stationers Hall, and in three-quarters of a year, finished their task. All which time they had from the Company of Stationers XXX[s] [each] per week[123] duly paid them: tho' they had nothing before but the self-rewarding, ingenious industry. Whilst they were imployed in this last businesse, he and he only, took notes of their proceedings: which notes he kept till his dying day.[124]

The report of the English delegates to the Synod of Dort also throws light on the activity of the translators. The

---

[122] As there were two groups each at Cambridge, Oxford, and Westminster, "two out of every company" would have meant twelve, nòt six. Two from each center must be meant.

[123] This sum—amounting to £702 for a board of twelve for "three quarters of a year"—could not possibly have been paid by the Stationers' Company. For a discussion of the payment of the revisers see *Records*, pp. 56–58.

[124] *Ibid.*, pp. 55–56.

English delegates included Samuel Ward, also, like Boys and Downes, one of the revisers of the Apocrypha. After explaining how the work was divided up, the report goes on to state that

Reverendissimus Episcopus Wintoniensis, Bilsonus, una cum Doctore Smitho, nunc Episcopo Glocestriensi, viro eximio, et ab initio in toto hoc opere versatissimo, omnibus mature pensitatis & examinatis extremam manum huic versioni imposuerunt.[125]

The report concludes with a list of eight rules laid down for the translators.

Selden has an interesting paragraph on the method of the translators:

The English Translacion of The bible is the best Translacion in the world and rend[r]s The Sence of the Originall best, takeing in for the English Translacion; The Bishops Bible as well as King James. The Translacion in King James time tooke an excellent way; That parte of the Bible was given to him who was most excellent in such a Tounge (as the Apocripha to Andrew Downes) and then they meet together; and one read The translacion The Rest holding in their hands some Bible either of The learned Tongues or ffrench, Spanish,Italian &c.—if they found any fault They speake if not he read on.[126]

The revision was completed by 1611, in which year it was issued in a handsome folio volume, the title reading:

The Holy Bible, Conteyning the Old Testament, and the New: Newly Translated out of the Originall tongues: & with the former Translations diligently compared and reuised: by his Maiesties speciall Commandement. Appointed to be read in Churches. Imprinted at London by Robert Barker, Printer to the Kings most Excellent Maiestie. Anno Dom. 1611.

[125] *Ibid.*, p. 337.
[126] *Table Talk of John Selden*, ed. F. Pollock (London, 1927), p. 10.

As far as we can tell, there was no real justification for the phrase "appointed to be read in churches." Later editions of the Bishops' Bible (from 1585 to the last in 1602) had borne the words "authorised and appointed to be read in churches"; and the folio of 1584 bore the phrase "Of that translation authorised to be read in Churches," but earlier editions had only "set forth by authority," and the phrase that was used in the later editions of the Bishops' Bible seems to have been warranted only by some lukewarm canons passed by the province of Canterbury in 1571.[127] The only version which had actually been appointed to be read in churches by royal command was, as we have seen, the Great Bible; but no injunction requiring the Bishops' Bible to be read in churches was ever passed by royal proclamation. Parker had, indeed, in his letter to Cecil accompanying the presentation copy for the queen, expressed the wish that "yf your honor wold obteine of the Queens highnes, that the edicion might be Licensed and only comended in publike reading in Churches, to drawe to one vniformitie, yt weare no greate cost to the most parishes and a Relief to him for his great charges susteined."[128] But

---

[127] E.g., "Quivis archiepiscopus et episcopus habebit domi suae sacra Biblia in amplissimo volumine, uti nuperrime Londini excusa sunt, et plenam illam historiam, quae inscribitur 'Monumenta martyrum' et alios quosdam similes libros ad religionem appositos" (E. Cardwell, *Synodalia* . . . . [Oxford, 1842], I, 115). Here the Bible is lumped together with Foxe's Book of Martyrs "et alios quosdam similes libros." And, later: "Curabunt etiam ut sacra Biblia sint in singulis ecclesiis in amplissimo volumine (si commode fieri possit) qualia nunc nuper Londini excusa sunt, ut liber publicarum precum, ut sacrae homiliae, quae nuper scriptae sunt contra rebellionem, sint in singulis ecclesiis" (*ibid.*, p. 123). Note the parenthetical phrase "if it can conveniently be managed," and contrast the tone of Henry VIII's proclamation.

[128] *Records*, p. 293.

no proclamation parallel to those of 1541, 1547, or 1559—
all of which commanded the Great Bible to be set up in
churches, providing penalties for omission to do so—was
issued with reference to the Bishops' Bible. Nevertheless,
the phrase "authorised to be read in Churches" had appeared in the later editions of the Bishops' Bible—and if the
canons passed by the province of Canterbury provided
"authorization" in any real sense the phrase was justified—
so the version of 1611, replacing the Bishops' Bible, naturally took over its claims.

But the word "authorised" does not occur on the title-
page of the 1611 Bible. "Appointed" is the word used, and
all this presumably meant was, as Pollard points out, "assigned" or "provided," so that the words "Appointed to
be read in Churches"' "literally expressed the facts that this
Bible was printed by the King's printer with the approval
of the King and the Bishops for use in churches, and that no
competing edition 'of the largest volume' was allowed to
be published."[129] And whatever theoretical authorization
the 1611 version may have lacked, it was the first English
Bible translation to have been initiated at a conference sum-
moned by the king and to have awakened the king's active
interest to the extent that it did. However eager Henry
VIII may have been to support English versions of the Bible
for personal and political reasons, he never for a moment
showed any interest in the inception and progress of any of
the translations that appeared in his reign, as James did in
the case of the 1611 Bible. But, apart from all this, the
superior merits of the 1611 Bible soon won for it a position
in the country which was as high as any authorization

[129] *Ibid.*, p. 60.

could have effected, and much higher than authorization could have effected had the translation been less successful. Nevertheless, it is as well to remember that the "Authorized Version" has never been authorized, as the Great Bible was in its day.

The Preface to the 1611 Bible, a fine piece of Elizabethan prose, begins with a general survey of the perversity of human affairs, whereby "the best things haue been calumniated," and proceeds, after giving many examples, from biblical and classical history, of noble persons whose good works brought them only infamy, to refer to the king's "constancie, notwithstanding calumniation, for the suruey of the English translations." Then follows "the praise of the holy Scriptures" which exceeds the Preface to the Geneva Bible in fervor and eloquence. It is the Protestant view of the Bible as the one source and origin of all good—a view whose beginnings we can trace in the writings of Wyclif and the activities of the Lollards in the fourteenth and fifteenth centuries—expressed finally and officially. No longer are safeguards and qualifications necessary before laymen can be allowed to read the Bible: from the reading of such a book can come nothing but good, in view of its nature and purpose. First come quotations from the Church Fathers in praise of the Bible and then the translators themselves take up the praise in an eloquent and picturesque passage.

A comparison of this preface with the Preface to the Douai Old Testament, which appeared only two years before, shows with startling clearness the different point of view with regard to the reading of the Bible reached by the professors of the reformed religion. Still more uncompromising is the attitude of the translators to Bible translation, and the Preface continues with an eloquent plea for "remooving the cover of the well." "How shall men meditate in that, which they cannot understand?" The question, like the answer, is rooted in Protestant individualism.

The Preface continues with a review of early translations of the Bible into Greek and Latin, then proceeds to refer to the views of the Fathers on Bible translation, following this with some controversial matter against "our chiefe Aduersaries." There follows an account of "the purpose of the Translators, with their number, furniture, care, &c." The Preface concludes with a technical discussion of the purpose of the marginal notes and a final exhortation to the reader.

The Preface is preceded by a dedication "to the most High and Mightie Prince, Iames by the grace of God King of Great Britaine, France and Ireland, Defender of the Faith, &c," a piece of writing as fulsome as dedications of the time usually were, for some reason still printed in modern editions of the Authorized Version. Tables, calendars, and similar apparatus follow the Preface. The title-page[130] was engraved by Cornelius Boel of Antwerp and is an elaborate piece of work showing various figures from the Old Testament and the New in allegorical postures, with a picture of the pelican feeding her young at the foot. The text is in black letter—a sharp, clear-cut type—with the words which today are printed in italics inserted in small roman type, as had been done also in the Bishops' Bible, though there the additional words were more numerous and often needlessly periphrastic. There are two columns to the

---

[130] This description refers to the title-page of the *first* of the two issues of 1611. The title-page of the second is a wood cut, much simpler in design.

page, inclosed within rules, with frequent decorations and type ornaments throughout.

There are various bibliographical problems connected with the first issue of the Authorized Version. Two separate issues, each bearing the date 1611, differ from each other in many small details. Of these differences the best known are the two readings in Ruth 3:15, where one issue reads "he went into the city," the other reading, correctly, "she went into the city." The "he"-Bible is most probably the earlier: unlike the "she"-Bible it is homogeneous, while the latter "is made up in a very remarkable manner, not only with reprints, but . . . . it is often mixed with the other Issue, with the preliminary leaves of 1613, 1617, and 1634."[131] The bibliographical problems connected with the first two editions of the Authorized Version are more complicated than this, but to enter into a discussion of them is no part of this study.[132] Our survey of the progress of English Bible translation from Tyndale to 1611 concludes with recording and describing the first issue of the "Authorized" or "King James" Version.

[131] Francis Fry, *A Description of the Large Folio Editions of the Authorised Version* (London and Bristol, 1865). Fry's conclusions were disputed by F. A. H. Scrivener (*The Authorised Edition of the English Bible* [Cambridge, 1884], pp. 5 ff.). But an article by W. E. Smith ("The Great 'She' Bible," *Library*, II [1890], 1–11, 96–102, 141–43) showed *inter alia* that Scrivener's method was unable to produce conclusive arguments, and later bibliographers accept the priority of the "he"-Bible as an established fact. Scrivener (Appen. B) gives a useful list of the variant readings in the two issues of 1611, and Fry has a facsimile collation of some interesting differences.

[132] For a summary of the problems and their suggested solution see *Records*, pp. 66–74.

CHAPTER II

BIBLE translation in England between the time of Wyclif and 1611 was mainly the product of two forces: the "back to the Bible" movement of the reformers and the disinterested scholarship that is a feature of the Renaissance. We have given some attention to the first of these two forces in its relation to Bible translation; it now remains to discuss the relation between humanism and the new attitude to the Bible, the growth of Greek and Hebrew scholarship in Europe, and the equipment of the English translators for their task.

Humanism in its first phase had no connection with Bible translation. The Italian humanists from Petrarch to Politian, as well as later in the more decadent days, never thought of employing their classical knowledge on the sources of Christianity, except in the attack on the Donation of Constantine begun by Laurentius Valla in 1440. Italian humanism in its most characteristic phase was pagan in spirit, devoting its energies to the re-creation of classical civilization. When Sadoleto turned his attention to Paul's epistles, to publish eventually a commentary on the Epistle to the Romans, Bembo reprimanded him for occupying himself with such trifling affairs, which would only corrupt his style. Study of the Bible is the last activity to be associated with Lorenzo de Medici's circle or with Pope Leo X— though Lorenzo's circle did include Pico della Mirandola, who acquired a knowledge of Hebrew and interested himself in Jewish cabalistic lore. Neither in its earlier nor in its later phases did humanism in Italy concern itself with the Bible.

But once humanism had crossed the Alps it changed greatly in tone. It was in northern Europe that the Renaissance became implicated in the Reformation, and the "New Learning" became an instrument in the hands of the reformers. The work of Reuchlin and Erasmus had implications for the history of religion and for the study of the text of the Bible that were totally absent from the work of Bembo or Manuzio or any other of the host of Italian scholars of the time. And this was because the northern scholars were at the same time more disinterested as scholars and more alive to the practical issues of their day. Their scholarship was not the handmaid of a neopaganism, and in this sense it was disinterested; nor was it isolated from contemporary life to dwell in a world of make-believe, as the work of the Italian humanists inclined to be.

In Germany particularly the influence of the Renaissance on the Reformation was evident. The activity of Reuchlin made him, against his own will, the center of a controversy where the new and the old ideas in religion were fiercely pitted against each other, though the new was not yet always identified with any split from the unity of Western Christendom. But we can see from the *Epistolae obscurorum virorum* how scholarship found itself in the camp opposed alike to obscurantism, ignorance, and religious conservatism. Erasmus—who cannot be taken to represent any one country, for, born though he was in Holland, his work had little connection with his native land, where he spent but a small part of his life—applied his scholarship to the text of the New Testament and of the writings of the Fathers and interested himself actively in the question whether the Bible should be translated into vernacular tongues. In the observations on the necessity for Bible translation scattered throughout his works we have the first clear indication that in this one respect humanism had led to the same point of view as the heretical movements which had sought the foundations of Christianity exclusively in the text of the Bible. Tyndale was no humanist in the popular sense of the word, though he was a considerable scholar and had imbibed much of the New Learning: his translation[1] of Erasmus' *Exhortation to the Diligent Study of Scripture* shows the affinity that one side of Erasmus' work had with the ideas of reformers such as Tyndale. The following extract from the *Exhortation* shows where humanist and reformer agreed:

I wold desire that all women shuld reade the gospell and Paules epistles/ and I wold to god they were translated in to the tonges of all men/ So that they might not only be read/ and knowne/ of the scotes and yryshmen/ But also of the Turkes and saracenes/ Truly it is one degre to good livinge/ yee the first (I had almoste sayde the cheffe) to have a little sight in the scripture/ though it be but a grosse knowledge/ and not yet consummatte (Be it in case that some wold laugh at it/ yee and that shuld erre and be deceaved) I wold to god/ the plowman wold singe a texte of the scripture at his plowbeme/ And that the wever at his lowme/ with this wold drive away the tediousness of tyme. I wold the wayfaringe man with this pastyme/ wold expelle the werynes of his iorney. And to be shorte I wold that all the communication of the christen shuld be of the scripture/ for in a maner soch are we oure selves/ as oure daylye tales are. . . . .[2]

[1] The translation may be by William Roy, Tyndale's secretary.

[2] *An Exhortation to the Diligent Studye of Scripture Made by Erasmus Roterdamus. And Translated into Inglissh* ([Antwerp], 1529).

Tyndale used almost the same words in putting the claims of scripture against those of the pope. The simple fact is that the scholarship of the humanists— the New Learning—had made it possible for the dreams of early heretics to be realized to a degree that the original advocates of Bible translation had not contemplated. The rise of Greek studies had made it possible for the original text of the New Testament to be examined, and even emended, before a translation was undertaken; and, together with the great improvement in Latin studies, it also made possible a new critical approach to the Vulgate. Similarly, the new Hebrew scholarship laid open the Old Testament in the original, and for the first time Christian translators did not have to depend entirely on the Vulgate. The present chapter being preliminary to a particular study of the Authorized Version of the Old Testament, the rise of Hebrew scholarship and the Hebrew learning of the translators is of more concern here than the progress of Greek studies, whose story has so often been told. But, that our survey may not lack perspective, a word must be said about the development of Greek scholarship in Europe before we proceed to discuss in more detail the study of Hebrew.

From the fifth century onward knowledge of classical Greek in western Europe rapidly declined. It formed no part of the university curriculum in the Middle Ages, as a rule, or of the corpus of knowledge acquired by the normal medieval scholar. It was studied in a few monasteries and by individual scholars, and occasional attempts were made to provide regular teaching, as the proposal of the Council of Vienne in 1312 to establish chairs of Greek in several universities. In England there were a few scholars who attained to some proficiency in Greek. There are traces, quite early, of a Greek learning in England which, however, was almost extinct by the seventh century, but which was revived in the eighth when it reached a comparatively high level. Aldhelm, bishop of Sherborne, and Tobias, bishop of Rochester, were known as eminent scholars, while the Venerable Bede must have been the most learned man not only of his own generation but of the generations immediately preceding and succeeding. And on the Continent at this time there were individuals who are credited with at least some knowledge of Greek. Charlemagne was reputed to have been able to read Greek, though not to speak it, and the same is told of Louis the Debonair.[3] Charlemagne wished to restore Greek, in order to facilitate intercourse with the East, as one of his capitularies testifies. But nothing seems to have been achieved as a result.

None of the scholars we have mentioned could have had more than a superficial knowledge of Greek at most. In the three centuries following the revival of the eighth century, Greek scholarship in England and in Europe generally disappeared almost completely. There was no intercourse with the Eastern churches, which alone could have supplied an impetus to Greek studies.

The time had arrived for the development and growth of that which came to be designated by the comprehensive term of "Latinitas." The Latin Vulgate had obtained the sole sanction of the Church, and came to be regarded in the light of the "sacred Text."[4] Even regarding the Old Testament, the term "Hebraica

[3] H. Hallam, *Introduction to the Literature of Europe in the 15th, 16th and 17th Centuries* (ed. 1854), I, 90.

[4] The Preface to the Rheims New Testament and to the Douai Old Testament restate this attitude with force and clarity.

Veritas," when employed by a mediaeval scholar, meant only Jerome's translation. The "Latin" ecclesiastic lived in a world of his own; he did not overstep the boundaries which circumscribed the field of his Latinity, he had occupations enough within. Foremost among them was the exposition of the Bible, the multiplication of copies of the "Text," its corruption and its correction. It frequently happened that corrupting and correcting were interchangeable terms. . . . . The ordinary corrector lacked the knowledge required for his undertaking, he could not refer to the Greek and Hebrew originals. On the rare occasions when this was done, it did not tend to restore Jerome's text—and this it was that was demanded—but to substitute new phrases. Such judicious efforts as were made by Stephen Harding and Nicholas Manjacoria were few and far between. Latin glosses, Latin homilies supplied all that was wanted for the exposition of the Bible, even to the references to the Greek and Hebrew. Doctrine and philosophy were studied from the Latin text-books, and, at length, the exposition of Peter Lombard's *Book of Sentences* supplanted the study of the text of the Bible. . . . . The Latin scholar had a sufficiency of scope in his Latinity, which was not transcended either by his aspirations or his ideals.[5]

This is the conventional view and is no doubt true of the great majority of medieval scholars. But even in the period of greatest decline Greek scholarship was kept alive by individuals. Greek was studied in the Abbey of St. Gall in the tenth century, and the names of Baldric, bishop of Utrecht, Bruno of Cologne, and Gerbert, among others, are recorded by the historians of St. Maur as having possessed some knowledge of Greek.[6] There is little record of any Greek learning in the eleventh century, and even the greatest names of the twelfth century are not associated with any

---

[5] *The Greek Grammar of Roger Bacon and a Fragment of His Hebrew Grammar*, ed. E. Nolan and S. A. Hirsch (Cambridge, 1902), Introd., pp. xl–xli.

[6] Hallam, *op. cit.*, p. 91.

Greek knowledge. Neither Bernard nor Abélard nor John of Salisbury shows any evidence of acquaintance with the language. In the thirteenth century there was something of a revival, and in England especially the names of Robert Grosseteste and Roger Bacon are associated with a more scholarly attitude to philology. We have it on the authority of Matthew Paris that Grosseteste, with the help of a Greek priest at St. Albans, translated the Testament of the Twelve Patriarchs from Greek into Latin. Grosseteste also translated the *Ethics* of Aristotle and the Pseudo-Dionysian writings and is reputed to have brought Greek books to England. Bacon's acquaintance with Greek is well attested in his own works, his Greek grammar alone being sufficient to place him above most other medieval scholars.[7] Other Greek scholars of the thirteenth century in England are John de Basingstoke, who learned Greek at Athens; Adam Marsh and Thomas of Wales (Thomas Wallensis), both of whom are praised as Greek scholars by Bacon; Michael Scot, who was in contact with the Hebrew and Arabic translators of Aristotle; and perhaps William de Mara.[8]

[7] Cf. C. B. Vanderwalle, *Roger Bacon dans l'histoire de la philologie* (Paris, 1929), which contains (pp. 19 ff.) a comprehensive bibliography of works on medieval philology. The sketch of the progress of Greek learning presented here makes no claim to completeness or detailed presentation; it is included merely to give a bird's-eye view of the field before we proceed to discuss the rise of Hebrew scholarship, with which we are more particularly concerned.

We may note here an extraordinary error in Vanderwalle's bibliography. He refers (No. 73) to Whiteford, "Bacon as an Interpreter of Scripture" in the *Expositor* (1897), pp. 349–60: this article is on *Francis* Bacon! This is typical of an extreme carelessness which mars an otherwise valuable work.

[8] The identification of the anonymous "homo sapientissimus," mentioned with praise by Bacon more than once, with William de Mara has been shown to be probable by P. Henreich Denifle, "Die Handschriften der Bibel-Correctorien des

The two pioneers were John de Basingstoke and Grosseteste, who by their introduction of Greek works into England and their collection of Greek codices provided the material for other scholars to work on.[9]
But these scholars are isolated examples, and their work does not form part of any sustained revival of Greek studies. There were, however, occasional attempts made throughout Europe to provide for regular teaching of Greek during the Middle Ages, such as the proposals of the Council of Vienne in 1312 to establish chairs of Greek, as well as of Hebrew, Chaldaic, and Arabic, at Paris, Oxford, Bologna, and Salamanca.[10]
In Italy, which maintained a closer contact with the East, knowledge of Greek was doubtless commoner than elsewhere in Europe, but even here there is no evidence of any considerable Greek knowledge in the Middle Ages. Naturally it was in Italy that the real revival of Greek learning, when it did begin, first manifested itself. The Calabrian scholar Barlaam, who had long resided at Constantinople, came to Italy in 1339 on a mission from the emperor Cantacuzenus. It was from Barlaam that Petrarch began to learn Greek, probably in 1342, though he soon gave up the study on account of "peregrinae linguae novitas

---

13ten Jahrhunderts," *Archiv für Literatur- und Kirchengeschichte des Mittelalters*, Vol. IV (1888). See also S. Berger, *Quam notitiam linguae Hebraicae habuerunt Christiani Medii Aevei temporibus in Gallia* (Nancy, 1893), p. 35; *Greek Grammar of Roger Bacon* . . . . , ed. Nolan and Hirsch, Introd., p. lviii.

[9] Cf. Vanderwalle, *op. cit.*, Art. III, pp. 37 ff.: "Le Movement scientifique philologique à l'Université de l'Oxford"; A. G. Little, *Studies in English Franciscan History* (Manchester, 1917), chap. vi.

[10] H. Denifle and E. Chatelain, *Chartularium Universitatis Parisiensis* (Paris, 1891), II, 154–55.

et festina praeceptoris absentia." Petrarch's abandonment
of his attempt to learn Greek throws some light on the difficulties which must have confronted anyone who wished
to attain a scholarly knowledge of classical Greek. There
were no grammars or dictionaries in any European language
or even in Latin. Students had to acquire the elements of
the language from Greek-speaking teachers from the East,
whose Greek was far different from the classical Greek
which the students desired to learn. Only a very few of the
Greek immigrants to Italy were competent to give instruction in classical Greek, and it was the fact that these were
invited as professors to Italian universities that was responsible for the revival of Greek in Italy in the fourteenth and
fifteenth centuries.

Boccaccio was more successful than Petrarch and acquired
a knowledge of Greek from Leontius Pilarus, one of Barlaam's pupils. Pilarus is known for his translations of
Homer into Latin prose; he was appointed teacher of Greek
in Florence in 1361. But there were few contemporaries of
Petrarch or Boccaccio who acquired any knowledge of
Greek; Petrarch himself reckoned the number to be ten in
all Italy—five at the most in Florence, one in Bologna, two
in Verona, one in Mantua, and one in Perugia. There were
none at Rome.[11]

The settling in Italy of Emanuel Chrysoloras at the very
end of the fourteenth century marks the beginning of wider
Greek learning in Europe. Chrysoloras was public teacher
of Greek at Florence from 1397 to 1400 and subsequently
lectured at several other Italian universities, numbering
among his pupils some famous humanists. An enthusiast

[11] Hallam, *op. cit.*, p. 98.

himself, he had the gift of imparting his enthusiasm to his hearers, and his lectures exerted a very great influence not only because of what they taught but because of the new attitude to Greek studies that they inspired. Other Greek teachers from the Eastern empire carried on the work of Chrysoloras between 1400 and 1453, when Constantinople fell to the Turks. Thus Greek studies were well established in Italy before the added impetus given by the presence of Greek refugees after 1453; indeed, the majority of the refugees did not wait until the final catastrophe before leaving Constantinople.

Among the famous Greek teachers who arrived in Italy during the first half of the fifteenth century are Georgius Trapazuntius; Theodore Gaza, who taught at Ferrara from 1441 to 1450; Gemistus Pletho, who did so much for Platonic studies; and, most important of all, John Argyropoulos, who occupied the chair of Greek in Florence from 1458 to 1471. About the same time Demetrius Chalcondylas was lecturing at Perugia.

Meanwhile Greek studies were progressing outside Italy. In 1458 Gregory Tiphernas was appointed teacher of Greek at Paris. He was succeeded by George Hermonymus, under whom Reuchlin studied Greek when he came to Paris in 1470. At the very end of the century John Lascaris taught at Paris, going later to Rome at the invitation of Leo X. Jerome Aleander arrived in Paris in 1508 with an introduction from Erasmus and lectured there for eight years. In 1529, with the publication of the first complete edition of Sophocles, and of the *Commentarii linguae Graecae* by Budaeus, Greek scholarship in France had justified itself and was now firmly established. From this time onward the number of French Hellenists increased steadily.

Rudolf Agricola (1444–85) was the pioneer of Greek studies in Germany, accomplishing much for the "humanizing" of that part of Europe before he died in 1485 at the early age of forty.[12] More famous than he was Johann Reuchlin (1455–1522), of whom we shall have more to say later. Reuchlin first learned Greek from Gregory Tifernas, and then from Hermonymus in Paris; and when he came to Rome he amazed Argyropoulos by his ready translation of Thucydides, causing him to exclaim, "Ecce, Graecia nostra exsilio transvolavit Alpes!" This was the beginning of the age of great German humanists who included, among many others, Melanchthon, Camerarius, and that romantic figure Ulrich von Hutten.

Erasmus, the greatest of all the humanists, belongs, as perhaps the German humanists also do, to the second stage of the Renaissance, when Italian humanism was already becoming decadent. He studied Greek in Paris during the first six years of the sixteenth century, spending the next five years in Italy. In 1510 he went to Cambridge, where he lectured in Greek and held the Lady Margaret Professorship of Divinity until 1513. In 1516 appeared his famous edition of the Greek text of the New Testament with a new Latin translation, which marked the beginning of a new epoch in biblical studies.

[12] Alexander Hegius (1433–98), the famous schoolmaster who made the school of Deventer the great center of humanism toward the end of the fifteenth century, was an older contemporary of Agricola and learned some Greek from him. Erasmus was a pupil of Hegius at Deventer. Rudolf von Langen (1438–1529) did for Münster what Hegius did for Deventer.

Meanwhile the New Learning was also making progress in England.

In the second half of the fifteenth century, a certain interest in Italian humanism was felt by men like John Tiptoft, Earl of Worcester (c. 1427–1470), William Grey, the future Bishop of Ely (d. 1478), John Free, Fellow of Balliol (d. 1465), and John Gunthorpe, the future Dean of Wells (d. 1498). All of these were Oxford men, all went on pilgrimages to Ferrara, all left Latin manuscripts to College libraries, and (notwithstanding their great merits) all of them failed to arouse any permanent interest in the Classics.[13]

It was not until the introduction of Greek learning into England that real enthusiasm for classical scholarship was aroused. Thomas Linacre was the earliest considerable Greek scholar in England at this period. He studied at Rome and Venice before returning to Oxford to pursue his work there. With the return from Italy of William Grocyn in 1490 the teaching of Greek in Oxford became regular. William Latimer is the third of this group of Oxford Hellenists, and a younger contemporary was William Lilly, who studied Greek at Rhodes. At Cambridge the teaching of Greek by Erasmus from 1510 to 1513 gave a great impetus to Greek studies. Richard Croke, who studied Greek at Oxford with Grocyn and subsequently studied at Paris and lectured in several Continental universities, returned to Cambridge in 1518 and began lecturing there in Greek, being officially appointed reader in Greek by the university in the following year. Sir Thomas Smith of Queen's College succeeded Croke as reader, and in 1540, when the five regius chairs were founded by Henry, Smith got that of

[13] J. E. Sandys, *Harvard Lectures on the Revival of Learning* (Cambridge, 1905), p. 197.

civil law, while Sir John Cheke was appointed to the professorship of Greek. The work of Sir Thomas Smith and
Sir John Cheke, especially that of the latter, set Greek
learning on its feet in England.

Thus by the beginning of the sixteenth century the revival of Greek learning throughout Europe had taken
place. It was not long before the New Learning, as the revived study of Greek and Hebrew was popularly called,
began to be applied to the chief documents of the Christian
religion. In Italy, as we have seen, classical scholarship was
employed mainly in an attempt to revive the culture embodied and implied in the literature of ancient Greece and
Rome; but north of the Alps the Renaissance was from the
beginning to a considerable extent moral and religious in
purpose. Not that there was complete lack of application
of scholarship to the documents of religion in southern
Europe. In Italy we have noticed Laurentius Valla (1406–
57), who was the first to employ historical criticism in
criticizing the style of the Vulgate, proving the Donation of
Constantine to be a late and forged document and proving
the spuriousness of the Apostolic Symbol. Italy produced
also that strange and brilliant scholar Pico della Mirandola,
whose importance for the revival of Hebrew studies will be
discussed later. In Spain the great Cardinal Ximenes
brought to his university at Alcalá scholars of Greek,
Hebrew, and Aramaic who produced the Complutensian
Polyglot, the first of the great polyglot editions of the Bible
and a landmark in biblical scholarship. By this time the
application of the New Learning to religious literature had
produced many important works. But before we proceed to
take a more careful view of the stage set for the production

of vernacular Bible versions in Europe, we must say something of the growth of Hebrew learning among Christian scholars.

The version of the Bible in general use by the Christian church until the Reformation, and by the Roman Catholic church since the Reformation, was the Latin translation made by Jerome, popularly known as the Vulgate. Jerome's work on Bible translation began with a revision of the Old Latin version—a version made throughout from the Greek —but his final and most important work was a new Latin translation made, so far as the Old Testament is concerned, directly from the Hebrew. This translation does not correspond exactly to the Vulgate of the Middle Ages. Parts of the Vulgate are Jerome's revision of the Old Latin. The Book of Psalms, for example, is in some texts the "Roman Psalter"[14] and in others the "Gallican Psalter" version, i.e., Jerome's revision of the "Psalterium Vetus," not a fresh translation from the Hebrew. In other books, too, the influence of the Old Latin version is obvious. So the Vulgate is not in its entirety a translation made from the original text; but the proportion of Old Latin text in it is very small, and the Vulgate is very largely Jerome's new translation from the original text.

Jerome, then, is the first important Christian Hebraist. And as his Hebrew learning gave the Christian church its Vulgate version of the greater part of the Old Testament, it is important that the sources and extent of his knowledge be known and the nature of this translation appreciated.

[14] The Roman Psalter was used in Rome and Italy down to the time of Pius V (1566–72), when it was displaced by the "Gallican Psalter," another of Jerome's revisions, based on a corrected Greek text with the aid of other Greek versions.

Translators of the Reformation period pitted the original
Hebrew against the Vulgate text, correcting the latter by
the former. But if it can be shown that Jerome was a more
competent Hebraist than later scholars, the value of this
procedure becomes a little doubtful.[15] Like many other
Christian students of Hebrew, Jerome learned his Hebrew
from Jews. He traveled in Syria and Palestine, finally settling in Bethlehem about the year 385, where he devoted his
attention to perfecting his Hebrew knowledge. We do not
know for certain who his Hebrew teachers were. He himself refers by name only to one—"Baranina," בר חנינא;[16]
called elsewhere by the general title of "Barrabanum,"
בר רבנן—who, being afraid to be seen teaching him, visited
him at night only. A second teacher is referred to as "Lyd-
daeus quidam praeceptor, qui apud Hebraeis primus haberi
putabitur." This teacher seems to have taught him not only
translation and exegesis but Jewish traditions and midrashic
interpretations. Jerome refers to him in his commentary
on Habakkuk (2:15): "Audivi Lyddae quendam de Hebraeis,
qui 'sapiens' (חכם) apud illos et δευτερωτης (תנא) vocabitur,
narrantem hujusmodi fabulam." This same teacher (probably) is referred to several times as "Hebraeus, qui me
in sacris Scripturis erudivit," and once as "eruditissimus
Hebraeorum." Jerome seems to have learned Aramaic from
a Jewish teacher whom he mentions as "Chaldaeus";
Aramaic was necessary before he could translate the Book of
Daniel and other Old Testament passages, as well as the

---

[15] We must remember, however, that the text of the Vulgate suffered considerable corruption—and correction—throughout the Middle Ages.

[16] Moritz Rahmer, *Die hebräischen Traditionen in den Werken des Hieronymus*
(Breslau, 1861). Rahmer identifies בר חנינא with the haggadist ר׳ חמא בר
חנינא.

books of the Apocrypha written in Aramaic. In his Preface
to *Daniel* Jerome says: "Coepi rursus esse discipula Chal-
daicus." It may be the same teacher to whom he refers
gratefully in Epistle 139: "Est vir quidam a quo ego plura
didicisse me gaudeo, et qui Hebraeum sermonem ita elima-
vit, ut inter scribas eorum Chaldeus existimetur." During
the forty years that he lived in Palestine, Jerome continued
to study with Jews.

Not only did Jerome learn the Hebrew language from
Jews but he absorbed many Jewish traditions as well as the
Jewish attitude to textual interpretation. His exegetical
methods are largely Jewish. Dr. Samuel Krauss has pointed
out cases where the language of the Haggadah appears in
his commentaries, e.g., when the explanation is given in the
form of question and answer (commentary on Dan. 2:12:
"Quaesunt Hebraei . . . . "); or when he says, in explaining,
"Hoc est quod dicitur" (זה הוא שנאמר), etc.;[17] and Dr.
Moritz Rahmer's careful examination of Jerome's commentaries[18] gives abundant proof of Jerome's dependence
on Jewish sources.

Like Reuchlin many centuries later, Jerome was fiercely
attacked for seeking knowledge from the Jews. But he defended his practice with boldness if not always with the
judgment shown by Reuchlin. He saw, as Reuchlin saw,
that the ignorance of Hebrew on the part of Christian
scholars made them unfit to argue on many important religious matters, that such ignorance bred prejudice, and that
no argument was possible with those who made the fan-

17 *Jewish Encyclopedia* (New York and London, 1904), VII, 117.

18 *Op. cit.* and *Hieronymus' Commentar zu den zwölf kleinen Propheten*, kritisch
beleuchtet von Dr. Moritz Rahmer (Berlin, 1902).

tastic assertions about the Hebrew text of the kind that were still being made by the translators of the Douai Old Testament in 1609. Again and again he stressed the fact that ignorance of Hebrew was a great danger to Christian theologians. "Sicubi dubitas, Hebraeos interroga," he wrote to Augustine (Epistle 99), and again in arguing against Ruffinus he stressed the same point: "Sicubi ergo editio mea a veteribus discrepat, interroga quemlibet Hebraeorum."[19] And once again in concluding his Preface to the Pentateuch he repeats, "Sicubi in translatione tibi videor errare, interroga Hebraeos."[20] But in his advocacy of Hebrew studies Jerome fought a rapidly losing battle.

Thus Jerome, learning Jewish traditional renderings from Jewish teachers, must have incorporated these into the Vulgate. And so it comes about that the Vulgate Old Testament differs much less from the traditional Jewish interpretation than might be expected. When sixteenth-century translators made use of Jewish commentators, such as David Kimchi, in order to clear up doubtful points in the Hebrew text, they did not realize that some of the traditional renderings which Kimchi records were already embodied in the Vulgate, owing to the Jewish sources of Jerome's Hebrew education. And when we realize that the translators of the Authorized Version of the Old Testament made great use of Kimchi's commentary and based their translation on versions which derived from the Vulgate as well as renderings from the Hebrew based on the Hebrew knowledge made available by the scholarship of the school of Reuchlin, who himself had Jewish teachers—when we see how at every

[19] *Adversus Ruffinum* i. 2.
[20] Rahmer, *Die hebräischen Traditionen* . . . . , p. 15.

stage English Old Testament Bible translation is reinforced by works embodying traditional Jewish interpretations, we begin to realize how dependent on Jewish sources Christian interpretation of the text of the Old Testament has been. It was not until a long time after the Authorized Version was completed that Christian Hebrew scholarship began to make itself independent of Jewish influence, so far as such independence was desirable or possible.

Jerome's Hebrew scholarship cannot, however, have been very profound. He seems to have been needing the help of Jews in his translation of the Old Testament to the very end, and perhaps he did not learn much more than the ordinary educated Jew of the time would know as a matter of course. On the other hand, the common belief that no really eminent Jewish scholar of the time would have acted as teacher to a Christian is unfounded.[21] A teacher whom Jerome records as being called δευτερωτης (i.e., תנא) must

---

[21] It is often said that throughout the Middle Ages and later Jews were prevented by a talmudical prohibition from teaching Hebrew to non-Jews. This is hardly accurate. There are one or two sayings in the Talmud (Tractate חגיגה 13a; Sanhedrin, 59a, etc.) which forbid the teaching of *Torah* to a Gentile (if he does not keep the seven noachide laws, ז' מצות בני נח) but not the teaching of the Hebrew language. The term "Torah" in this connection obviously means the body of civil and criminal law (mainly the oral law), but would not include the prophets, Psalms, etc., or the historical parts of the Pentateuch. In any case, the "prohibition" is only the view of certain rabbis and was never generally accepted. Thus, while in view of the social and other conditions prevailing, it is unlikely that either in the time of Jerome or in the Middle Ages the most distinguished Jews would have taught Christians—though this is not true of Spain and Italy at certain times—yet Jews were not prevented from teaching Hebrew to Christians, and in numerous cases (e.g., that of Reuchlin) they did so. Cf. D. Kaufman, "Elia Menachem on Jews Teaching Hebrew to Non-Jews," *Jewish Quarterly Review*, IX (1897), 500 ff.; and the statement of R. Yechiel of Paris, ספר ויכוח רבינו יחיאל מפריס (Thorn, 1873), p. 10, which shows that Jews taught Hebrew to non-Jews in medieval Paris.

have belonged to the distinguished and select company of
תנאים, while the title בר רבנן, also recorded by Jerome
as being that of one of his teachers, indicates a high
level of prestige and scholarship. Nevertheless, there can be
little doubt that in the hundred years from Reuchlin to the
Authorized Version a greater body of Hebrew learning than
Jerome ever acquired was made available to Christian
scholars.

After Jerome, Hebrew scholarship among Christians was
very rare indeed for well over a thousand years. But we do
find traces of it throughout the Middle Ages. In England
Bede is credited with having possessed some knowledge of
Hebrew: Bacon referred to him as "literissimus in gram-
matica et linguis in originali." In his commentary on Genesis, chapter 10, Bede notes the difference between the Hebrew letters ש and ס.[22] The evidence afforded by his exposition of Hebrew names in the *Expositio nominum* does not
necessarily point to a direct knowledge of Hebrew—the
information probably came from Jerome's similar work.
Alcuin seems to have had some knowledge of Hebrew,
though his references to the Hebrew text (e.g., in his note
on Eccles. 10:12) may well have been derived from intermediate sources.[23] We know, however, from a poem of his
that the episcopal library at York contained works in
Greek, Hebrew, and Arabic.[24]

[22] "Filii Regma, Saba et Dadan: hic Saba per *schin* litteram scribitur; supra vero
per samech. . . . . Nam in LXXI psalmo, ubi nos habemus: *Reges Arabum et Saba*
. . . . , in Hebraeo scriptim est: *Reges Saba*, primum nomen per *schin*, secundum per
samech" (*Patrologia Latina*, Vol. XCIII, col. 300). The *Quaestiones super Genesim* are,
however, only doubtfully ascribed to Bede.

[23] Cf. S. A. Hirsch, "Early English Hebraists," *JQR*, XII (1899), 40.

[24] L. Maître, *Les Ecoles episcopales et monastiques de l'Occident, 768–1180* (Paris,
1866), p. 4.

Rabanus Maurus (776–856), abbot of Fulda and archbishop of Mainz, incorporated into his commentary on the Book of Kings passages embodying Hebrew traditions. These were taken from the *De quaestionibus in libris regum et Paralipomenon*, a work for long attributed to Jerome but now known to be a Christian redaction of a work written by a (baptized?) Jew at the beginning of the ninth century.[25] Rabanus Maurus himself acknowledges the help he received from a Hebrew scholar, referring to him as though he were a contemporary.[26] Many other medieval writers have passages which at first sight appear to exhibit evidence of Hebrew knowledge, but which actually come either from this work or from Jerome's works on the etymology of Hebrew place names. Paschasius Radbertus, in his biblical commentaries, has references to the Hebrew text which indicates that he had some direct help from a contemporary Jewish scholar. His biographer records that he was learned in Greek and Hebrew.[27] His comments on Matt. 27:46[28] present some interesting problems, but it seems clear that the help of a Jewish scholar was invoked— as indeed he himself states[29]—and that he did not depend,

[25] Berger, *op. cit.*; Jules Soury in *Bibliothèque de l'Ecole des Chartes*, LIV (1893), 734.

[26] J. B. Hablitzel, *Hrabanus Maurus: Ein Beitrag zur Geschichte der mittelalterlichen Exegese* (Freiburg, 1906); Reiger, "Wer war der Hebräer dessen Werke Hrabanus Maurus benutzt hat?" *Monatschrift für Geschichte und Wissenschaft des Judentums*, LXVIII (Frankfurt, 1924), 66; S. A. Hirsch, *Transactions of the Jewish Historical Society of England*, Vol. VII (London, 1915); *Patrologia Latina*, Vol. CXII.

[27] *Patrologia Latina*, Vol. CXX, col. 22C: ". . . . In his porro lucubrationibus omnibus apparet auctorem Graece et Hebraice doctum fuisse." Paschasius, in addition to the references noted above, interprets (in his own fashion) Hebrew letters in his commentary on Lamentations.

[28] *Ibid.*, col. 957.

[29] *Ibid.*, col. 957: ". . . . Et ut nuper audivi a quodam Hebraeo lamazapathani sonare videtur, ut quid perexquisisti me. . . . ." Cf. J. B. Hablitzel, "Der 'Hebraeus

like Rabanus Maurus, on the *De quaestionibus* merely. Agobard, the anti-Semitic archbishop of Lyons (d. 840), and his like-minded successor Amolo (d. 851) seem to have had some knowledge of talmudical traditions which, in the case of the former at least, may have been picked up in verbal intercourse with Jews.[30] In the eleventh century Abbot Sigo of St. Florent de Saumur (d. 1070) is credited with a knowledge of Greek and Hebrew.[31] It is perhaps rash to deduce a knowledge of Hebrew on the part of the author of the Latin religious poem *De divinis nominibus* merely because he begins successive paragraphs with an invocation to God, each using a version (generally garbled) of one of the Hebrew names for the Deity, and includes in the poem an account of the tetragrammaton:

> Nomenque anecfoneton
> Quod fronte tulit Aaron
> Sculptum per tetragrammaton
> Quatuor gemmis in petalon:
> Joth, He, Vau, Heth Hebraicum.[32]

Such vague and inaccurate information might have been picked up anywhere and implies no real acquaintance with

---

quidam' bei Paschasius Radbertus," *Hist. Jahrbuch d. Görresgesellschaft*, 1927, pp. 340–41; Reiger, *op. cit.*

[30] B. Altaner, "Zur Kentniss der hebräischen im Mittelalter," *Biblische Zeitschrift*, XXI (1933), 290. Cf. Berger, *op. cit.*, and the review of this by Jules Soury in *Bibliothèque de l'Ecole des Chartes*, LIV (1893), 734.

[31] "Abbas Sigo, vir valde venerabilis . . . . et insuper litteris Ebraicis et Graecis peritissimus legendi et scribendi" (Martène and Durand, *Thesaurus novus anecdotorum* [Paris, 1717], Vol. III, col. 848). J. Ebersolt (*Orient et Occident, recherches sur les influences byzantines et orientales 'n France avant les croisades* [Paris and Bruxelles, 1928]), accepts this eulogy at its face value and states simply that Sigo "pouvait lire et écrire le grec et l'hébreu" (p. 83).

[32] *Analecta hymnica Medii Aevi*, ed. G. M. Dreves (Leipzig, 1893), XV, 14.

Hebrew. Other lines of the poem—such as "Abba pater, Ben filius" (1. 13)—support the view that the author was merely flaunting what little knowledge he had. He seems to have known some Greek and shows off occasionally with whole lines consisting of Greek words written in Latin characters.

Stephen Harding (St. Etienne), the English-born third abbot of Cîteaux, completed in 1109 an important revision of the Vulgate text: in revising the Old Testament he enlisted the help of Jews who knew Hebrew and Aramaic, as we know from a note of his at the end of the second volume of the Cîteaux Bible (now in Dijon).[33] Though he does not appear to have known Hebrew himself,[34] he realized its importance for the study of the Old Testament. Peter the Venerable (d. 1156), translator of the Koran and one of the most erudite of medieval scholars, has some quotations (in Latin) from the haggadic portions of the Talmud in his *Tractatus contra Judaeos*.[35] Nicholas Manjacoria, the author of *Suffrageneus bibliotheciae*, obtained the help of a Jewish scholar in comparing the text of the Old Testament with the Hebrew original, and, as a result, in his work there is a considerable amount of Jewish traditional matter.[36] Nicho-

---

[33] Cf. Ebersolt, *op. cit.*, II, 12; *Histoire littéraire de la France*, XI (Paris, 1759), 222–23; Berger, *op. cit.*, cap. iv; J. P. P. Martin, *Saint Etienne Harding et les premiers recenseurs de la vulgate latine, Theodulfe et Alcuin* (Amiens, 1887).

[34] Cf. *Revue des études juives*, XII (1889), 131–33.

[35] E.g., *Patrologia Latina*, Vol. CLXXXIX, cols. 625–26, 631 ff. The *Tractatus* contains a translation of a מעשה דר׳ יהושה בן לוי which differs from the same tale as told in the different Hebrew redactions which have come down to us (cf. *Revue des études juives*, XII [1889], 43).

[36] Berger (*op. cit.*, p. 13) gives some interesting examples of talmudic and midrashic influence on Nicholas' work, as well as echoes of Rashi, all coming, doubtless, from his Jewish helper.

las—who is rather a shadowy figure altogether—probably wrote at the end of the twelfth century. Robert of Cricklade, prior of St. Frideswide's, Oxford, in the middle of the twelfth century, is credited by Giraldus Cambrensis with a knowledge of Hebrew, but there is no further evidence. The definiteness of Gerald's language seems to indicate at least some Hebrew knowledge on Robert's part.[37] Godfrey of Viterbo (*ca.* 1120–91) has long had a knowledge of oriental languages, including Hebrew, attributed to him, but the only ground for assuming his knowledge of Hebrew seems to be two passages in his own works where he speaks vaguely of his wide reading and multitude of foreign instructors.[38] It is fairly evident, however, that Godfrey's statements about his own width of learning are not to be taken too literally; even his knowledge of Greek is very doubtful.[39] Real evidence of the existence of some Hebrew knowledge among Christian scholars of the twelfth century is provided by the twelfth-century version of the Psalms (Codex Casinensis 557)[40] based partly on Jerome's *Psalterium*

[37] *Giraldi Cambrensis opera*, VIII ("Rolls Series" [London, 1891]), 65. For Robert of Cricklade cf. C. H. Haskins, *Studies in the History of Mediaeval Science* (Cambridge, Mass., 1924), pp. 168–71.

[38] "Saepe enim Graeci a Constantinopoli et Saraceni a Babilonia et Persae a Perside et Armeni ab Armenia ad Curiam imperialem et papalem venientes et magnas legationes ferentes me instruxerunt et sua scripta aliquando tradiderunt mihi." "Sum perscrutatus ex omnibus armariis et Latinis et Barbaris et Graecis et Judaicis et Chaldaicis" (cited by Altaner, *op. cit.*). Basilio Eroldo, in his Preface to an edition of Godfrey's *Pantheon* (Frankfurt, 1584), affirmed that Godfrey knew Latin, Greek, Hebrew, Chaldee, and many other tongues. This is typical of the uncritical statements about Godfrey made by early writers.

[39] Cf. M. Manitius, *Geschichte der lateinischen Literatur des Mittelalters*, III (Munich, 1931), 393.

[40] *Liber Psalmorum iuxta antiquissimam Latinam versionam nunc primum ex Casinensi cod. 557 curante D. A. M. Amelli in lucem profertur* (Rome, 1912).

iuxta Hebraeos. The author of this version clearly referred to the original text. There is, however, some doubt as to whether the version really does belong to this period.[41]

Alexander Neckam (more properly, Nequam) (1157–1217), abbot of Cirencester, gives some evidence of Hebrew knowledge in his *De naturis rerum* in the section "De initio Geneseos secundum Hebraicam veritatem." He quotes the first sentence of Genesis in Hebrew (Latin characters) and does some pretty juggling, something in the manner of the Christian cabalists, to prove the doctrine of the trinity from the arrangement of the letters.[42] In the second part of the same author's *Corrogationes Promethei* there are also references to the Hebrew text of the Bible.[43]

Throughout the twelfth century there are indications that the study of Hebrew is coming to be regarded by individual scholars as desirable for a proper understanding of the Old Testament, though this is by no means the general view even of the scholars of the time. We have noticed the importance attached to the Hebrew text of the Old Testament by Stephen Harding in his recension of the Vulgate: two other significant indications of the same attitude are provided by a short injunction in the *Decretum Gratiani* (Pars I,

[41] Cf. A. Allgeier, "Die mittelalterliche Überlieferung des Psalterium iuxta Hebraeos von Hieronymus und semitische Kentnisse in Abendland," *Oriens Christianum*, IV (3d ser.; Leipzig, 1930), 200 ff.; and the same writer's note in *Römische Quartalschrift*, XXXVII (Freiburg, 1929), 439.

[42] Alexander Neckam, *De naturis rerum*, ed. Thomas Wright ("Rolls Series" [London, 1863]), pp. 7 ff.

[43] An elaborate summary of this work, together with many quotations (including passages with the references to the Hebrew), is given by Paul Meyer, "Les *Corrogationes Promethei* d'Alexandre Neckam," *Notices et extraits des MSS de la Bibliothèque nationale*, XXXV (Paris, 1896), 641–82. There are several manuscripts of the *Corrogationes* in the Bodleian.

Distinctio X, cap. vi) stressing the importance of the original text[44] and—a more casual reference but for this very reason important as indicating an attitude that cannot have been wholly unusual—a letter of Abélard to the nuns of the Paraclete recommending the study of Greek and Hebrew as well as Latin and pointing to Eloise as an example of one who had knowledge of the two former languages, neither of which Abélard knew himself.[45] Michael Scot had some acquaintance with both Hebrew and Arabic. Gregory IX, writing about Scot to the Archbishop of Canterbury, praises him for his knowledge of these two languages.[46] Scot, as the astrologer of the emperor Frederick II, must have come into close contact with the scientific and philological activity that was so great a part of the "brilliant and precocious" culture[47] of Frederick's Sicilian kingdom. Scot seems to have had some relations with Jacob Anatoli (Jacob ben Abba Mari ben Simson),[48] the Hebrew translator of Arabic scientific and philosophic literature. His work, however, cannot be taken as in any way representative of general European learning of the time: his contacts with Hebrew and Arabic literature

[44] "Ut ueterum librorum fides de ebreis uoluminibus examinanda est, ita nouorum greci sermonis normam desiderat" (*Corpus iuris canonici*, ed. Aemilius Friedberg, Vol. I [Leipzig, 1879], col. 17).

[45] "Magisterium habetis in matre quae non solum latinae verum etiam tam hebraicae quam Grecae non expers, sola hoc tempore illam trium linguarum adepta peritiam videtur" (cited by Maître, *op. cit.*, p. 244).

[46] Denifle and Chatelain, *op. cit.*, No. 54, p. 110: " . . . . hebraice et arabice insudavit laudabiliter et profecit. . . . . "

[47] Haskins, *op. cit.*, p. 272. Cf. *ibid.*, chaps. xii and xiii.

[48] Cf. M. Steinschneider, *Die hebräische Übersetzungen des Mittelalters* (Berlin, 1893), pp. 57–58 *et passim*.

were due to the special character of Sicilian culture at that time.

There seem to have been several Christian theologians in the twelfth century who applied to Jewish scholars for help in interpreting passages of the Old Testament. Latin-Hebrew glossaries of the period survive, e.g., at Avranches and Tours. Mention must also be made of the unidentified author of the *Isagogue*, extant in an early thirteenth-century manuscript in the library of Trinity College, Cambridge, which contains biblical passages in Hebrew with a Latin translation. The passages are the so-called "christological" passages of the Old Testament, and the Ten Commandments. The identity of the author is unknown, but he appears to have been a twelfth-century ecclesiastic.

With the foundation of the Franciscan and Dominican orders we find in the thirteenth century a great increase in missionary activity, and with this a growth of interest in linguistic studies. Missionary activity could be properly carried on among Jews and Mohammedans only if the missionaries knew the language of those whom they wished to convert. Accordingly, the study of oriental languages became for a time a feature of Dominican and Franciscan studies. Greek, too, was necessary for work in the Eastern empire.[49] Humbert de Romans, who was general of the Dominican order from 1254 to 1263, gave an impetus to the establishment of missionary schools where languages were

[49] Cf. B. Altaner, *Die Dominikanermissionen des 13 Jahrhunderts* (Habelschwerdt, 1924), pp. 9–19. For the Dominican mission to the Mohammedans in Spain and the consequent study of Arabic (which generally took precedence over Hebrew) by members of the order cf. *ibid.*, pp. 93–94.

taught,[50] and for another fifty years we hear of the founding of such schools, particularly in Spain. In 1281 Hebrew and Arabic studies were instituted at Barcelona, Raymund Martini being the "lector ad studium ebraicum"; and in 1291 a "studium" for Arabic and Hebrew was founded at the monastery of Xativa in Catalonia.[51] Raymund Martini is an important figure in the history of both Hebrew and Arabic studies. He seems to have had a fair acquaintance with Hebrew and rabbinic literature. His polemical *Pugio fidei*[52] shows some acquaintance with the Hebrew Bible, the Talmud, and with a fair amount of Jewish exegetical and homiletical literature. The range of references and quotations is quite surprising: he quotes from Talmud and Midrash, from Rashi and Ibn Ezra, from David Kimchi's commentary on the prophets and from the same writer's *Michlol* and *Sefer Hashorshim (Liber radicum)*, from Maimonides' *Guide to the Perplexed*, and from many other rabbinical works such as the *Seder Olam*. He knows something of both the Babylonian and the Jerusalem Talmuds, though it is interesting that nearly all his quotations from the former (which greatly preponderate) are from "Sanhedrin." Rashi is cited as R. Salomo Jarchi or simply R. Salomo. Though Raymund Martini may have had less scientific knowledge of Hebrew

---

[50] See "Littera magistri ordinis fratris Humberti," in Martène and Durand, *op. cit.*, Vol. IV, cols. 1707–8. Humbert points out that missionary activity among Jews and Saracens is hindered by the missionaries' lack of languages among other causes.

[51] Altaner, *Die Dominikanermissionen* . . . . , p. 94. Cf. H. Denifle, *Die Entstehen der Universitäten des Mittelalters* (Berlin, 1885), pp. 496–97.

[52] I have used the edition edited by de Voisin (Paris, 1651). The references to the Hebrew books mentioned are too numerous to be cited, occurring on almost every page.

than Bacon (which is very doubtful), he certainly had read,
if in a misty and muddled fashion, more in Hebrew literature than any other Christian writer of his time. All his
quotations from Hebrew books are in the original Hebrew,
and he gives a Latin translation of his own. Raymund seems
to have taught Hebrew to Arnold of Villanova, distinguished physician and lay theologian.[53]

The place of study in the activity of the Dominicans was
indicated clearly by Humbert de Romans: "Studium est
ordinatum ad praedicationem, praedicatio ad animarum
salutem, quae est ultimus finis."[54] Knowledge of languages
such as Greek and Hebrew was not an ultimate end but an
important means to an end which was itself the means to
the final end, the salvation of souls. In this sense, of course,
all branches of knowledge were but handmaids of theology,
but the study of languages came to be regarded by the
Dominicans and Franciscans of the thirteenth century as
more directly bound up with theology than any other science; for their duty as missionaries was to understand the
documents of their religion and explain them to foreign
peoples. St. Francis himself was no scholar and unfavorably
disposed to learning. A friar, he maintained, had no need of
books, nor indeed of any belongings save his habit; a man's
piety is assessed by his works, not his knowledge.[55] But it
was not long before the Franciscans, like the Dominicans,

[53] H. Finke, *Aus den Tagen Bonifaz VIII*, 1902, *apud* Altaner in *Biblische Zeitschrift*,
XXI (1933), 304.

[54] *Opera omnia*, ed. Vivès (Paris, 1876), XXIX, 29: "Contra impugnantes Dei
cultum." Cf. *Archiv für Literatur- und Kulturgeschichte des Mittelalters*, herausgegeben
von P. Heinrich Denifle, S.J. (Berlin, 1885), I, 190.

[55] L. Wadding, *Scriptores ordinis minorum* (Rome, 1731), p. 346. Cf. J. S. Brewer,
Monumenta Franciscana (London, 1858), Preface, pp. xx–xxxiv.

found that their missionary activities demanded learning and study, and accordingly the development of Franciscan studies proceeded apace throughout the thirteenth century. St. Francis died in 1227, and his view of the futility of learning did not survive his death.[56]

The Franciscans came to Oxford in 1224,[57] and it was not long before the English Franciscans became pre-eminent among the order for their learning and philosophic ability. The first great teacher of the Franciscans at Oxford was Robert Grosseteste, who left to become bishop of Lincoln in 1235; he seems to have been mainly responsible for directing attention to the study of languages. Grosseteste's learning drew an eloquent tribute from Roger Bacon,[58] himself the most distinguished of the learned men of the order. Neither Grosseteste nor any of the three lecturers to the Franciscans at Oxford who followed him were themselves members of the order; they were simply distinguished ecclesiastics who were called in to help them with their studies, and it says a great deal for their enthusiasm for learning that they should

[56] Cf. A. G. Little, "Franciscans at Oxford," *Franciscan Essays* (Aberdeen, 1912), pp. 75–76. Speaking of the growth of learning among the Franciscans, Little re-marks: "A revolution had taken place, a revolution so rapid and striking that it was fully recognised by contemporaries both inside and outside the Order, and which was denounced by some, lamented by others, defended by others. . . . . Some such development was inevitable . . . . and it was hastened by the friars settling in university towns." The relations between Franciscan scholars and the universities of Europe constitute an interesting phase of the history of medieval universities.

[57] *Tractatus Fr. Thomae vulgo dicti de Eccleston de Adventu Fratrum minorum in Angliam*, ed. A. G. Little (Paris, 1909), p. 3. This date (1224) has been disputed (see Little, *The Grey Friars in Oxford* [Oxford, 1892], p. 1, n. 1).

[58] *Fr. Rogeri Bacon opera quaedam hactenus inedita*, ed. J. S. Brewer ("Rolls Series" [London, 1859]), pp. 91, 472.

have adopted this procedure. Grosseteste's successor was, as we learn from Thomas of Eccleston, "magister Petrus qui postmodum in episcopum in Scotia promotus est,"[59] and he was succeeded by Roger de Wesham (or Weseham), who later became bishop of Lichfield. Thomas of Wales, later bishop of St. David's, was the fourth lecturer. After Thomas the lecturers to the Franciscans ceased to be in the rather anomalous position of independent tutors in a university community: their connection with the university was regularized, and henceforth they were regent masters in theology belonging to the Franciscan order.[60] Adam Marsh, pupil and friend of Grosseteste and scholar of repute, was the first regent master among the Oxford Franciscans.[61]

Since Grosseteste might be called the founder of the tradition of learning that existed among the Oxford Franciscans, any inquiry into the Hebrew studies of the Franciscans at this time must be prefaced by some account of Grosseteste's ability in this field. Bacon's testimony is vague, and the sum of it seems to be that Grosseteste had some reading knowledge of Greek and Hebrew, never attaining to the ability to translate in the latter, though becoming proficient enough for translation in the former toward the end of his life.[62] Of his enthusiasm for having both languages taught there can be no doubt.

[59] *Eccleston*, ed. Little, p. 61. Probably, as Little suggests, Peter of Ramsay, who became bishop of Aberdeen in 1247.

[60] Little, *The Grey Friars in Oxford*, p. 29.

[61] *Eccleston*, ed. Little, pp. 63-64. Both Thomas of Wales and Adam Marsh received high praise from Bacon as teachers and scholars, and both may have had some knowledge of Hebrew (*Opus majus* [ed. Brewer], p. 73; *Opus tertium*, p. 88; *Compend. stud.*, p. 428).

[62] *Opus tertium*, ed. Brewer, pp. 88, 91; *Compend. stud.*, ed. Brewer, p. 472.

It is highly probable that such knowledge of Hebrew as
Grosseteste acquired he got from Jews. Jews had come from
Normandy—chiefly Rouen—in the wake of the Conqueror,
and at Oxford at this time there existed one of the largest
Jewish communities in the country. There is a tradition
that Grosseteste studied Hebrew with an Oxford rabbi.[63]
We know from such of his writings as the *De cessatione
legalium*[64] and his letter to the Countess of Winchester[65] as
well as from references in other of his works and from his
actions[66] that Grosseteste was much more humane and reasonable in his attitude toward the Jews than most of his
contemporaries, and this fact may be taken as further evidence of his having had personal association with Jewish
scholars.

It was not long before the Franciscan school at Oxford
became famous throughout Europe for its philological
studies as for many of its other activities. But it is difficult

[63] Tovey, *Anglia Judaica* (Oxford, 1738), pp. 244 ff. This tradition, whose truth
is probably, though by no means certainly, established, has been made the basis of
airy generalizations about Oxford Jews teaching Hebrew to Christians by J. Felten,
Robert Grosseteste, Bischof von Lincoln (Freiburg-im-Breisgau, 1887), pp. 12 ff., and
C. B. Vanderwalle, who, following Felten, states confidently that "[les juifs à
Oxford] donnèrent des cours d'hébreu à des étudiants chretiens" (*op. cit.*, p. 353).
Bacon's own testimony is definite but ambiguous, e.g., "Doctores . . . . non desunt.
Ubique sunt Hebraei . . . ." which seems to refer to what might be done rather than
to what has been done. The relations between Jews and Christians at Oxford were
clearly such as to permit of such teaching of Christians by Jews, at least on occa-
sions. Cf. A. Neubauer, *Notes on the Jews in Oxford*, in *Collectanea* of the Oxford
Historical Society (2d ser., 1890), p. 287, and F. M. Stevenson, *Robert Grosseteste,
Bishop of Lincoln* (London, 1899), pp. 21–23, 97 ff.; also L. M. Friedman, *Robert
Grosseteste and the Jews* (Cambridge, Mass., 1934), *passim*.

[64] Printed in abridged form (London, 1658).

[65] Reprinted in an English translation by Friedman, *op. cit.*, pp. 12 ff.

[66] Friedman, *op. cit.*, p. 23; Stevenson, *op. cit.*, pp. 224, 269, *et passim*.

to estimate to what extent Hebrew was taught regularly as a result of Grosseteste's efforts. Bacon, whose writings provide us with most of the evidence concerning the study of Hebrew among the friars, is himself a very exceptional case, and we are not justified in making any generalizations from the knowledge he displays. Indeed, Bacon often criticizes his teachers and contemporaries, complaining, for example, that too much attention is paid to the *Liber sententiarum* and not enough to the original text of the Bible, while he frequently points out deficiencies in linguistic knowledge.[67] That some Hebrew studies were carried on among the Franciscans at Oxford in the thirteenth century is beyond doubt, but it was probably erratic and unsystematic. The library of the Gray Friars seems to have contained a certain number of Hebrew texts, though the bulk of these may not have been acquired until after the expulsion of the Jews in 1290.[68] We know that it was part of the policy of Franciscan scholars at this time to encourage the study of Hebrew at the universities. Raymund Lull wrote to the University of Paris recommending the foundation of "studium Arabicum, Tartaricum et Grecum" (for missionary purposes),[69] and both Raymund Lull and Roger Bacon proposed the introduction of oriental studies throughout the universities of Europe. Raymund was the chief person responsible for the resolution passed in 1312 by the Council of Vienne recommending the establishment of chairs of Greek, Hebrew, Arabic, and

[67] *Opus minus*, ed. Brewer, pp. 328–29; etc.

[68] Anthony Wood, *Survey of the Antiquities of the City of Oxford*, ed. A. G. Clark (Oxford, 1889–90), II, 380.

[69] Denifle and Chatelain, *op. cit.*, I, 84.

Chaldee in Paris, Oxford, Bologna, and Salamanca.[70] Whether the recommendation of the Council of Vienne reinforced the efforts of the Franciscans to have Hebrew taught at Oxford to any practical extent is difficult to ascertain. It does appear, however, that at the beginning of 1321 there was a converted Jew teaching Hebrew at the University of Oxford, as a tax of one farthing in the pound was levied on ecclesiastical goods in the province of Canterbury in February, 1320–21, "pro stipendiis Conversi Docentis Oxonie linguam Ebraicam atque Grecam, et pro negociis aliis communibus ecclesie Anglicane."[71] The fact that it was a Jewish convert who was teaching Hebrew at Oxford in 1321 is one among innumerable indications that Hebrew scholarship in medieval Europe never became established as a regular study independent of contemporary Jewish help.

Some action seems to have been taken at Paris, too, as a result of the Council of Vienne. Johannes Salvati de Villanova, a convert from Judaism, was appointed to the University of Paris in 1319 and taught Hebrew and Syriac there.[72]

[70] L. Wadding, *Annales minorum seu trium ordinum a S. Francisco institutorum*, VI (Rome, 1733), 199.

[71] *The Registers of John de Sandale and Rigaud de Asserio, Bishops of Winchester*, ed. F. J. Baigent (London, 1897), p. 389. "Atque Grecam" here appears to have slipped in as part of the stock association "Lingua Hebraica et Graeca." No convert who taught Hebrew could have been an authority on Greek: if a Greek teacher is referred to also, it must have been another person, and no convert. Some effort appears to have been made to collect the tax at least in the diocese of Lincoln and Winchester. In 1321 the cathedral priory of Worcester paid 17½d. out of the church revenues of Oakham toward the expenses of the teacher of Hebrew, Aramaic, and Chaldee at Oxford (A. G. Little, *Studies in English Franciscan History*, p. 217; *Westminster Abbey Monuments*, No. 29465).

[72] Altaner in *Biblische Zeitschrift*, XXI (1933), 305; *Zeitschrift für Kirchengeschichte*, 1933, pp. 231–32.

In 1326 we find Pope John XXII ordering Hugo, bishop of Paris, to investigate the students of Hebrew, Greek, Arabic, and Chaldee at Paris,[73] and we have evidence that Hebrew was being taught at Paris in the beginning of the fifteenth century, though there is no trace of such teaching after the middle of the century.[74] Apart from such indications of activity at Oxford and Paris, there is no trace of the constitution passed by the Council of Vienne having been carried out by any of the other universities.

But to return to the English Franciscans of the thirteenth century. By far the most distinguished of these, and to some extent standing apart from them, was Roger Bacon, whose knowledge of Hebrew, however limited on modern standards, seems to have been greater than that of any other Englishman, and perhaps any other Christian, of his time. Throughout his writings Bacon exhibits a veneration for the Hebrew tongue displayed by no other medieval Christian scholar, regarding it as the language in which God first revealed his philosophy to his saints:

Revelavit igitur Deus primo philosophiam sanctis suis, quibus et legem dedit; nam philosophia utilis est legi Dei, ad intellectum, ad promulgationem, ad probationem, ad defensionem, et multis aliis modis, ut patet per opera qua scribo. Et ideo primo tradita est principaliter et complete in lingua Hebraea.[75]

This philosophy, Bacon held, is the basis of all knowledge. Familiarity with the Hebrew language, therefore, is essential for a true understanding of any branch of knowl-

[73] Denifle and Chatelain, op. cit., II, 293–94.

[74] C. Jourdain, "De l'enseignment de l'hébreu dans l'Université de Paris de XVᵉ siècle," Excursions historiques et philosophiques à travers le Moyen Age (Paris, 1888), pp. 233–45.

[75] Opus tertium, ed. Brewer, p. 32.

edge whatsoever. In the Hebrew writings are found the foundations of all wisdom. Bacon constantly expresses his distrust of translations and stresses the dangers of ignorance of the original text.

Bacon gives four main reasons for the study of languages, in particular of Hebrew, Greek, and Arabic. The first is "propter studium sapientiae absolutum";[76] the second is for the better carrying-out of affairs of state, in the spheres of commerce, justice, and international relations; the third is "conversio infidelium"; and the fourth, "reprobatio eorum qui converti non possunt."[77]

Though, like his fellow-Franciscans, Bacon stressed the conversion motive in pursuing Hebrew studies, he was equally if not more interested in the critical and textual aspect. On many separate occasions he expresses his desire for a really scholarly investigation of the text of the Bible made with a knowledge of the original tongues. He attacks the errors of the Vulgate texts and equally the copyists who multiply error. "Nam textus est pro majori parte corruptus horribiliter in exemplari Vulgato, hoc est Parisiensi."[78] His

---

[76] In association with this primary reason, Bacon puts forth the further reason "propter sapientiam comparatam ad Dei Ecclesiam," and notes that words of Greek and Hebrew origin are used in the liturgy, that "Ecclesiae Dei necessaria est cognitio linguarum propter sacramenta et consecrationes," and that the proper carrying-out of Christian rites in foreign lands where the Latin church has established itself demands a knowledge of languages (*Opus majus*, ed. Brewer, p. 115).

[77] Bacon also gives many other reasons for the study of Greek, Hebrew, and Arabic throughout his writings, as well as remarking frequently on the advantages of linguistic study in general—e.g., *Opera hactenus inedita*, ed. Brewer, pp. 33, 102, 433–44, etc. For Bacon's view of the biblical text as the source of all knowledge see P. T. Witzel, "De Fr. R. Bacon eiusque sententia de rebus biblicis," *Archivum Franciscanum historicum* (Quaracchi, 1910), pp. 3–22, 185–213.

[78] *Opera hactenus inedits*, ed. Brewer, p. 330.

reason for attacking the Paris Correctorium[79] is made quite clear: "Quia non sequuntur antiquas Biblias, et quia ignorant Graecum et Hebraeum, oportet quod sit error infinitus, quia textus a Graeco et Hebraeo descendit, et de linguis his habet vocabula infinita."[80]

Thus Bacon leaves no doubt of his belief in the necessity of Hebrew and other linguistic studies for Christian scholars and ecclesiastics. How much knowledge he himself actually possessed is another question. He mentions his own knowledge of Hebrew and other languages, as in that passage of the *Opus tertium* which sums up the contents of the *Opus maius:*

> Transeo igitur ad partem tertiam in Opere Majori, et illa est de linguis, seu de utilitate grammaticae, secundum linguas praecipue tres, scilicet, Hebraeam, Graecam, et Latinam. De Arabica tango locis suis; sed nihil scribo Arabica, sicut Hebraee, Graece et Latine; quia evidentius et facilius ostenditur propositum meum in his.[81]

Besides referring several times to his knowledge of Hebrew, Bacon boasted that he could teach Hebrew to a zealous student in three days.[82] It has been argued with plausibility that a man who could undertake to teach He-

---

[79] I.e., the revision carried out by Dominican scholars in Paris in the beginning of the thirteenth century under the leadership of Hugo de S. Caro. Hugo displays some knowledge of Hebrew in his notes.

[80] *Opera hactenus inedita*, p. 333. There is a certain mutual conflict between Bacon's opinions here. Both "antiquae Bibliae" and the original languages are authorities. But often there has to be a choice between the two. Bacon both condemns "Andraeas quidam" for substituting his own translation from the Hebrew *and* praises him for his use of the original Hebrew (cf. S. A. Hirsch in *Roger Bacon Commemoration Essays*, ed. A. G. Little [Oxford, 1914], pp. 146–47).

[81] *Opera hactenus inedita*, ed. Brewer, p. 88.   [82] *Ibid.*, p. 65.

brew in three days must have had a very elementary conception of what constituted a knowledge of a language. And it is probably true that we interpret Bacon's references too generously if we understand him to be boasting of a knowledge that would be regarded as at all adequate by modern scholars. An elementary reading knowledge based on a limited vocabulary and familiarity with the main grammatical principles of the language was probably all that any medieval scholar meant in claiming to "know" a language other than Latin or his own vernacular. Unfortunately, the Hebrew grammar which Bacon is traditionally supposed to have written[83] is not extant; but a fragment containing the Hebrew alphabet and some elementary notes on Hebrew grammar was discovered by Rev. Edmund Nolan at Cambridge University Library at the beginning of this century. This fragment is almost certainly by Bacon and may have been a draft for a section of his lost grammar.

It is chiefly because of the ambiguity of all medieval references to "knowing" a language like Greek or Hebrew that it is impossible to give anything like an exact estimate of Bacon's Hebrew knowledge. We know that he stressed the importance of philology, that he adduced particular reasons for venerating Hebrew, that he wrote an elementary Hebrew grammar, that he discusses some Hebrew terms in his other works, and that he might well have been in contact with Jewish scholars at Oxford.[84] We know too that

[83] The first reference we have to Bacon's Hebrew grammar is that of Bale, who in his list of Bacon's works includes a "Grammaticam Hebraicam" (*Index Britanniae scriptorum* . . . . , ed. R. Lane Poole [Oxford, 1902], p. 397).

[84] "Doctores non desunt . . . ." etc., see above, p. 105, n. 63. Hirsch (*JQR*, Vol. XII [1899]) notes the complete lack of any disparaging reference to Jews in all Bacon's works and his unusual "sentiments" of tolerance with regard to Jews.

he was influenced by Grosseteste,[85] whose attitude to languages we have discussed, that he was the culminating figure in a brief revival of learning which included linguistic studies, and that there is no a priori reason why he should not have attained some proficiency in Hebrew. The case against his Hebrew knowledge has been put forcibly by Jules Soury:

> Que Roger Bacon, en dépit de la tradition, n'ait plus su l'hébreu que l'arabe, c'est ce que démontre manifestement la connaissance de ses livres. [Soury wrote, however, before the discovery of the fragment of Bacon's Hebrew grammar.] Des déclarations de principe en faveur de l'étude de ces langues pour l'intelligence de la Bible, on en trouve chez Bacon comme chez nous les Pères et docteurs de l'Eglise, fussent-ils, comme saint Augustin, les plus étranges à la connaissance des langues hébraïque et chaldaïque. Bacon avait certes l'étoffe d'un linguiste, mais l'idée qu'il se faisait encore d'un helléniste ou d'un hébraïsant montre assez qu'ici le sens des mots est tout, et que, pour ce moine franciscain comme pour tous ses contemporains, "savoir le grec et l'hébreu" n'a jamais signifié ce que nous entendons par ces expressions. ... Bacon reconnait et témoigne hautement que, de son temps, la science du grec, de l'arabe et de l'hébreu etait toute en la possession exclusive des Grecs, des Arabes et des Juifs. Il en gémit naturellement. ...[86]

Hirsch forgets Bacon's attack on the Jews for "corrupting" the Hebrew text of the Bible, which Soury, *op. cit.*, interprets as arising from Bacon's resentment at the Jewish monopoly of Hebrew knowledge.

[85] For a discussion of Grosseteste's possible influence on Bacon's rules and principles of translation see Ludwig Bauer, "Der Einfluss des Robert Grossetestes auf die wissenschaftliche Richtung des Roger Bacon," in *Roger Bacon Commemoration Essays*, esp. p. 41.

[86] *Op. cit.*, p. 736. Soury refers frequently to "le caractère illusoire et purement légendaire d'une connaissance réelle de l'hébreu chez les theologiens et les exégètes bibliques de notre race en moyen âge. De Saint Jerome à Reuchlin cette science est demeurée l'apanage et la patrominie des Juifs" (*ibid.*, p. 732). Soury, of course, is right on the whole, though this need not prevent us from seeking exceptions to this general rule.

Perhaps the fairest estimate is that of S. A. Hirsch, who, while illustrating the deficiencies in Bacon's knowledge of Hebrew, points out indications of sufficient knowledge to elevate Bacon above most other Christian claimants to Hebrew scholarship of his time.

Bacon founded no school of Hebrew studies, though the Franciscan revival of learning of which he was such a distinguished representative had some interesting results. First, however, we may mention a predecessor of Bacon, a biblical commentator to whom Bacon himself attributes a knowledge of Hebrew. This is "Andraeas quidam" whom Bacon charges with having altered the Vulgate text in accordance with the Hebrew.[87] This Andrew is a shadowy figure: he is perhaps the Englishman of that name who lived *ca.* 1150 and was a pupil of Hugo de Sancto Victore.

Perhaps the influence of the Franciscan study of languages is also discernible in the thirteenth-century *correctoria* of the Vulgate text, many manuscripts of which contain notes on the text of the Old Testament which indicate some definite Hebrew knowledge. A resemblance between these notes and the principles of textual revision advocated by Bacon in the *Opus minus* has been observed by several scholars, so that Bacon has been put forward as their author by some, and by others Bacon's contemporary whom he refers to only as "homo sapientissimus"[88] has been suggested.[89] The "homo sapientissimus" has been doubtfully identified with the anti-Thomist Franciscan William de Mara, whose *Correc-*

---

[87] *Compend. stud.*, ed. Brewer, p. 482. As we have noted, there is something self-contradictory in Bacon's attitude here.

[88] *Opus tertium*, ed Brewer, p. 80; *Opus minus*, ed. Brewer, pp. 317, 320.

[89] Denifle, "Die Handschriften des Bibel-Correctorien des 13ten Jahrhunderts," *op. cit.*, pp. 263 ff., 471 ff.; Little, *Studies in English Franciscan History*, pp. 213 ff.

toria (not a textual work, but a criticism of Aquinas) appeared about 1282. If Denifle's double identification of the "homo sapientissimus" with both the author of the *Correctorium Vaticanum* and William de Mara is right, then William must be added to the list of medieval students of Hebrew, for this *correctorium* displays considerable familiarity with Hebrew texts.[90] Denifle makes a further identification of William de Mara with the author of replies to certain questions relating to the text and interpretation of the Bible contained in a manuscript now in Toulouse. These replies are by a writer who was obviously conversant not only with the Hebrew language but also with the rabbinical writings and especially Rashi's commentary. The respondent seems to have lectured for some time in Paris and was perfectly familiar with French. His identification with William de Mara is possible; he seems at least to have been either French or English.[91]

There are English manuscripts of the thirteenth and fourteenth centuries which contain evidence of elementary knowledge of Hebrew and Greek, some of which certainly, and others probably, were written by Franciscans. The Hebrew, as well as the Greek, in these manuscripts is transliterated into Latin characters and is generally in small scraps. Matthew of Paris mentions Robert of Arundel as a Hebrew scholar and a translator of Hebrew works into

[90] Denifle, "Die Handschriften des Bibel-Correctorien des 13ten Jahrhunderts," *op. cit.*

[91] Berger, *op. cit.*; Hirsch, in *Transactions of the Jewish Historical Society of England*, Vol. VII (1915); Little, *Studies in English Franciscan History*, p. 214, n. 2; *Roger Bacon Commemoration Essays*, ed. Little, pp. 140–41. It is not certain, though it is probable, that William de Mara was English (cf. Little, *Grey Friars in Oxford*, p. 215).

Latin.[92] Gregory of Huntingdon is another thirteenth-century Englishman to whom an unverifiable knowledge of Hebrew has been attributed.[93] Robert of Reading was led by a love of Hebrew to embrace the Jewish religion; he was described by Florence of Worcester as "lingua Hebraea eruditissimus," and embraced Judaism in 1275.[94] There is a fifteenth-century manuscript now in Christ's College, Cambridge, and originally from the charter-house at Coventry, the second part of which contains a commentary on the Psalms by the Franciscan Henricus de Costeseye (Henry of Costessey or Cossey, near Norwich) which shows some knowledge of Hebrew and refers to Jewish commentators. Henry studied with the Franciscans at Oxford and later became teacher of divinity to the Cambridge Franciscans, appearing forty-sixth on Eccleston's list of teachers there.[95] He died *ca.* 1336. With the subsequent decay of learning among the English Franciscans and the decay of their library, Hebrew knowledge among them passed away completely. Almost a century later the solitary name of Richard Brinkley, provincial of the English Franciscans, is associated at least with some interest in the Hebrew text of the Bible: in 1502 he borrowed a Hebrew psalter from the Abbey library at Bury St. Edmunds, and himself added to

---

[92] *Matt. Parisiensis Chronica majora,* ed. H. R. Luard, IV (London, 1877), 553.

[93] K. A. Neumann, *Über orientalische Sprachstudien seit den 13 Jahrhundert mit besonderer Rückseit auf Wien* (Vienna, 1899), p. 110.

[94] *Florenti Wigorniensis Chronicon,* ed. B. Thorpe (London, 1849); H. Graetz, *Geschichte der Juden* (3d ed., 1894), VII, 421 ff.

[95] MS Christ's Coll. Camb., F.1. 17; *Eccleston,* ed. Little, p. 73. Cf. M. R. James, *A Descriptive Catalogue of the Western MSS in the Library of Christ's College* (Cambridge, 1905), pp. 28–36.

the manuscript a note on the Hebrew names of God.[96] There is no real continuity between the Franciscan studies of Hebrew and the revival of such studies at the Reformation.

The insistence of both Dominicans and Franciscans on Hebrew, Arabic, and Greek studies in the thirteenth century led to a series of papal and other recommendations between 1248, when Innocent IV arranged for the upkeep of ten boys skilled in Arabic and other oriental languages at the University of Paris,[97] and 1312, when the Council of Vienne passed the resolution that we have noted. Thus individual action by Dominicans and Franciscans, such as Raymund Martini and Raymund of Pennafort[98] among the former and Raymund Lull and Roger Bacon among the latter, was supplemented both by papal and by conciliar action, though neither achieved anything permanent. However, throughout the remainder of the Middle Ages echoes of the friars' demands are heard, and it is sporadically pointed out that Greek and Hebrew knowledge is necessary both for missionary purposes and—this aspect is oftener stressed—for the promotion of biblical exegesis. Perhaps some slight thread of continuity between the activity

[96] The manuscript is now in Bodley. Cf. M. R. James, *On the Abbey of St Edmunds at Bury* (Cambridge, 1895), pp. 87–88. Richard of Bury (1281–1345), bishop of Durham and noted bibliophile, though no great scholar himself, recognized the importance of Greek and Hebrew studies and procured Greek and Hebrew grammars and manuscripts for his library.

[97] Denifle and Chatelain, *op. cit.*, I, 212–13. The boys were to study theology and then go out East and act as missionaries. Innocent's decree was repeated with modifications at intervals by his successors up to and including Honorius IV (*ibid.*, pp. 372 and 368).

[98] Cf. C. Douais, *Essai sur l'organisation des études dans l'ordre des frères precheurs au treizième et au quatorzième siècle* (Paris and Toulouse, 1884), pp. 135–40.

of the Dominicans and the later revival of Hebrew studies at the Reformation can be seen in the *studia Biblia* of the Dominicans which continued at least in theory to include Hebrew, Arabic, and Greek studies and which were to this extent the inspiration of the "trilingual colleges" founded in the sixteenth century.[99]

In the second half of the thirteenth century a work was begun in England which shows that there must have been a certain amount of interest in Hebrew at that time. This was a literal translation of the Old Testament into Latin from the original Hebrew. A large part of this translation is extant is several manuscripts; the extant part may represent

[99] Cf. Rashdall's *Mediaeval Universities*, ed. Powicke and Emden (Oxford, 1936), I, 371. Another possible link between the thirteenth-century revival of philosophical and other studies and the Renaissance and Reformation might be found in the literary history of fourteenth-century Naples. A. G. Little has this interesting suggestion: "Were the seeds so carefully sown and tended by Grosseteste and Roger Bacon lost, or were they transplanted to a more fruitful soil? Did they come to fruit in the Italian Renaissance? It might be worth while to investigate from this point of view the literary history of the court of King Robert of Naples, and an examination of the Neapolitan archives might give valuable results. Robert of Naples forms a link between the Franciscans and the early Italian humanists. With the Franciscan school at Oxford he had some slight connection. William of Alnwick, who preceded the Baconian, William of Naples, as lecturer to the friars at Oxford, was later called to the University of Naples, and finally appointed bishop of Giuvenazzo by King Robert. [Cf. *Eccleston*, ed. Little, p. 69.] It will possibly be found that King Robert's youthful essay on the *Dicta et opiniones philosophorum* (never printed) owes something to the *Compendoloquium*, or to the *Breviloquium de virtutibus antiquorum principum et philosophorum* of John of Wales; the latter treatise . . . . attracted the educated laity of Italy of the fourteenth century. To King Robert Arnold de Villeneuve dedicated his book, *De conservatione juventutis et retardatione senectutis*, which is largely based on Bacon's medical treatises. Among the books transcribed for King Robert we note a *De perspectiva* (perhaps the fifth part of Bacon's *Opus Majus*) and several translations from Greek, Arabic and Hebrew. If we could find the catalogue of King Robert's library, it might throw new light on the origins of the Renaissance" (*Studies in English Franciscan History*, pp. 218–19).

all the work that was accomplished, or it may be that some
is lost. In the Bodleian Library (formerly in the library of
Corpus Christi College) there are: (1) a manuscript con-
taining the Pentateuch written in Hebrew and Latin, that
Latin being the Vulgate text in a column between the two
columns of Hebrew, the Hebrew text having an interlinear
Latin translation literally rendered from the Hebrew; (2) a
manuscript containing the books of Joshua, Judges, Samuel,
Ecclesiastes, and Esther in Hebrew, part of Samuel having a
Latin gloss, with a few Latin glosses on Joshua; (3) a manuscript containing the books of Samuel and Chronicles in
Hebrew with the Vulgate version of Samuel in the margin,
an interlinear Latin gloss on I Samuel to verse 54 of chapter
17 and on I and II Chronicles, and a few Latin glosses on
single words in the rest of I Samuel; (4) a manuscript containing the Book of Psalms in Hebrew, with two Latin
renderings—Jerome's "Gallican" and "Hebrew" versions
—in parallel columns and a third interlinear Latin translation, rendered literally from the Hebrew, and also an English gloss; (5) a manuscript containing the Psalms and
Proverbs in Hebrew, the Psalms being accompanied by
Jerome's "Hebrew" version and many marginal notes;
Proverbs has a Latin gloss on the first few words. There is
also in the library of St. John's College a manuscript containing the books of Joshua, Judges, Canticles, and Ecclesiastes, with the Vulgate version in the margin and an
interlinear Latin translation rendered literally from the Hebrew; and in Trinity College, Cambridge, there is a manuscript containing the Psalter in Hebrew with both Jerome's
Latin versions and an interlinear Latin gloss over the He-

brew text. These manuscripts are thirteenth to fourteenth century, and some appear to be in identical hands.

In all these manuscripts the interlinear Latin translation of the Hebrew is the work of one man, as is evident from certain peculiarities occurring in all the glosses. As for the nature of the gloss:

Glossa haec est, non interpretatio, neque verisimile est, nostram versionem continua serie et quasi currente calamo unquam descriptam esse. Nam superest in ea quasi nota artificis, singulae particulae orationis indicantur, quae ab ingenio Latinorum prorsus abhorrent. . . . . Non plane novum illud opus [est], sed translationem nostram ex hieronymiana ita excrev[it], ut vix aliud esse videatur quam perpetua vulgatae versionis ad hebraicam litteram accomodatio. Undequis quaeret, num illud in Judaeum virum bene cadat, cum Hieronymianum opus ecclesiae catholicae quasi vexillum fuerit. Neque nos Hebraeum nostrum aquae baptismi expertem fuisse crederimus.[100]

Whoever the author was—and we have no means of making even an approximate guess—we can at least say of him that he did his work in England, probably in the latter half of the thirteenth century, and that he may well have been a follower of Roger Bacon. If, as seems certain, Jewish help in some form or other was utilized, it cannot have been done after the expulsion of the Jews from England in 1290. It is possible, as Berger and Soury suggest,[101] that the whole was done by a converted Jew, which might put the possible date some years later were not most of the manuscripts of the thirteenth century.

The controversy over the Talmud in France in the middle of the thirteenth century provides some interesting evidence of Hebrew knowledge among Christians. Nicholas Donin

[100] Berger, op. cit., p. 53.   [101] Soury, op. cit., p. 735.

of La Rochelle, a converted Jew, actuated by motives of spite rather than of theology,[102] brought a series of detailed charges against the Talmud before Gregory IX. As a result the pope sent bulls throughout Europe ordering the seizing and burning of all copies of the Talmud on a fixed day.[103] This was done only in France, and the seized books were handed over for examination to a commission consisting of members of the Franciscan and Dominican orders. On June 25, 1240, a public disputation took place, where the Talmud was defended by Jechiel of Paris, Judah ben David of Melun, Samuel ben Solomon of Château-Thierry, and Moses of Soucy, while Nicholas Donin led the attack.[104] Both sides claimed the victory, but the result was a foregone conclusion, and the Talmud was condemned to be publicly burned. How much Hebrew, if any, did the members of the commission that examined the Talmud know? They had the help of Donin, who as a former Jew certainly knew some Hebrew. And when in 1248 a re-examination of the Talmud was ordered by the pope, followed by a second condemnation by Odo of Châteauroux, there is a reference made in Odo's condemnation to the members of the second commission as versed in Hebrew matters.[105] But in this case probably the only member of the commission who knew Hebrew was the Dominican Theobald of Sezanne, a baptized Jew.[106] The *Extractiones de Talmut*, which was com-

[102] S. Grayzel, *The Church and the Jews in the XIII Century* (Philadelphia, 1933), Appen. A.

[103] Denifle and Chatelain, *op. cit.*, I, 204; Grayzel, *op. cit.*, p. 240.

[104] Wagenseil, *Tela Ignea Satanae* (Altdorf, 1681), Vol. II.

[105] ספר ויכוח רבינו יחיאל (Thorn, 1873).

[106] Quetif-Echard, *Scriptores ordinis praedicatorum* (Paris, 1719–21), I, 166 f.; Berger, *op. cit.*, p. 31.

piled between 1248 and 1255 on the orders of Odo of Châteauroux as a justification of the condemnation, contains in the Prologue a statement by its author that he was helped by "duos interpretes catholicos in hebrea lingua quam plurimum eruditos."[107] As, however, the author of the *Extractiones* seems, according to the heading of one of the manuscripts,[108] to have been the above-mentioned Theobald, we might wonder what need he would have of non-Jewish help in translating the Talmud. All we can say is that, while on the whole knowledge of Hebrew among Christians at this time seems to have been confined to converts from Judaism, there is some evidence of Christian theologians in Paris in the middle of the thirteenth century having learned some Hebrew from Jewish teachers. This is clearly suggested by a remark of Jechiel of Paris in his defense of the Talmud, where he asserted that Jewish scholars were teaching Hebrew to Christians.[109] The dependence of Christian scholars on Jews for such knowledge of Hebrew as they might possess, even when that knowledge was used against the Jews, is clear evidence of the complete lack of any regular study of Hebrew by Christians at this time.

Further examinations of Jewish writings by Christian theologians are recorded in the thirteenth and fourteenth centuries, at most of which Hebrew knowledge was supplied by converts from Judaism. Thus Pablo (Paulus) Christiani, formerly a Jew, repeated at Aragon in 1257 the part that Donin had played at Paris in 1239–40; a further com-

---

[107] N. Valois, *Guillaume d'Auvergne, évêque de Paris* (Paris, 1880), p. 134, n. 2.

[108] Altaner in *Biblische Zeitschrift*, Vol. XXI (1933).

[109] ... ‏רבכל יום אנו .. מלמדים תורה לגי שהרי יש כמה גלחים‎
‏יודעים לקרוא בספר יהודית .. (ויכוח רבינו יחיאל מפריס‎ .10 ‎p.)

mission to inquire into Jewish books was set up in Aragon in 1264, and this commission included Pablo Christiani and Raymund Martini, whose knowledge of Hebrew has been discussed. Raymund Martini may have taught Hebrew to some Christian theologians; he is known to have taught Arabic to at least one—Frater Arnold de Guardia.[110] There were examinations of Jewish books ordered at Aragon once more in 1296,[111] in Toulouse in 1319 (when two wagonloads of Talmuds were burned),[112] at Avignon in 1320—which explains the presence of 120 Hebrew codices in the papal library at Avignon[113]—at Calatayud in Catalonia in 1326,[114] and at Aragon again in 1391.[115] But these examinations do not necessarily imply a knowledge of Hebrew on the part of the examiners, who often knew nothing of what they were supposed to be inquiring into. It is probable, however, that the Aragon examinations were conducted by men one or two of whom knew some Hebrew.[116]

At the beginning of the fourteenth century in France there was one writer whose knowledge of Hebrew is indisputable. This is Nicholas de Lyra, the popular exegete,

[110] Altaner, in *Biblische Zeitschrift*, Vol. XXI.

[111] Rubio y Lluch, *Documents per l'historia de la cultura catalana migeval*, II (Barcelona, 1921), 9–11.

[112] C. Devic and J. Vassette, *Histoire générale de Langedoc*, IX (Toulouse, 1886), 393 f.

[113] *Historia Bibliothecae romanorum pontificum tum bonifationae tum Avenionensis*, enarrata . . . . a Francisco Ehrle, I (Rome, 1890), 362 (No. 980), 376 (No. 1184), 398 (No. 1183 and n. 455).

[114] Lluch, *op. cit.*, p. 50.   [115] *Ibid.*, p. 337.

[116] Cf. *ibid.*, p. 50. Fra Ramón de Miedes was granted some Hebrew books in 1326, from those confiscated from the Jews. The letter of James II granting him the books says of him that "aliqualem linguae hebraicae habetis noticiam."

who was born at Lyre, Normandy, about 1270 and lived until 1340. His *Postillae perpetuae, sive brevia commentaria in universa biblia* shows clear evidence of his Hebrew knowledge. Lyra's characteristic as a Bible scholar is his insistence on the literal meaning of the original. In his *Prologues* he deplores the tendency to find false and fanciful meanings in the sacred text and states his own aim clearly: "Intendo non solum dicta doctorum catholicorum: sed etiam hebraycorum: maxime Rabbi Salomon qui inter doctores hebreos locutus est rationalibus ad declarationem sensus literalis inducere."[117] That is, not only has Lyra gone to the Hebrew text but he has also gone to the Jewish commentators. "Rabbi Salomon" is Solomon ben Isaac, generally known among Jews as "Rashi," whose commentary on the Bible has been for centuries the most popular of Hebrew exegetical works. Throughout the *Postillae* we find abundant evidence of a knowledge of the Hebrew text and of Rashi's commentary. Indeed, Rashi's aim was very similar to Lyra's: both commentators paying more attention to the literal meaning of the text—the "sensus literalis" of Lyra— than to the allegorical or mystical meaning—the "sensus mysticus vel spiritus"—though neither denied the existence of the second kind of meaning. It is interesting to note that Luther borrowed considerably from Lyra's *Postillae*, thus bringing into his work at second hand some traditional Jewish interpretations.[118] Lyra himself is important for familiarizing Christian theologians with traditional Jewish

[117] Bible with Nicholas de Lyra's *Postillae* [no title-page] (Nuremberg, 1585), Prologus secundus, sig. (*a*)^v. (Bodl. Bib. Lat. c.1-3.)

[118] See Siegfried, "Raschi's Einfluss auf Nicolaus von Lira und Luther," *Archiv für wissenschaftlichen Erforschung des Alten Testaments*, ed. Merx, I (1869), 428.

interpretations of the Old Testament. The theory that he was of Jewish origin has never been proved; but he was certainly in touch not only with Jewish scholarship but with contemporary Jewish scholars. Thus at every turn we find the Hebrew tradition in the Christian study of the Bible being reinforced. Paul of Burgos is another name to be noted in connection with Christian Hebrew scholarship. He lived almost a century after Lyra and continued the latter's work. Born a Jew, he became converted to Christianity in 1391. His additions to Lyra's commentary give many evidences of Hebrew knowledge and familiarity with rabbinical traditions.

We have not discussed the sporadic knowledge of the Hebrew alphabet which is evidenced in medieval manuscripts or the occasional glossaries and interpretations of Hebrew names. These prove little or nothing. Often they are the work of copyists who copied blindly with no understanding of Hebrew whatsoever; and the originals of the works on place names derived in almost every case from Jerome's *De interpretatione Hebraicorum nominum* and *De situ et nominibus locorum*.

Biblical scholarship in Spain presents a rather isolated phenomenon, this isolation dating from the very beginning of the Middle Ages. The Visigothic texts were already different in character from other European texts of the Bible,[119]

119 "Les textes visigoths, soigneusement conservés tant que l'Espagne garda son particularisme intellectual et réligieux, diffèrent beaucoup de tous les autres textes bibliques. Disposés, comme l'avait voulu saint Jérome, suivant l'order du canon des Hébreux, remplis de leçons parfois excellentes et primitives, plus souvent d'origine suspecte, ils constituent un groupe extrêmement cohérent et sont inséparables de l'ancienne forme de culte dans la Péninsule, de la liturgie mozarabe. Ils affirment le charactère indépendant de l'Espagnol, ils conservent les traditions

while throughout the Middle Ages the influence of Jewish Hebrew scholarship on Spanish Bible translation was evident. As early as the middle of the thirteenth century a Castillian version of the Psalter, ascribed to Herman el Aleman (the German), was made apparently from the Hebrew. The title-page in the manuscript runs: "Esta es la translacion del Psalterio que fizo maestro Herman el Aleman, segund cuema esta en el ebraygo."[120] The translation does not, however, appear to have been made directly from the Hebrew, but from Jerome's *Psalterium Hebraicum*, though occasionally Herman corrects Jerome from the original Hebrew, of which he must have had some knowledge.[121] In the two following centuries translations of the Old Testament into Castillian were made directly from the Hebrew. Two manuscripts, representing the same text, exist: one in the library of the Escorial and one in the library at Evora, the first dating from the second half of the fourteenth century and the second dated 1429. The Escorial manuscript, decorated by work probably of a Jewish artist, contains the whole

locales d'une Eglise que la domination des Arabes avait isolée de Rome et du continent, et qui s'est maintenue par un prodige de tenacité. Par eux, l'esprit de la litterature hébraique s'est perpetué bien mieux dans le monde espagnol, où les juifs tennaient tant de place, que dans nos pays où la civilisation chrétienne avait tout nivelé. ... A mésure que la croissant se rétire, l'originalité réligieuse de l'Espagne diminue. ... De même, au XIVe et au XVe siècle, l'esprit d'independence nationale et du fidéleté aux traditions continue a s'affirmer dans les traductions castillanes, les seules dans tout le moyen âge pour lequelles le texte hébreu ait fait autorité" (S. Berger, "Les Bibles castillanes," *Romania*, XXVIII [1899], 360 ff.).

[120] Berger, "Les Bibles castillanes," *op. cit.*, p. 388. The author is probably the same as Hermannus Alemanus (*fl.* 1240–56), who translated Aristotle into Latin (*ibid.*, p. 390; Jourdain, *Recherches sur les anciennes traductions latines d'Aristote* [Paris, 1843], pp. 135 f.).

[121] Berger, "Les Bibles castillanes," *op. cit.*, pp. 389 ff.

Old Testament, and the books are in the Hebrew order, with some slight exceptions, which are generally features of Spanish Hebrew biblical texts. Proper names are in their Hebrew, not the Latin, form. The Evora manuscript is incomplete but otherwise is very similar; it contains the latter prophets and the Hagiographa in the order of the Hebrew Bible, again with a few slight exceptions. The translation represented by both manuscripts seems to be a revision of an earlier Castillian translation made with constant reference to the Hebrew text. There is a third manuscript, also in the library of the Escorial, related to the other two.

The Bible of the House of Alba, a magnificently illuminated manuscript, preserves a translation of the Old Testament into Castillian from the Hebrew, begun in 1422. This famous translation was made for Don Luís de Guzman, grand master of the Military Order of Calatrava, by Rabbi Moses Arragel. We cannot dwell here on the history and nature of this translation, full of interest though the subject is; it must suffice to note its existence as a translation made from the Hebrew, for a Christian but by a Jew. The translation was based on the Vulgate, the Hebrew being followed where the Vulgate differed from the Hebrew text, and many Jewish glosses and comments being given, among others.

It was not until the latter half of the fifteenth century that Hebrew learning among non-Jews really began to take root in Europe. Pico della Mirandola (1462–94) was one of the first to interest himself in cabalistic literature, an approach to Hebrew studies which became fairly common in the fifteenth and, more especially, the sixteenth centuries. Mirandola's study of Hebrew was made possible by the good relations which existed between Jews and Christians at this time, in spite of the fierce hostility of the monastic orders. At a time when Jechiel of Pisa, banker and philanthropist, was one of the leading figures in Tuscany, and the celebrated Jewish doctor Gugliemo di Portaleone was physician to Duke Ludovico Gonzaga, after first having served Ferdinand of Naples and then Duke Galeazzo Sforza of Milan in a similar capacity, the social standing of educated Jews in Italy was bound to be high. Intercourse between Jews and Christians was, for a brief period, more general than in any other part of Europe. Foremost among the Italian Jewish scholars of the time was Elias del Medigo (1463–89). He it was who taught Mirandola Hebrew. Mirandola was initiated into the mysteries of the Cabala by another Jew, Jochanan Aleman, who had come to Italy from Constantinople. Aleman himself was a mystic and something of a fanatic, and under his influence Mirandola came to believe that the Cabala was the repository of all wisdom, its secrets having been handed down from earliest antiquity. Adapting Aleman's teaching to serve his own views, Mirandola applied the methods and formulas of the Cabala to prove the essential dogmas of Christianity. This he was able to do to his own satisfaction, and accordingly translated certain of the cabalistic writings from Hebrew into Latin, to acquaint Christians with the power of this great new teaching. Thus it was that Hebrew scholarship in the Renaissance became entangled with the fantastic doctrine of the Cabala—an entanglement which had unfortunate results in deflecting the attention of such a great scholar and otherwise clear thinker as Reuchlin from more profitable branches of Hebrew literature.

It was from Mirandola that Reuchlin first got his interest in cabalistic lore, but Reuchlin's interest in Hebrew and Hebrew literature, though it may have originated in a desire to understand the Cabala, was much wider and deeper than Mirandola's and had much greater practical results. Before we go on to discuss the Hebrew scholarship of Reuchlin and his contemporaries, however, a word must be said about Johann Wessel (1419–89), an earlier student of Hebrew. Born at Gröningen, Wessel studied at Cologne, Heidelberg, Louvain, Paris, and in several towns in Italy. In the course of his travels in search of knowledge he acquired some acquaintance with Hebrew, though where and how is not quite clear. At Cologne he studied Greek with Greek refugees who had settled there. Perhaps he also found there an instructor in Hebrew,[122] but wherever he learned the language he undoubtedly did obtain a certain knowledge of it and was known among his contemporaries as a scholar of Latin, Greek, and Hebrew, in all of which languages he appears to have given instruction at Cologne, Heidelberg, and Basel. Rudolf Agricola learned Hebrew from Wessel, and after having forgotten most of what he had learned took up the study again in his old age.[123]

[122] C. Ullman, *Reformers before the Reformation*, trans. Robert Menzies (Edinburgh, 1855), II, 287: "Whether he was at the same time instructed by monks ('a monachis qui vixerant in transmarinis regionibus') in the Hebrew, Chaldee and Arabic, must be considered doubtful. He had previously been taught Hebrew by educated Jews. A knowledge of Chaldee and Arabic must, however, be reckoned among the exaggerations on the subject of his erudition; at least not a single clear trace of it is to be discovered in his writings." I know of no authority for Ullman's assertion that Wessel had been taught Hebrew by educated Jews; perhaps baptized Jews were his teachers.

[123] L. Geiger, *Das Studium der Hebräischen Sprache in Deutschland vom Ende des XV. bis zur Mitte des XVI. Jahrhunderts* (Breslau, 1870), p. 21.

Sebastian Murrho of Colmar also appears to have had some knowledge of Hebrew, but our information on this point is scanty.[124] Other names known to us in connection with the study of Hebrew in the late fifteenth century are those of Peter Negri, whose *Tractatus contra perfidos Judaeos* was of such assistance to Conrad Pellican, Paul Scriptoris—Pellican's companion in his early travels in search of knowledge—and Conrad Summenhart, under whom Pellican studied at Tübingen.

The Hebrew studies of Conrad Pellican are closely connected with those of Reuchlin, of whom he was a younger contemporary. Pellican turned to Hebrew studies as a preliminary to his later work on the Bible and published his *De modo legendi et intellegendi Hebraea* in 1504, a slight and elementary work, soon rendered out of date by Reuchlin. Johann Reuchlin is generally known as the father of Hebrew studies in Europe, and the title is not unmerited. He it was who first put non-Jewish Hebrew scholarship in Europe on a firm basis, and his work was the immediate cause of the rapid development of Hebrew studies which took place during the sixteenth century and made possible the scholarly translation of the Old Testament from the original. Others, within a comparatively short period, developed his work and reached a standard of scholarship to which he was unable, owing to the conditions under which he worked, to attain. But Reuchlin was to a large extent the pioneer, the first Christian to examine Hebrew grammar and literature methodically and intensively, recognizing as he did the supreme importance of Hebrew studies for an adequate understanding of a great part of the documents

[124] Cf. *ibid.*, p. 25, n. 1.

of Christianity. Throughout his life he was subject to attacks from the conservative element in the church, and his long struggle with the apostate Jew Pfefferkorn and the Dominicans of Cologne, which so troubled his later life, is a tribute to the independence and courage with which he maintained the cause of disinterested scholarship against a bigoted and frightened clericalism.

Reuchlin was born in Pforzheim in 1455 and spent his youth studying at various universities—Freiburg, Basel, Paris, Orleans, Poitiers. He seems quite early to have developed a desire to learn Hebrew, but for long he was unable to find a teacher. It is very doubtful if there was a teacher of Hebrew in Paris when Reuchlin came there and almost certain that Reuchlin got as little Hebrew knowledge from Paris as from any of the other universities which he visited.[125] But in 1492 Count Eberhard, in whose service he was, sent Reuchlin to the emperor Frederick III to negotiate on a question concerning Eberhard's territory, and there he met Jacob Jehiel Loans, the emperor's Jewish physician. In Geiger's phrase, "Dieses erste Begegniss Reuchlins mit einem jüdischen Arzt ist ein Moment von welthistorischer Bedeutung." In the state of Würtemberg, where he had studied first, there had been comparatively few Jews, among whom none were both able and willing to give Reuchlin the instruction he desired. But Reuchlin found in Loans a Jew of a high level of general culture, possessing social and intellectual advantages as well as a special knowledge of Hebrew; of him he could and did make a real friend. Loans

[125] L. Geiger, *Johann Reuchlin, sein Leben und seine Werke* (Leipzig, 1871), p. 103. Geiger's is the authoritative biography, except for his interpretation of the struggle between Reuchlin and Pfefferkorn and the Dominicans, where his views are not now accepted.

taught Reuchlin Hebrew.[126] Reuchlin found a second
teacher in 1498 on one of his numerous journeys to Rome;
this was Obadiah ben Jacob Sforno, a distinguished Jewish
physician and philosopher, who gave him lessons daily so
long as the delegation of which he was a member remained
in Rome.[127] It was in Rome that Reuchlin first had the opportunity of purchasing Hebrew books and manuscripts,
the lack of which had hitherto so seriously hampered him
in his studies. Already in 1497 Reuchlin had sufficient Hebrew to give private instruction in that language in Heidelberg, and now after a further course of study and the ac-
quiring of some Hebrew books and manuscripts his proficiency must have increased considerably.

Reuchlin's first published work that is at all relevant to
Hebrew studies is his *De verbo mirifico* (Basel, 1494), a treatise on cabalistic wisdom in the form of a discussion between Baruchias, a Jew, Capnion (Reuchlin himself), a
Christian, and a Greek. The outcome is praise of Jewish
wisdom and a glorification of the Hebrew language through
which that wisdom is expressed. As we have noted, Christian interest in Hebrew in the Renaissance came through
mystical pursuits, which provided the incentive to the
study of Hebrew. But once that study had got under way it
largely freed itself from these mystical interests, though
this beginning in cabalistic literature did have some permanent effect on the course of Hebrew scholarship in Eu-

---

[126] J. Reuchlin, *De rudimentis Hebraicis* (Pforzheim, 1506), p. 3. This book has
no title-page, and the title is given only in the dedication to his brother (in the form
of a letter), which begins, "Johannis Reuchlin Ll. Doc. ad Dionysium fratrum
suum germanum de Rudimentis Hebraicis." The first page, otherwise blank, contains the words "Principium Liber."

[127] *Ibid.*

rope throughout the fifteenth and sixteenth centuries. Thus in James's Bodleian catalogue of 1605 there is listed a very high proportion of cabalistic works among the Hebrew books in the library.

Reuchlin, however, while he derived his enthusiasm for the Hebrew language from this dubious source, soon proceeded to a more critical study of the language. His *De rudimentis Hebraicis* (Pforzheim, 1506) began a chapter in the history of Semitic studies in Europe. Though not the first Hebrew grammar written by a Christian—Pellican's brief grammar had preceded it[128]—it was the first to make a real impression on contemporaries. A slight enough affair on modern standards, consisting of meager instruction in pronunciation and etymology, a brief treatment of Hebrew grammar, and a fairly elaborate vocabulary, the *De rudimentis* represented much hard work in the face of great difficulties on the part of the author. The grammatical portion derives largely from David Kimchi's ספר מכלול, while the vocabulary is dependent on the same author's ספר שרשים, though Reuchlin arranges the words alphabetically and not entirely by roots, as Kimchi had done. Reuchlin himself acknowledged his indebtedness to Jewish sources, in particular to the Jewish grammarians.[129] There are many references to rabbinical writings, though at this stage Reuchlin probably knew them only through Kimchi. Even in this early work Reuchlin shows an independence of judgment that is quite surprising. In his endeavor to find the exact meaning of a Hebrew word or phrase he compares the

---

[128] Conrad Pellicanus, *De modo legendi et intellegendi Hebraea* (Strassbourg? 1504?). (Probably not 1503, nor at Basel, as Geiger has shown.)

[129] *De rudimentis*, p. 223.

interpretations of several rabbinical authorities and chooses the one he finds most convincing. He refers frequently to the Vulgate, often in disagreement with its rendering of a Hebrew phrase, with such a remark as "nescio quid nostra translatio sonniauit dicens"; of an interpretation of Augustine that does not agree with the Hebrew text, he remarks: "Beautus Augustinus nescio quo somno motus . . . ."[130] His frequent outbursts concerning mistranslations in the Vulgate and elsewhere show how closely related to the new study of the Bible text is Reuchlin's pursuit of Hebrew learning. Here we see the new critical attitude toward the Vulgate and a demand for an accurate translation from the original texts springing directly from scholarship, with no doctrinal implications. This disinterested demand grew side by side with the Protestant desire for new Bible translations from the original, which had more specifically theological motives. Reuchlin, like Erasmus, was interested in religion but not in theology, and his scholarship is never doctrinaire.

Reuchlin's next contribution to the study of Hebrew was a practical exercise for those studying his first book, consisting of the Hebrew text of the seven penitential psalms (Psalms 6, 32, 38, 51, 102, 130, and 143) with a Latin translation and grammatical explanations (Basel, 1512). After

[130] *Ibid.*, pp. 571, 523. Reuchlin's attitude to the Hebrew text of the Bible can be seen from this note on the verb חסר and the Vulgate rendering of לא וחסרון יוכל להמנות as "et stultorum infinitus est numerus": " 'Et stultorum infinitus est numerus.' quodsic omnes aetate nostra theologi hactenus allegauerunt, sed nusquam haec sententia reperitur. est enim recitatus textus ita de uerbo ad uerbum in linguam latinam traducendus. 'Et defectus non poterit reparari.' Considerabis aliquando circa hoc vocabulum defectus nostros in scriptura sacra, ut hyperbolice loquar, infinitos defectus. de quibus utinam nobis deus misericors largiatur tempus coposius differendi" (*ibid.*, sub. vb. חסר).

this his Hebrew knowledge progressed rapidly. His next work, *De accentibus et orthographia Hebraeorum* (Hagenau, 1518), deals in some detail with points of grammar, accentuation, and punctuation and assumes some initial knowledge of the language on the part of the reader. While the *De rudimentis* taught only an elementary reading knowledge of the language, the *De accentibus* taught how to write also. Here, again, the influence of Reuchlin's Jewish teachers is obvious throughout, a particularly interesting piece of evidence being the musical notation for the chanting of the Torah with which he concludes the work: this could only have come from a contemporary Jewish source.

Reuchlin's influence made itself felt at least as much by his personal teaching as through his published works. Though throughout his life he remained a student, he was also a keen teacher and taught Greek and Hebrew both privately and publicly, sometimes under the most difficult conditions. His success as a teacher is indicated by the reverent and even affectionate attitude of his disciples, many of whom—such as Johann Böschenstein and John Cellarius— dedicated their own works to their master.

It was well for Reuchlin that he had the regard and support of his contemporary humanists, for it was not long before his novel studies drew upon himself the fierce hostility of the conservative element in the church. The story of his struggle with the Dominicans of Cologne has been told too often to require detailed repetition here.[131] The

---

[131] See especially *Epistolae obscurorum virorum: The Latin Text with an English Rendering, Notes, and an Historical Introduction*, ed. Francis Griffin Stokes (London, 1909); H. Graetz, *History of the Jews*, trans. B. Lowy (London, 1892), Vol. IV, chap. xiv.

baptized Jew Pfefferkorn, who had joined the Dominican
order after his conversion, pressed for the destruction of all
Hebrew books possessed by the Jews of Cologne and Frankfurt and succeeded in obtaining an order from the emperor
Maximilian for that purpose. With the support of the Dominicans of Cologne, Pfefferkorn confidently asked for
Reuchlin's support in putting this order into effect. But
Reuchlin the jurist was also Reuchlin the enthusiastic student of Hebrew. After a certain period of delay, during
which Reuchlin tried to dismiss Pfefferkorn's scheme by
charging technical irregularities in the emperor's mandate,
Reuchlin received an imperial summons to express his view
on the destruction of the Jewish books. His opinion, dated
from Stuttgart, October, 1510, was on the whole highly
favorable to Hebrew literature. He divided Hebrew literature into six classes (excluding the Old Testament), of
which only one, and a small one at that, contained books
offensive to Christianity. For the rest, he argued with real
conviction that the literature of the Jews was very necessary for an adequate understanding of the documents of
Christianity. He concluded his eloquent and scholarly plea
by advocating that their books should not be taken away
from the Jews, but that two professors of Hebrew should be
appointed at every German university, where Hebrew
books, including rabbinic works provided by the Jews,
should be studied. This plea met with the furious opposition of Pfefferkorn and the Cologne Dominicans, headed by
their ignorant and bigoted prior, Jacob van Hoogstraten,
who did not leave Reuchlin in peace for the rest of his life.
The battle continued on various fronts. The universities decided against Reuchlin; the humanists, in his favor. Pfeffer-

korn, as his contribution, circulated a highly abusive pamphlet about Reuchlin, the *Handspiegel* (1511), which declared that Reuchlin had been bribed by the Jews to give his opinion in their favor. To this Reuchlin replied in his *Augenspiegel* in the same year. Hoogstraten thereupon ordered Reuchlin to appear before the Dominican court at Mainz on the charge that the *Augenspiegel* contained heresy and succeeded in getting the book banned by an imperial order. In 1514 the pope put the case in the hands of the youthful Bishop of Speyer, who acquitted Reuchlin and ordered Hoogstraten to pay costs. But the Dominicans refused to accept this verdict and appealed to the pope. For six years they managed to hold up a decision, until finally Leo X, for political reasons as well as for the sake of peace and quiet, decided against Reuchlin. But by this time public interest in the case had died down, and Reuchlin's moral victory had been won.

This controversy between Reuchlin and the more reactionary elements of his day was in reality a pitched battle between humanism and antihumanism in Europe. All the foremost humanists of the time were on Reuchlin's side, as is witnessed by the *Epistolae clarorum virorum* (1514), a series of letters addressed by contemporary scholars to Reuchlin in his support. A more effective weapon was the *Epistolae obscurorum virorum*, a series of letters purporting to be written by some of his students to Ortwin de Graes (Ortwinus Gratius), professor at Cologne and archreactionary, the "poetistam asinum, lupum rapacem, si non potius crocodilum" described by Luther. The first volume of these letters, probably written by John Jaeger (Crotus Rubeanus), appeared in 1514; the second, by Ulrich von Hutten and

many other humanist friends of Reuchlin, in 1517. By illustrating their complacent ignorance and obscurantism in letters written in execrable dog Latin, the *Epistolae* poured
Rabelaisian ridicule on Reuchlin's enemies, whose humilia-
tion became complete after it was realized that some of the
victims themselves took the letters to be genuine and saw
nothing wrong in them. From the point of view of the history of culture and scholarship, the *Epistolae obscurorum
virorum* represented the climax of the battle, and the humanists won.

And so, in spite of Reuchlin's enemies, Hebrew studies in
Europe progressed. In 1537 Sebastian Münster brought out
a revised edition of Reuchlin's *De rudimentis*, with many
additions and alterations. Münster, who left the Franciscan order about 1529 to become a Lutheran, became one of
the most distinguished Hebraists of his time. He taught
Hebrew and Old Testament exegesis at Heidelberg and
Basel, where he died in 1552. His original Latin translation
of the Hebrew Bible (Basel, 1534–35; with his own edition
of the Hebrew text) is of great importance in the history of
Bible translation, and his work in Semitic grammar and
lexicography is of equal account. He brought out, as well
as Hebrew grammars, an Aramaic grammar, an Aramaic
dictionary, and a Latin-Greek-Hebrew dictionary, and edited and translated several rabbinic works. In addition to
Reuchlin's influence, the teaching of Elias Levita, the Jewish grammarian and poet, was of great help to Münster.
Levita, whose many works on Hebrew grammar and the
massoretic text were of great importance in the history of
sixteenth-century textual criticism, led a wandering life in
the course of which he taught Hebrew to many Christian

scholars. His influence on the development of Hebrew studies among Christians is second only to that of Reuchlin. John Immanuel Tremellius was another Jewish Hebraist who greatly helped the development of Hebrew learning. The son of a Jew of Ferrara, Tremellius became converted to Christianity about 1540. He came to England on Cranmer's invitation in 1547, and later taught Hebrew at Cambridge. His Latin version of the Old Testament and of the Syriac New Testament appeared in 1579. But by that time there had been many others in the field. Santes Pagninus had translated the Old Testament afresh from Hebrew into Latin as early as 1528: the translation appeared in that year along with his rendering of the New Testament from the Greek. There was also Leo Juda's Latin Bible of 1543. It was Pagninus' Latin version, revised by Arias Montanus, that appeared in the Antwerp Polyglot of 1584. But let us go back once again to Reuchlin for a final view of sixteenth-century Hebrew studies before proceeding to discuss the situation in England.

CHAPTER III

REUCHLIN'S conflict with the Dominicans made the position of the supporters of the New Learning quite clear. The "Reuchlinists" included all those who wished to put the rapidly growing fruits of linguistic and other scholarship at the service of religion, believing that religion could only gain as a result. Their opponents, content with their "Latinitas" and the Vulgate tradition, were suspicious of the critical apparatus which the New Learning brought in its wake, and suspicion grew to the fiercest hostility. It was a simple issue and a fundamental one; and, looking back from a later century, we can see that it was never for a moment in doubt. It was not in textual matters only that the time had come for a re-examination of fundamentals in Europe, and Reuchlin's controversy with Hoogstraten was but one aspect of a movement which affected every branch of European civilization. The spate of Bible translation which followed was a natural development, for Reuchlin's underlying purpose was to make more available for the public, in more accurate versions, and with more possibility of their being adequately understood, the chief documents of the Christian religion. Reuchlin and his followers were not "pure" scholars in the sense that they pursued their studies for the sake of the studies alone; they pursued them for the sake of the religion and the civilization in which they believed. That is perhaps the reason why the scholarship of the Renaissance, though no greater, even relatively, than that, say, of the nineteenth century, produced so much more brilliant monuments. The Authorized Version is a case in point.

In England most of the men who counted in the world of scholarship were, with greater or less explicitness, on Reuchlin's side: Fisher and More (for More was essentially a humanist, and his controversy with Tyndale was altogether different in its implications from that of Hoogstraten with Reuchlin), Linacre, Grocyn, Colet, Latimer, Tunstall. Tyndale, who combined the Wyclifite and the humanist traditions, showed by his work, if not so clearly by his attitude, that the two were essentially compatible. His scholarship derived from the humanist tradition—his knowledge of Greek was quite profound for the time, and his Hebrew knowledge, the sources of which it is impossible to trace in detail, considerable—while his zeal for translation sprang in large part from a democratic religious viewpoint which Wyclif shared with Protestantism generally. This combination of the humanist and the democratic (Wyclifite) traditions persisted in English Bible translation until it had produced the Authorized Version.

Erasmus, whose edition of the Greek Testament, with his own Latin translation, first appeared in 1516, encouraged biblical studies as much by his general attitude as by his work on the Greek text. It was he who first used the words which were echoed soon after by Tyndale: "I should wish that all good wives read the gospel and Paul's Epistles; that they were translated into all languages; that out of these the husbandman sang while ploughing, the weaver at his loom; that with such stories the traveller should beguile his wayfaring.''[1] Painstaking philology was important as a means to this end:

Why are we so precise as to our food, our clothes, our money-matters, and why does this accuracy displease us in divine literature alone? He crawls along the ground, they say, he wearies himself out with words and syllables! Why do we slight any word of Him whom we venerate and worship under the name of the Word? But be it so! Let whoever wishes imagine that I have not been able to achieve anything better, and out of sluggishness of mind and coldness of heart, or lack of erudition have taken this lowest task to myself; it is still a Christian idea to think all work good that is done with pious zeal. We bring along the bricks, but to build the temple of God.[2]

If Reuchlin's *De rudimentis Hebraicis* "helped to define and determine the religious tendencies in Teutonic humanism, to change the fanciful mysticism that had begotten the book into a spirit at once historical, critical and sane,"[3] his later work, and the work of his successors, completed this change. The nature of the movement as it began to develop throughout Europe is indicated by the number of trilingual colleges which sprang up in Germany, England, France, and Spain at this time. Hebrew, Greek, and Latin were the three languages necessary for a proper understanding of the Bible: Europe moved back to the position of Jerome, whose great work had been, in one sense, an equally great obstruction to knowledge and understanding, for the Vulgate had stood throughout the Middle Ages as a wall which bounded the study of the biblical text. But more and more the six-

---

[1] Erasmus, *Letters*, in J. Huizinga, *Erasmus* (New York, 1924), p. 140. See above, p. 2.

[2] Erasmus in Huizinga, *op. cit.*, p. 142.

[3] A. M. Fairbairn, "Tendencies in European Thought in the Age of the Reformation," *Cambridge Modern History*, II, 696.

teenth-century scholars came to hold, as Jerome had done, that the original languages must be studied by all serious theologians.

The most famous of all the trilingual colleges was that founded by Cardinal Ximenes at Alcalá. Fray Francisco Jiménez de Cisneros found himself in 1495, not altogether willingly, primate of Spain and one of the most powerful and wealthy churchmen of his day. Moved partly by a revival of that independent tradition of biblical scholarship which had persisted in Spain for many centuries and which remained to the end free of any flavor of Protestantism, Ximenes decided to use his wealth to found a university at the city called by the Romans Complutum and by the Moors Alcalá, whose first purpose was to study the original texts of the Bible and bring out a polyglot edition. The university was founded about 1500, and the trilingual college of St. Jerome was established as a part of the university in 1528. The biblical work, however, did not wait for the founding of the college, and the great Complutensian Polyglot was completed in 1517, though the papal license to publish it was not obtained until 1520, three years after Ximenes' death.[4]

In England the trilingual movement was felt at both Oxford and Cambridge. At Oxford, Bishop Fox founded Corpus Christi College, completed in 1517. The three public

[4] Volume I (N.T.) was completed on January 10, 1514, as the colophon tells us. Volume II was completed the following year; it contains a Hebrew and Aramaic dictionary and other similar textual aids. The other four volumes, containing the O.T., were completed on July 10, 1517. As a result of the three years' lag in publication, Erasmus' Greek Testament, though begun later, was published some years earlier. The Aldine edition of the Greek Testament also anticipated the Complutensian, appearing in 1518.

readerships which he established were in Latin, Greek, and Divinity, but it seems probable that Divinity was substituted for Hebrew because of a lack of Hebrew books and teachers, and also, possibly, because Wolsey appointed a Hebrew reader at Cardinal College, making a similar readership at Corpus unnecessary.[5] The foundation of Cardinal College by Wolsey at this time was partly the result of the trilingual movement. Robert Wakefeld, the first Hebrew reader at Oxford of whom we have definite information, was attached to this college after it had changed its name on being refounded by Henry VIII after Wolsey's fall. Wakefeld, who carried on the work of Reuchlin, seems to have had, for the time, a very competent knowledge of Hebrew. It was he who put Hebrew studies on their feet at Oxford—as his brother did at Cambridge—and henceforth Hebraists were to be found in increasing numbers in England until the eighteenth century, after which Semitic scholarship declined considerably until toward the end of the last century. At Cambridge, Bishop Fox, enthusiastic for the study of Greek and Hebrew, persuaded the Lady Margaret to found Christ's and St. John's, where the three languages were to be especially fostered.

Francis I encouraged the trilingual movement in France, and the royal professorships which he founded at Paris in 1531 included a regius chair of Hebrew. The first occupant of the chair was Francis Vatablus (d. 1547), whose publications (a great number of which were produced after his death from the notes taken by his students) included careful notes on the Hebrew text and an edition of David Kimchi's

[5] P. S. Allen, "The Trilingual Colleges of the Early Sixteenth Century," in *Erasmus, Lectures and Wayfaring Sketches* (Oxford, 1934), pp. 138 ff.

commentary on the twelve minor prophets accompanied by
his own explanatory notes. In 1545 Robert Stephens
brought out at Paris a parallel text of the Vulgate and Leo
Juda's Latin translation of the Bible, together with notes
from the lectures of Vatablus: this, and other of his works,
were of great use to the translators. He had many distinguished pupils, including Jean Mercier (Johannes Mercerus)
(d. 1570), who succeeded him in the professorship in 1546.
Mercier translated the Targum Jonathan into Latin,
brought out an Aramaic dictionary, Hebrew and Syriac word
lists, additions to Pagninus' Hebrew lexicon, and, most important of all, selections from rabbinical writings. Reuchlin had recognized the importance of the rabbinical traditions in the interpretation of the Hebrew text of the Bible,
but Mercier went further and, by collecting the passages
from the Talmud that bear on the Bible text, provided a
storehouse for later translators themselves unfamiliar with
the Talmud. His edition of the prophets with the Hebrew
commentaries was a valuable source for scholars who followed. David Kimchi was already well known to non-Jewish students of the Bible text, but Mercier seems to have
been the first to make considerable use of Ibn Ezra. (Kimchi, however, always remained the most popular by far of
Jewish exegetes among Christians, while Ibn Ezra was
largely neglected, except at Cambridge at the end of the
sixteenth and beginning of the seventeenth centuries.)[6]
Among Vatablus' pupils was Antoine Chevalier (1523–

---

[6] Edward Lively (1545–1605), regius professor of Hebrew at Cambridge from
1575, quotes from Ibn Ezra in his compendious *Annotationes in quinque priores ex
minoribus prophetis* (London, 1587), but not so often as he quotes from Kimchi.
All of Lively's quotations from Ibn Ezra may well have come from Mercier or
Tremellius. The same is true of his quotations from Rashi.

72), the French Protestant Hebraist. Chevalier was one of those Continental Hebrew scholars who came to England in the reign of Edward VI. Encouraged by Cranmer, he lectured unofficially in Hebrew at Cambridge, where he stayed with Tremellius. He spent the rest of Edward's reign at Cambridge, living on a pension granted by Cranmer and the Bishop of Ely. He left England on Edward's death in 1553 and later was appointed professor of Hebrew at Strassbourg. After further vicissitudes he returned to England in 1568 where he lectured in Hebrew at St. Paul's Cathedral and, in May, 1569, became the official Hebrew professor at Cambridge. Among his pupils were John Drusius and Hugh Broughton.[7]

Jerome Busleiden founded a trilingual college at the University of Louvain. The college seems to have been established shortly after Busleiden's death in 1517, provision for its foundation having been made in his will. Robert Wakefeld taught Hebrew here for a few months as a young man, and he was succeeded by another Englishman, Robert Shirwood, who taught for one month in 1519. Shirwood enjoyed a considerable European reputation as a Hebrew scholar; his one published work, a Latin translation of Ecclesiastes rendered literally from the Hebrew, with notes making use of the Aramaic and of the rabbinical commentaries, shows an impressive familiarity with Hebrew idiom to an extent rare among non-Jewish Hebrew scholars of the century. After Shirwood, Johannes Campensis occupied the Hebrew chair at Louvain for eleven years.

The trilingual movement also had its effect at Wittenberg, which was founded by the Duke of Saxony as essen-

[7] *DNB*, *s.v.* "Chevalier, Anthony Rodolph."

tially a trilingual college; at Vienna, where Bishop Faber founded the college of St. Nicholas; and elsewhere. By the time the movement had spent itself, Hebrew studies were firmly entrenched in the universities of Europe.

But the development of Hebrew studies was not confined to the trilingual colleges. A view of what was happening can perhaps best be gathered from a survey of the work done on the Hebrew text of the Bible at this time.

It would be beyond the confines of this study to give an account of the printed Hebrew Bibles that appeared throughout the sixteenth century, but some reference must be made to the editions available for those working on the Hebrew text at this period. There were many separate parts of the Bible printed in the late fifteenth century, and it is worth noting that the first of these was an edition of the Psalms with David Kimchi's commentary, which appeared in 1477, printed probably at Bologna. Editions of the Pentateuch and other parts of the Bible were fairly numerous from 1482 (when the first printed Pentateuch was published at Bologna). The first complete edition of the printed Hebrew Bible was brought out at Soncino by Joshua Solomon Israel Nathan Soncino. A complete Hebrew Bible appeared in 1494 at Brescia, from the press of Gerson ben Moses Soncino, and this is the text used by Luther in his German translation; but more important than this were the rabbinical Bibles, the first of which was published at Venice in 1517–18, edited by a Christian convert from Judaism, Felix Pratensis. This edition, like the later rabbinical Bibles, contained, in addition to the Hebrew text, Targum Onkelos to the Pentateuch; Rashi on the Pentateuch; Targum Jonathan and Kimchi on the Prophets; the Targum to the

Psalms, with Kimchi's commentary; and rabbinical commentaries on other parts of the Bible. In 1525 the second rabbinical Bible appeared, also published by Bomberg at Venice. This was a more elaborate undertaking than the former. Edited by the Jewish scholar Jacob ben Chayim of Tunis, it contained an elaborate introduction to the Massorah by the editor, the texts of both the greater and the lesser Massorah, the Targumim, Ibn Ezra's introduction to the Pentateuch with other rabbinical works on the Hebrew text, and the commentaries of Rashi, Ibn Ezra, Levi ben Gershon, and others. This edition and the Hebrew text of the Complutensian Polyglot are the two bases of the greater number of later editions of the Hebrew Bible until quite recent times. A smaller number descends from the Soncino Bible of 1488, through Sebastian Münster's Basel edition of 1536 and that brought out by Robert Stephens at Paris, 1539–44.

The polyglot Bibles provided another source of the original texts. The first of these, the Complutensian, has already been referred to. It appears from the introduction to this work that the Hebrew text was based on a collation of manuscripts procured in Spain and is thus independent of the Soncino Bibles. Each page of the Old Testament contains the Hebrew, the Vulgate, and LXX (the last with an interlinear Latin translation), and, at the foot of the page, the Targum and a Latin translation of it in parallel columns. Word-for-word correspondences between the Hebrew and the Latin of the Vulgate are indicated by identical letters placed at the top right-hand corner of the word. The Antwerp Polyglot, edited for Christopher Plantin by Arias Montanus, bases its Hebrew text largely on the Complutensian Polyglot. The Antwerp edition included, besides the text of the Complutensian, a revision of Pagninus' Hebrew dictionary by Francis Raphelengien, Plantin's son-in-law, later professor of Hebrew at Leiden.

What, then, can be said of the state of Hebrew scholarship in England at the time when the Authorized or King James Version was undertaken? And what of the Hebrew scholarship of those who produced the earlier versions, from Tyndale's to the Bishops' Bible, on which the Authorized Version was built? We have seen what European scholars in general had produced throughout the century in the way of helps to the study of Hebrew, and the extent of Hebrew knowledge which might be expected to result. Let us now turn more specifically to the English scholars of Hebrew, considering first what we can learn from the works of English Hebraists throughout the sixteenth century.

Robert Wakefeld, as we have noticed, is the first English Hebraist of the time of whom we have definite knowledge. His *Oratio de laudibus* . . . . *triarum linguarum, Arabicae, Chaldaicae, & Hebraicae* (London, 1525) was the first book printed in England with Hebrew and Arabic characters. This book, like the *Kotsur codicis R. Wakefeldi* (London, 1532?) and its continuation, the *Syntagma de Hebreorum codicum incorruptione*, shows little more than a rudimentary knowledge of the language, but all his works give evidence of a real enthusiasm for Hebrew studies. He published, without place or date, a Latin translation of Ecclesiastes, which provides some indication of the extent of his Hebrew knowledge. It is difficult to tell from Wakefeld's works exactly how much Hebrew he knew. Robert Shirwood,

Wakefeld's successor at Louvain, seems to have acquired a more profound knowledge of the language. In particular, his familiarity with Aramaic and with the rabbinic idiom (the latter of which was very imperfectly known to Christian scholars at this time) gives him a special claim to distinction. He, too, translated Ecclesiastes "ad veritatem Hebraicam" (Antwerp, 1523) and incorporated parts of rabbinical commentaries.

That Tyndale translated what he did of the Old Testament from the Hebrew is apparent from an examination of his text, which often agrees with the Hebrew against the Vulgate and against other secondary sources that were available to him. There are cases where Tyndale, A.V., and the Hebrew agree against all the intermediate English versions, and others, more numerous, where the Geneva Bible restores the Hebrew rendering obscured by Coverdale and the Great Bible. It seems clear that Tyndale knew more Hebrew than did the translators of any of the other English versions except the Geneva Bible, the Bishops' Bible, and A.V., and the Bishops' Bible is a doubtful exception.[8] There is abundant internal evidence that Tyndale had a firm grasp of the essentials of Hebrew syntax and vocabulary.

Paul Fagius (1504–49) studied Hebrew with Wolfgang Capito and Elias Levita and, after having made a European reputation as a Hebraist, came to England with Bucer in 1549 on the invitation of Cranmer. He died at Cambridge the same year, presumably before he had time to exert any

---

[8] E.g., Isa. 12:5, where Tyndale reads "that is knowen" beside "this is knowen" of A.V., GenB, against "as it is knowne" of C, GB, BB, and "announce this" of Vulg. and LXX. Hebrew is מוּדַעַת זֹאת, "this is known."

influence on Hebrew studies there. Richard Pace (1482?–1536) brought out, probably in 1530, *Praefatio in Ecclesiastem recognitum ad Hebraicam veritatem*, which appears to draw heavily on Shirwood's Latin edition of Ecclesiastes. Pace's active career as a diplomat and later as dean of St. Paul's can have left him comparatively little time for study; yet he was appointed reader in Greek at Cambridge in 1520, though he does not seem to have given any lectures. His Greek knowledge seems to have been sounder than his knowledge of Hebrew, which was not profound.

Thomas Wakefeld, brother of Robert, was the first occupant of the regius chair of Hebrew at Cambridge. It is impossible to estimate the extent of his Hebrew scholarship, for the one work that he is known to have written, the *Locutiones seu phrases in Novo Testamento quae videntur secundum proprietates linguae Hebraeae*, never seems to have seen the light. John Immanuel Tremellius, the converted Jew who did so much for Hebrew studies in Europe, came to England in 1547 and after 1549 took over, at intervals, Wakefeld's lecturing. The inference has been drawn that Wakefeld had to suspend his lectures owing to his adherence to the old religion.[9] It is perhaps some gauge of Wakefeld's scholarship that such distinguished Hebraists as Fagius and Tremellius were invited to substitute for him.

William Turner (d. 1568), dean of Wells, seems to have had some knowledge of Hebrew. He translated the "Comparison between the Old Learning and the New" of Urbanus Rhegius in 1537 and offered to revise the Great Bible. Rhegius' defense of the New Learning in the work translated by Turner takes the form of an argument that the so-

[9] Cf. *DNB, s.v.* "Wakefeld, Thomas."

called new learning is really the old learning restored, and, on the other hand, what is "new" is what the Roman Catholic church claims as the old learning, for it consists of unwarranted additions to and modifications of scriptural authority: the *real* old learning, Rhegius maintains, is the New Learning, and it is this that he is defending, while he attacks the spurious old learning, which is in reality new and lacking in all authority. This argument finally emerges as a defense of the authority of the original biblical text against Roman Catholic accretions and misinterpretations. It is worth noting that there were two editions of Turner's translation brought out in 1537, another in 1538, and a fourth in 1548. Turner himself, whose main occupations were botanizing and theological controversy, probably had little more than a smattering of Hebrew, but it is significant that a botanist with no pretensions to philological scholarship should have been aware of the importance of Hebrew knowledge and, apparently, acquired some himself.

Richard Taverner, whose revision of "Matthew's" Bible, as we have seen, is no part of the direct ancestry of A.V., seems to have had a competent knowledge of Greek, but very little if any knowledge of Hebrew. He seems to have revised "Matthew's" Old Testament with the help of the Vulgate and his imagination: there is not the slightest indication of any recourse to the Hebrew text.

James Pilkington, bishop of Durham (d. 1576), had some knowledge of Hebrew. His *Aggeus the Prophete Declared by a Large Commentarye* (London, 1560) and *Aggeus and Abdias Prophetes, the One Corrected, the Other Newly Added, and Both at Large Declared* (1562) constitute all the evidence we have of his familiarity with the language, which appears to have been tolerable.

William Fulke (1538–89), the Puritan divine, shows considerably more knowledge of Hebrew than most theological controversialists in England of his time. His *Defense of the Sincere and True Translation of the Holie Scriptures into the English Tong* (London, 1583) consists of a point-for-point refutation of Gregory Martin's attack on the vernacular translations. Fulke stresses the importance of the original Hebrew and Greek text and makes some display of his own Hebrew knowledge.

John Udall (1560?–1592), the Puritan scholar, was one of the most competent English Hebraists of the sixteenth century. He was responsible for the first Hebrew grammar to appear in English. This was his מפתח לשון הקדש *That Is the Key of the Holy Tongue: Wherein Is Conteined, First, the Hebrue Grammar out of P. Martinius. Secondly, a Practize upon the Psalmes. Thirdly, a Short Dictionary.* Together with a translation of Martinius' grammar, Udall's book contained exercises on Psalms 25 and 65 and a vocabulary of biblical Hebrew. The work is illuminating as showing what was meant by a knowledge of Hebrew in Europe at this time. A man who "knew" Hebrew well had a good vocabulary of the words occurring in the Bible, was familiar with all the main rules of grammar and syntax, but was somewhat confused about the nature of the Hebrew tenses and was liable to fall down completely and frequently on matters of Hebrew idiom. This is true of Udall, as it is true of the translators of A.V. Udall's commentary on Lamentations (1593) shows the Hebrew knowledge we should expect from his grammar.

Edward Lively (1545–1605), appointed regius professor of Hebrew at Cambridge in 1575, was one of the A.V. translators, whose Hebrew knowledge as a whole is discussed in the following chapter. But as he died in 1605 and left works where his Hebrew knowledge is more explicit, the evidence afforded by these may be discussed here. His *Annotationes in quinque priores ex minoribus prophetis, cum Latina eorum interpretatione* (London, 1587) is a scholarly work, showing a very competent knowledge of Hebrew and a wide range of reading. The authorities he refers to—many of them at second hand—included the Hebrew text, LXX, Symmachus, Theodotion, Vulgate, Targum Onkelos, Syriac; Kimchi (Quimquius), Rashi (Iarchius), Ibn Ezra (Aben Ezra); Arias Montanus, Tremellius, Pagninus, Calvin, Oecolampadius. He is one of the few commentators of the time to make considerable use of the commentaries of Nicholas de Lyra. For points of grammar and vocabulary he refers frequently to David Kimchi's *Liber radicum* ("Quimquius in radicibus suis"). Kimchi himself he refers to as "doctissimus Hebraeus," an opinion which was shared by all his contemporaries, for the A.V. translators as a whole depended on Kimchi to a quite surprising degree: he was the only Jewish commentator whom they used continuously. Lively's procedure in discovering the exact shade of meaning of Hebrew phrases and idioms is worth noting, for it was probably the method adopted by the other A.V. translators also. He would cite as many passages as he could where the same phrase occurred and, by careful examination and comparision, draw a conclusion. We note in Lively's scholarship a humility that is lacking in most scholars of the time. This trait, together with his habit of using illustrations from Latin and Greek literature, reflect an Anglican rather than a Puritan temper. There is about his work a suavity and a tolerance which is not to be found in the Puritan theologians. His writing has at times an almost eighteenth-century flavor.

Nicholas Gibbens in his *Questions and Disputations concerning the Holy Scripture* (London, 1601) shows himself a scholar similar to Lively in ability and temper. He quotes the Hebrew text, the Targumim, and LXX in the original. He, too, makes much use of Kimchi ("Rab. Dauid"), both the *Liber radicum* and the commentaries. He quotes Rashi, whom he frequently cites as "Rabb. Solom. et alii Rabbini," the "alii Rabbini" merely serving, apparently, to indicate that Rashi would naturally be in agreement with rabbinical traditions. He has some references to the Talmud which do not appear to be at first hand. He refers frequently to patristic literature: Jerome, Augustine, Cyprian, Basil, Ambrose, Athanasius, Hilary, Tertullian, Clement of Alexandria, Chrysostom, Aquinas, Justin Martyr, Cyril, Peter of Lombard, Origen—to take the order as it occurs in the first few pages of the first volume—are all cited repeatedly. Other writers frequently referred to are Calvin, Luther, and Oecolampadius. He has a few quotations from Josephus. He quotes from Aristotle, Plato, and Homer in Greek, and of Latin authors quotes Cicero, Ovid, and Pliny among others. The catholicity of his references is more striking even than Lively's; he ranges through the original texts, Targum, LXX, rabbinical literature, classical literature, medieval and patristic literature, and the New Learning. In spite of his numerous references to medieval writers, he is strongly anti-Catholic, as the "errors and slaunders of Atheists, Papists . . . ." of the title shows.

Gibbens, like Lively, displays Anglican scholarship at its best. These writers have a grace and a versatility that the Puritans lacked, though the latter often possessed more detailed scholarship on particular points.

Hugh Broughton (1549–1612) was one of the very best of the Puritan scholars, though he was not included among the A.V. translators, to his great annoyance. He studied Hebrew with Antoine Chevalier when the latter lectured in Hebrew at Cambridge. His Hebrew knowledge was perhaps the most profound of all the English Hebraists of the period. He seems to have had friendly relations with Jews, which would account for his familiarity with Jewish learning and traditions. He traveled in Germany in 1589 and 1590, where he made some Jewish contacts. In 1593 he offered, with five others, to revise the Bishops' Bible, but his offer, made in a letter to Lord Burghley, was not accepted. His *Epistle to the Learned Nobilitie of England Touching the Translation of the Bible* (Middleburg, 1597) gives the principle of translation which he would have applied:

The holy text must be honored, as sound, holy, pure: hede must be taken that the translater neither flow with lyes nor haue one at all: prophecies spoken in doubtfull termes, for sad present occasiones, must be cleared by sad study and stayd safty of ancient warrant: termes of equivocation witty in the speaker for familiar and easy matters, must be looked vnto, that a translater drawe them not vnto foolish & ridiculous senses: Constant memorye to translate the same often repeated in the same sort is most nedeful. Facility of phrase, defended by the new Testament, the Septuagint, and writers old indifferent for all nations, must be had. And herein, the stately words of the new Testament, in Greeke, taken from the Septuagint may stand profitable in the margent through the old. Also where the later repeat the former holy writers, therein as it were commenting vpon them, that should in al clearnes be expressed and noted. These be poinctes of necessitie. Some others of ornament in the end of our speach may be consydered.[10]

Broughton's works, which include commentaries on Ecclesiastes and Daniel and a violent attack on the A.V., which doubtless had its origin in his resentment at being excluded from the company of translators, display a very genuine scholarship inflamed and often perverted by rabid partisanship and violently controversial purposes. He quotes the Hebrew text and LXX frequently and also shows himself familiar with talmudic traditions. He, too, draws heavily on David Kimchi, to whom he refers as "the king of grammarians."[11] But even Broughton stumbles badly with certain Hebrew idioms, though it is not easy to say when his mistranslations are not deliberate, as part of a piece of special pleading.[12]

Broughton joins in the usual attack on the Jews for deliberately corrupting the text of the Hebrew Bible.[13] Yet he takes a great deal from Jewish sources and was on friendly terms with Jews throughout his life.[14] Further, he shared

[10] *Epistle to the Learned Nobilitie*, pp. 3–4.

[11] *Ibid.*, p. 12.

[12] *Ibid.*, pp. 18–19, where he seems to show ignorance of a very common idiom, the use of בן together with a number of years to give a man's age. But in this case it is clear that he prefers the mistranslation, which helps him in his argument, and his error is thus conscious and deliberate.

[13] *Ibid.*, p. 27: "For bad Iewes invented all this disturbance of very malice."

[14] Hugh Broughton, *An Epistle to an Ebrew* (n.p., n.d.); *A Petition to the King To Hasten Allowance for Ebrew Institution of Ebrewes* (London? 1608?), etc.

in general the Jewish attitude to the massoretic text, which he defends vigorously against the Catholics.[15] He went so far as to affirm the divine origin of the points.

Broughton exhibits the virtues and defects of a typical Puritan scholar of his time. He is unusually learned in Hebrew language and literature, yet his is an explosive and spluttering scholarship. He has none of Lively's urbanity or Gibbens' universality. Perhaps his exclusion from the A.V. translators was wise.

Henoch Clapham, an Englishman who seems to have spent some time as the minister of an English congregation in Amsterdam, possessed some knowledge of Hebrew, as we gather from his אלהים or *Ælohim-triune, Displayed by His Workes* (London, 1601): his earlier *Briefe of the Bible Drawen into English Poesy* (Edinburgh, 1596) gives no certain evidence of his knowledge of the language. Clapham's learning must have been typical of that of hundreds of English ministers, and thus his knowledge of Hebrew, even if superficial, is worth noting.

Finally, we may mention Andrew Willet (1562–1621), whose work on the textual criticism of the Bible shows him to be a scholar of at least the caliber of Lively or Gibbens. His *Hexapla in Genesin* (London, 1605) is a polyglot edition containing LXX, Targum, Vulgate, the Latin of Tremellius, GB and GenB, with selected phrases carefully compared with the Hebrew and also with the translations of Pagninus and Arias Montanus, and a great deal of other textual apparatus. It is the most impressive work on the purely textual side that any English scholar had yet produced. An interesting point is that Willet admits getting

[15] *Epistle to the . . . . Nobilitie*, p. 11.

his references to rabbinical writers out of Mercier, which is additional evidence for what one is led to suspect independently, namely, that Lively, Gibbens, and most of the other biblical scholars of the time who have references to Jewish commentators besides Kimchi very probably took these references out of Mercier and not directly from the works of the commentators themselves. Kimchi alone, as we know from his continuous use by the GenB and A.V. translators, was quoted directly by non-Jewish scholars of the sixteenth and early seventeenth centuries.[16]

From this brief account of English writers who published works which give evidence of a knowledge of Hebrew (leaving the post-Tyndale Bible versions for separate consideration), we may draw some conclusions concerning the state of Hebrew studies in England by the end of the sixteenth century. By this time, knowledge of Hebrew had ceased to be a rare or isolated phenomenon; most of those who wished to write about the Bible as scholars, and even some who wrote solely as controversialists, deemed it necessary to show some acquaintance with the original tongues. The degree of that acquaintance varied greatly. At best, it was impressive, comprising a fairly complete knowledge of Hebrew vocabulary, a good knowledge of the general structure of the language from the point of view of grammar and syntax, and some acquaintance with other Semitic tongues

---

[16] Why Willet was not among the A.V. translators is rather difficult to understand. He was perhaps the best textual critic of his day. DNB (s.v. "Willet, Andrew") suggests that it was owing to his Puritan leanings; but Willet was throughout his life a Church of England man, in spite of holding certain Calvinistic ideas, and stronger Puritans than he were included. More plausible is the other suggestion, that he lost official favor after his quarrel with King James over the latter's proposed Spanish marriage.

—Aramaic, sometimes also Syriac, rarely (before William
Bedwell) Arabic. The greatest weakness was consistently a
certain confusion about the nature of the Hebrew verb
forms (Reuchlin, misled by Latin and Greek, had started
off with some major blunders here, and though these were
rectified it was long before later scholars recognized the
precise nature of, for example, the Hebrew "imperfect")
and a lack of understanding of the flexibility of Hebrew
idiom. It is significant that David Kimchi was the one Jewish commentator who was universally used by Christian
scholars at this time. Rashi, who was far the most popular
exegete among the Jews themselves, was rarely used by non-
Jewish writers, while Ibn Ezra was employed more rarely
still. Kimchi's Hebrew is simple and straightforward compared with that of Rashi, while Ibn Ezra's more philosophical prose presents even greater difficulties. Thus the way in
which the English Bible translators used Hebrew commentators provides a very interesting index of their Hebrew
knowledge.

There are other types of evidence concerning the knowledge and ability of the translators themselves which we
might use before proceeding to examine the internal evidence provided by the actual translation. In the list of forty-seven translators that has come down to us[17] there are
the names of scholars whose reputation and ability can be
assessed independently of their work on A.V. Lively, we
have already discussed: he died in 1605, soon after A.V.
got under way, and so cannot have had very much influence
on even his section of the translation (I Chronicles to

[17] E. Cardwell, *Documentary Annals of the Reformed Church of England* (2d ed.;
Oxford, 1844), II, 144 ff.

Ecclesiastes). But among those who worked on the translation for a longer period there are many whose knowledge of the original tongues can be estimated from other of their works.

Lancelot Andrewes, who is first on the list of translators, headed, as dean of Westminster, the group which met at Westminster and translated Genesis to II Kings (inclusive). Better known as a preacher than as a linguist, Andrewes nevertheless seems to have possessed a knowledge of Hebrew that compared favorably with that of any of his contemporaries. His works provide abundant evidence of his knowledge of Hebrew vocabulary and grammar, though it is difficult to discover from his numerous references to Hebrew words and phrases just how deep this knowledge went. He was known to his contemporaries as a brilliant linguist, especially in oriental languages, and there is no doubt of the diversity of his linguistic knowledge. He probably knew more of patristic literature than any scholar of his day. He was a man of extraordinarily wide learning, and in general the breadth rather than the depth of his knowledge fitted him to preside over his fellow-translators.

John Overall, dean of St. Paul's (later bishop of Coventry and Lichfield and finally bishop of Norwich), is the second on the list of the translators of the first part of the Old Testament. Much less of a scholar than Andrewes, Overall was nevertheless known to his contemporaries as a brilliant Latinist.[18] In his Cambridge days he had held the post of "praelector Graecus" and "praelector mathematicus." In 1596 he succeeded William Whittaker as regius professor of

18 Fuller, *Worthies* . . . . (ed. 1662), p. 61.

divinity at Cambridge. More of a theologian than a linguist, Overall has left little evidence on which to form a judgment of his knowledge of Hebrew. References in his works are insufficient to afford grounds for any definite opinion.

Adrian de Saravia, the third in this group, is another whose knowledge of Hebrew it is difficult to assess. Born in Artois of Spanish-Flemish stock, he eventually became professor of divinity at Leiden in 1582 and later settled permanently in England, where he acquired a reputation as a scholar of modern languages. In 1595 he was appointed a prebendary of Canterbury and in 1601 prebendary and later in the same year dean of Westminster. His published works, all of a theological nature, provide little opportunity for investigating his Hebrew knowledge.

Richard Clarke, fellow of Christ's College, Cambridge, is the fourth of this group. Contemporary references to him are few and inconclusive. He was at one time vicar of Minster in the Isle of Thanet.[19] His only published works are his *Sermons* (London, 1637), which reveal a certain amount of scholarship but tell us little or nothing about his Hebrew knowledge.

John Layfield, fellow of Trinity College, Cambridge, is the fifth of this group. He appears to have been a better Greek than Hebrew scholar, holding the position of "lector linguae Graecae" at Cambridge in 1593. Little more is known of him. Of Dr. Teigh, the sixth of the Westminster translators, not much is known besides the fact that he was archdeacon of Middlesex, and the extent of his Hebrew

[19] John Lewis, *The History and Antiquities, Ecclesiastical and Civil, of the Isle of Tenet in Kent* (London, 1736), I, 62, 101.

scholarship must remain conjectural. As little is known of the next on the list, Francis Burleigh, of Pembroke Hall, Cambridge. Geoffrey King, next on the list, was professor of Hebrew at Cambridge after Robert Spalding, Lively's successor, and must therefore have been a competent Hebraist.

The ninth on the Westminster list, Richard Thomson, known to his contemporaries as "Dutch Thomson"—he was born in Holland, though of English parents—had a reputation both as a drunkard and as a linguist. Lancelot Andrewes seems to have thought highly of him, for he presented him to the living of Snailwell in Cambridgeshire. He seems to have been a Hebraist of some ability; his works give some indication of Hebrew knowledge.

The list of the translators of Genesis to II Kings concludes with the name of the Arabic scholar William Bedwell. His works, as well as his reputation, provide abundant evidence of his ability as a scholar of Semitic languages. Among his many other works, he compiled the first Arabic lexicon produced in England and was perhaps the most distinguished Orientalist of his day.

The group at Cambridge who translated I Chronicles to Ecclesiastes (inclusive) was headed by Edward Lively, whom we have already discussed. The second member of this group was John Richardson, appointed regius professor of divinity at Cambridge in 1607. He had a considerable contemporary reputation as a Hebraist but left no works on which a judgment of his Hebrew knowledge might be based.

Laurence Chaderton (or Chatterton), master of Emmanuel College, was the third of this group. He, too, was recognized by his contemporaries as a Hebrew and classical scholar, but has left no published works.

Fourth of this Cambridge group was Francis Dillingham of Christ's College, a better Greek than Hebrew scholar, so far as we can gather from his works. Thomas Harrison of Trinity, who follows Dillingham on the list, was a distinguished Puritan Hebraist who enjoyed a great reputation as a biblical scholar, on which his lack of published works makes it impossible to comment. Roger Andrewes, sixth of this group, was a brother of Lancelot, though not such a distinguished scholar. Robert Spalding, the seventh, was Lively's successor at Cambridge, which alone attests to his competence as a Hebraist. This Cambridge group concludes with Andrew Byng, who succeeded to the same chair in 1608.[20]

The Oxford group, who translated Isaiah to Malachi (inclusive), was headed by John Harding, professor of Hebrew at Oxford. There is no conclusive evidence of the extent of Harding's scholarship, but there is some reason to believe that Oxford Hebrew scholarship at this time was slightly below the level of Cambridge.

John Rainolds (or Reynolds), Puritan scholar of note, worked with this group until his death in 1607. Rainolds' knowledge of Hebrew, as is evident from his published works, was considerable and probably at least equal to that of any member of the group. Though this Oxford group was nominally led by Professor Harding, Rainolds seems actually to have been its leader: it was he who had pressed most strongly the original proposals for the revision at the

[20] After Lively's death in 1605, Spalding, King, and Byng held the regius professorship of Hebrew at Cambridge in rapid succession.

Hampton Court Conference, and until his death it was at his house that the other members of the group met weekly when engaged on the translation.

The third member of this group was Thomas Holland, regius professor of divinity at Oxford; though there is little evidence in his published works, Holland's scholarship in Greek and Latin—especially the former—seems to have been considerable. He had a contemporary reputation as a linguist and a Bible scholar.

Richard Kilbye was the fourth member of the Oxford group. He succeeded Harding as professor of Hebrew in 1610. Unfortunately, his Latin commentaries on Exodus and his continuation of Mercier's commentary on Genesis[21] were never published, but they suggest a sound Hebrew knowledge: no one who was not a competent Hebraist could have presumed to continue one of Mercier's biblical commentaries.

Miles Smith, later bishop of Gloucester, was the fifth in this group. Smith, who enjoyed a great reputation as a scholar of the oriental tongues, took a specially prominent part in the translation of the Old Testament: he was one of the two who undertook the final revision of the complete text, and it was he who wrote the Preface.[22] His sermons (London, 1632) give some evidence of his knowledge of Semitic languages.

Richard Brett, the next on the list, seems to have spent most of his career before 1604 perfecting himself in classical

---

[21] Wood, *Athenae Oxonienses*, ed. Bliss, II [London, 1815], 287: "The chief part [of the commentary on Exodus] is excerpted from the monuments of the rabbins and Hebrew interpreters."

[22] *Ibid.*, p. 359.

and Semitic tongues. He had a great contemporary reputation as a scholar of Latin, Greek, Hebrew, Aramaic, and Arabic.[23] His published works, however, are inconclusive as evidence. The identity of Mr. Fairclough of New College, the last name on the list, remains obscure.

These are those of the translators of the Old Testament whose names have come down to us. There were doubtless many others who assisted in various ways, giving opinions on points that were submitted to them or substituting for one of the official translators. Old age and death wrought considerable changes in the personnel of the translators, of which the above list does not entirely take account.

Bodley's first librarian completed his catalogue of books in the library in 1605.[24] A.V. was commenced in 1604, the very year when James was compiling his catalogue. The Hebrew items in James's catalogue should therefore be fairly representative of the material available for English translators at this time. Apart from college and private libraries, the books in Bodley should suggest the kind of Hebrew items accessible to the Christian scholar, comprising as it were a cross-section of such material. The items are surprisingly varied. There are several Hebrew texts of the Old Testament, of which the two most used by Bodleian readers were almost certainly those in the Complutensian and Antwerp polyglots. Copies of these survive in good condition, though obviously much used. There are copies of almost all the available Hebrew grammars, including those of David Kimchi, Moses Kimchi, Reuchlin, Münster, Ber-

---

[23] *Ibid.*, pp. 611–12.

[24] Thomas James, *Catalogus librorum bibliothecae publicae quam T. Bodleius in academia Oxoniensi nuper instituit* . . . . (Oxford, 1605).

tram, and Martinius. There are also the Aramaic grammar and dictionary of Münster and the Aramaic and Syriac grammar of Tremellius. There are copies of Targum Onkelos and Targum Jonathan, both in the original and in the Latin translation (apart from the texts in the polyglots). There is a fair number of rabbinical works, including some complete Talmud sets; but these were most probably little used. The biblical commentaries of Lyra, Arias Montanus, Conrad Pellican, and John Drusius are listed, and, of Jewish commentaries, those of David Kimchi (several editions), Rashi, Levi ben Gershon, Abarbanel, and a few minor commentators. Of Hebrew dictionaries, in addition to those included in the grammars already mentioned and David Kimchi's *Liber radicum*, there are those of Avenarius, Celepinus, and Pagninus, and the Hebrew-Latin-Italian dictionary of David de Pomis. There is quite a disproportionate number of minor cabalistic works.

These are the items relevant only to a study of the Hebrew text of the Bible, and they naturally comprise but a small fraction of the biblical material in Bodley at the time. They would provide ample scope for those translating from the original Hebrew, even if the translators began with but the slightest knowledge of the language. For a complete study of the material available for the A.V. translators, it would be necessary to examine the contents of all contemporary libraries, both public and private. It would be an interesting, if lengthy, task to compare these results with the internal evidence yielded by a comparison of the different sections of the A.V. text.

CHAPTER IV

W̲E ARE fortunate in knowing the declared methods of the A.V. translators as well as in possessing a list giving the names of most of the translators themselves. How far the declared methods were followed is another matter, but, except for those of the rules which an examination of the text shows the translators not to have followed, it is reasonable to suppose that they were adhered to. At any rate, it would be well to start an investigation of the A.V. text with an examination of these rules, which were drawn up probably by Bishop Bancroft for the guidance of the translators.[1]

First, the translators were to follow BB. Bancroft—or whoever it was who drew up the rules—could hardly help himself here. BB was the "authorized version" in 1604, though not officially; GenB, if a more scholarly as well as more popular translation, was a Puritan version outside the tradition of Anglican translations. As we shall see, this rule was not strictly adhered to. In view of the admitted inferiority of BB to GenB in point of scholarship and accuracy, it is probable that the translators regarded the rule

[1] The text of the rules has been printed many times, with some slight variations. Gilbert Burnet, *History of the Reformation*, II, 368 (ed. 1681), gives them "ex MS D. Borlase," and Westcott gives them from Burnet. There is also a very summary list, omitting many of the points, in the report of the English delegates to the Synod of Dort, 1618 (*Acta synodi nationalis . . . . Dordrechtianae . . . .* [Dort, 1620]).

as a mere diplomatic gesture.[2] In matters of *style*, it is true, BB was more the model, but not where questions of accuracy arose.

Second, proper names were to be in the form "as nigh as may be, accordingly as they were vulgarly used." This provision not only had for its purpose the differentiation of proper names in A.V. from those in the Douai version, which used the Latin forms; it was also in the tradition of English Bible translation, whose main purpose was to make the Bible *familiar* to English readers.[3] This tradition was opposed to that of the Roman Catholic church, which endeavored even in its vernacular versions to stress the esoteric character of the book and the inadequacy of the ordinary layman to understand the bare text. But Erasmus—though no Protestant—and Tyndale had wished the plowman to sing Bible texts at his work, and this attitude, fundamental to English Protestant Bible translation from Wyclif to A.V., is responsible for many features of the sixteenth-century versions and, to some extent at least, for the magnificent style of A.V. itself. For the English translators always insisted that their version should be pleasant to read, familiar yet impressive, simple yet dignified, and it is this combination of qualities—we find it even in Tyndale—that makes the style of A.V. what it is.

The third rule, that the old ecclesiastical words were to be kept ("church," e.g., was not to be replaced by "congre-

[2] Such as King James's description of GenB as "the worst of all," and his pretense that he had not seen GenB until his attention had been drawn to it by "an English lady" (see above, p. 65).

[3] We must remember, however, that owing to the medieval tradition a great many biblical names were still popular in their Latin forms. The Puritans were largely responsible for the decline of this tradition.

gation''), had a similar purpose in view: the English Bible must be kept familiar to the people. It was also directed against the Puritan tendency to abandon the traditional terms which had associations with Catholic ritual and is an interesting reflection of the essentially Anglican nature of A.V. Other aspects of this tendency are seen in the fourth rule, which provides that where a word has several meanings the one to be used is that "which hath been most commonly used by the most of the ancient fathers, being agreeable to the propriety of the place and the analogy of the faith''; and in the fifth, which deprecates any unnecessary interference with the customary division of the chapters.

The sixth rule prohibited the employment of marginal notes except in cases where the explanation of the original Hebrew or Greek "cannot, without some circumlocution, so briefly and fitly be expressed in the text." This was natural after the Church of England's experience of the controversial violence of Puritan notes. The seventh provided for cross-references to be indicated in the margin.

Rules 8–11 are concerned more specifically with the procedure in translating. Each individual in each group was to translate the same portion, go over it until it satisfied himself, and then submit it to the other members of the group who were to confer together and agree on what parts should stand and what should be emended further. When each group had completed any one book in this manner, it was to be sent to the other groups to be "seriously and judiciously" considered once again; "for his majesty is very careful in this point." Any doubts or differences which arose at this stage must be communicated with full particulars to the group which originally translated that passage, and if they did not agree to a further emendation the question must be decided at a final general meeting "of the chief persons of each company." Any special obscurity might be referred "to any learned man in the land for his judgment of such a place."

The twelfth rule provided that every bishop should inform his clergy of the work that was being undertaken and encourage all those who were "skilful in the tongues" to send to the group of translators concerned such observations on the text as they might desire to make.

Rule 13 states that the directors in each company were to be "the Deans of Westminster and Chester for that place; and the king's professors in the Hebrew or Greek in each university."

The fourteenth gives the translations to be used when they agree better with the meaning of the original than BB—"Tindale's, Matthew's, Coverdale's, Whitchurch's, Geneva." A final rule, which seems to have been added later, provided that "three or four of the most ancient and grave divines in either of the universities, not employed in translating" were to be assigned by the vice-chancellor "upon conference with the rest of the Heads, to be overseers of the translation as well Hebrew as Greek, for the better observation of the fourth rule above specified." This was to provide an authoritative ruling concerning the application of the rather vague provisions of Rule 4.[4]

The translators did not hurry. As the Preface informs us, they scorned to follow the practice traditionally ascribed to the translators of the Septuagint: "The worke hath not

4 B. F. Westcott, *History of the English Bible*, rev. W. Aldis Wright (3d ed.; London, 1905), p. 116.

bene hudled vp in 72. dayes, but hath cost the workemen, as light as it seemeth, the paines of twise seuen time seuentie two dayes and more." Their aim, as the Preface again tells us, was not to prepare a new translation—though the title does say "Newly Translated out of the Originall Tongues"—"but to make a good one better, or out of many good ones, one principall good one, not iustly to be excepted against."

Neither did wee thinke much to consult the Translators or Commentators, *Chaldee, Hebrewe, Syrian, Greeke,* or *Latine,* no nor the *Spanish, French, Italian* or *Dutch;* neither did we disdaine to reuise that which we had done, and to bring backe to the anuill that which we had hammered: but hauing and vsing as great helpes as were needfull, and fearing no reproch for slownesse, nor coueting praise for expedition, wee haue at the length, through the good hand of the Lord vpon vs, brought the worke to that passe that you see.

To determine exactly and in detail the sources of A.V. would be an impossible task, as the combinations of possible sources which would have yielded the same results are almost infinite in number. Even if we confine ourselves to the Old Testament, and to the Book of Isaiah in particular, as this study seeks to do, the problem is still impossibly complex. Let us briefly consider the versions of the Old Testament which the A.V. translators might have consulted. Of English versions, there were portions of the Old Testament translated by Tyndale, Coverdale's Bible, "Matthew's" Bible, the Great Bible, Taverner's Bible, the Geneva Bible, and the Bishops' Bible. Most of these show differences in different editions. Of translations into languages other than English, there were—in chronological order of their first editions—the Complutensian Polyglot, Luther's

Bible, the Zurich Bible, the Latin Bible of Pagninus, the Latin Old Testament of Münster, Lefèvre's French Bible, Olivetan's French Bible, Leo Juda's Latin Bible, Castalio's Latin Bible, Cassiodoro de Reyna's Spanish Bible, Arias Montanus' Latin-Hebrew Bible, Tremellius' Latin Old Testament, the revised French Bible of 1588, Cypriano de Valera's Spanish Bible, and Giovanni Diodati's Italian Bible. And these are only the translations noted by Westcott[5] as having "a direct literary bearing on the history of the Authorised Version."

Thus, though we know the declared principal sources of A.V., it is impossible to give definitely the source of an A.V. rendering which differs from most or all of the declared principal sources but yet agrees with, say, Tremellius and the commentary of David Kimchi; or with Pagninus and the Targum; or with Leo Juda and one of the French versions. We are faced with the fact that, while we know the chief sources as a whole, any given rendering might have come from one of many available sources. Was it Kimchi or Tremellius that suggested the rendering in the first of the cases just cited? Was it Pagninus or the Targum in the second? And where A.V. agrees with GenB and some other source against the other English versions, has A.V. gone to GenB or is the agreement a coincidence? One might prove that Kimchi has influenced the rendering of all the principal cruxes in a certain book, yet because Kimchi's influence runs through most of the European versions of the sixteenth century, this would be no conclusive evidence of the use of that commentary by A.V. When faced with a crux, we might expect the translators to go anywhere at all for help, and it

---

[5] *Op. cit.*, Appen. II.

is this wealth of possible sources for the rendering of any given difficult passage which makes any definite conclusions about A.V. sources impossible—at least impossible without a painstaking textual collation which no individual could hope to achieve in a lifetime. Of course, the A.V. translators did not choose a rendering blindly; if they did accept an interpretation from a given source, it was because they were convinced that it was right, so ultimately the version does reflect their own scholarship in the original tongues. In no case did they accept an interpretation from a given source solely on account of the prestige of that source. Yet even this statement needs some qualification, for there is evidence that in the case of Kimchi's commentary—which was regarded by Christian scholars of the time as the work of the most competent of the Jewish grammarians and which consequently enjoyed tremendous prestige among them—the name of the author was in some cases sufficient to justify the adoption of his rendering, other things being equal. In the case of a genuine crux, where the translators found the meaning thoroughly obscure, this would almost certainly apply. But it is not always easy to say what was considered by the A.V. translators to be a genuine crux.

Throughout English Bible translation from Tyndale to A.V. new influences were constantly making themselves felt. That Tyndale used the Hebrew text, as we have already mentioned, is fairly clear. Not only does he stress in his writings the necessity of following the original, but internal evidence shows that where the Vulgate and the Hebrew disagreed he followed the latter. And though Tyndale most probably knew Luther's translation, there is a sufficient number of cases of agreement with the Hebrew against both Luther and the Vulgate to prove Tyndale's independence.[6] A surprising amount of Tyndale's Pentateuch and *Epistles Taken Out of the Old Testament* remains in A.V. text: the reason is simply that both are translated from the Hebrew. Where Tyndale had the true sense of the Hebrew, his rendering is nearly always to be found in GenB, and A.V. follows GenB when it agrees with the Hebrew against BB and the other English versions. (At least, it appears to do so: this and any following generalization about the sources of the A.V. text must be taken to indicate a tendency rather than a rigid law, for, as the foregoing remarks have indicated, we cannot be *certain* of the source of any given rendering, though we may establish a very strong probability.) Even Tyndale's Jonah, though not in the direct line of ancestry of A.V., is much less different from the A.V. of Jonah than might be expected.[7] Some of the passages from Isaiah which Tyndale translated in his *Epistles*, with an indication of the renderings preserved in A.V., will be found in Appendix I.

Coverdale made no claim to originality in his translation. The title-page of the first edition states that his Bible is "faithfully and truly translated out of Douche and Latyn into Englishe," and in the dedication he speaks of "fyue sundry interpreters" whom he followed in his rendering; and again, further on in the dedication, he tells us that "I haue had sondrye translacions, not onely in latyn, but also of the Douche interpreters: whom (because of theyr syn-

6 Tyndale appears to have used Luther more in his translation of the N.T. than in his Pentateuch and other O.T. translations (see collation in Westcott, *op. cit.*, pp. 148 ff.).

7 See D. Daiches, *William Tindale's Version of the Book of Jonah* (London, 1937), for a collation of Tyndale's Jonah with A.V. and an explanation of their relation.

guler gyftes & speciall diligence in the Bible) I haue ben the
more glad to folowe for the most parte, accordynge as I
was requyred." The "fyue sundry interpreters" followed
by Coverdale were almost certainly the Vulgate, Pagninus'
Latin version of 1528, Luther's German Bible, the Zurich
Bible of Leo Juda, Zwingli, Pellican, and others, and Tyndale's New Testament and Pentateuch. For the Old Testament, except the Pentateuch, the Zurich Bible is certainly
Coverdale's primary source,[8] with occasional renderings of
Pagninus and Luther preferred to those of the Zurich version. The basis of his Pentateuch is Tyndale's, and Tyndale
also influenced Coverdale's rendering of Jonah.[9] Coverdale's
New Testament is a revision of Tyndale largely by the
Zurich text. When his other authorities left him in genuine
doubt, Coverdale almost always resorted to the Vulgate,
which was for him the ultimate text. He gives no evidence
of any knowledge of Hebrew. Westcott's assertion[10] that
he "had some knowledge of Hebrew by which he was
guided at times in selecting his rendering" rests on no other
foundation than Coverdale's expressed intention of preparing for the Great Bible a table giving the variant readings
of the Hebrew, Aramaic, Greek, and Latin texts. But (1)
this table was never published; (2) there is no reason to
believe that Coverdale prepared it himself from an examination of the original texts, and every reason to believe that,

[8] See the collation in Westcott, *op. cit.*, Appen. VII, pp. 311 ff., and "An Examination of the Sources of the Notes in Coverdale's Bible of 1535," *ibid.*, Appen.
IV, pp. 298 ff.

[9] Though not to the degree that Westcott (*op. cit.*, p. 164, n. 1) thinks. Westcott draws his conclusions from a collation of one verse. A complete collation
shows more important variations.

[10] *Ibid.*, pp. 163 and 75.

if indeed it was completed, it was a secondhand compila-
tion; and (3), in any case, this would not show that Coverdale knew Hebrew at the time he was preparing his Bible of
1535.

Coverdale's own sense of style often led him into rather
diffuse paraphrase, guided by no other authority than his
own ear. But this fluency of his had a permanent effect on
the style of A.V., for it was he more than any other single
writer whose sense of rhythm gave English Bible translation that musical quality which is particularly evident in
A.V.[11] It is easy, however, to exaggerate Coverdale's contribution to the style of A.V. and to minimize the work of
later translators. The truth is, Coverdale's ear was not un-
erring; it frequently led him to monotony and prolixity,
and his work had to be severely pruned by later translators.
Sometimes, again, following the concise diction of the German or the Latin, he is led into quite abrupt passages,
which had to be expanded by revisers.[12]

"Matthew's" Bible, as we have seen, was a conflated
version made up of Tyndale's New Testament and Pentateuch, the Old Testament from Ezra to Malachi from Coverdale, the Apocrypha from Coverdale, and the Old Testament from Joshua to II Chronicles in a hitherto unpublished

---

[11] Coverdale's style was based on an innate sense of rhythm, on a sense of the
rhythm required by the meaning, rather than on any attempt to imitate the rhythm
of the original, of whose precise nature he was unaware. There is some evidence
that the translators of GenB first made some attempt to reproduce the rhythm of
the Hebrew in the English and that in this they were followed by the A.V. translators.

[12] E.g., the difficult phrase גוי קו־קו ומבוסה is rendered by C. "a desperate
and pylled folke" (cf. Zurich). GenB has "a nacion litle and litle, euen troden
vnder fote;" BB, "a nation troden downe by litle and litle;" and A.V., "a nation
meted out and trodden down."

translation, most likely that on which Tyndale was engaged between the completion of his Pentateuch and his death.[13] Coverdale's, and not Tyndale's, Jonah is included, and Tyndale's version of the *Epistles Taken Out of the Old Testament* are not used. The translation of the Old Testament from Joshua to II Chronicles has many of the characteristics of Tyndale's other Old Testament translations and bears evidence of an adherence to the original Hebrew in preference to all other texts. It is probable that Tyndale had extended his knowledge of Hebrew after completing the Pentateuch: in a letter from prison at Vilvorde he asks for a Hebrew Bible, a Hebrew grammar, and a Hebrew dictionary.[14] Rogers, who put together and edited "Matthew's" Bible, did very little revision of text himself; such additions and alterations as are his work seem to come from the French versions of Lefèvre and Olivetan. Rogers' chief contribution was his host of marginal notes, which are doctrinal rather than textual.

GB is Coverdale's revision of MB, so far as the Old Testament is concerned, largely with the help of Münster's new Latin translation from the Hebrew which was completed just after Coverdale's first Bible. The second (1540) edition of GB shows further revision after Münster, particularly in the Prophets. Curiously enough, the third edition reverts in many parts to the text of the first. In GB Coverdale has disciplined his sense of style, and some of his experiments in phrasing and word order are brilliantly successful—particu-

---

[13] Cf. Westcott's arguments, *op. cit.*, pp. 170–79.

[14] "Maxime ante omnia tuam clementiam rogo atque obsecro ut ex animo agere velit apud dominum commissarium quatenus dignari velit mihi concedere bibliam hebreicam, grammaticam hebreicam et vocabularium hebreicum, ut eo studio tempus conteram" (Tyndale's Pentateuch, ed. Mombert, p. li).

larly in the Psalter, of which the GB version is used in the
Book of Common Prayer. The New Testament of GB is also
a revision by Coverdale, after the Vulgate and the Latin
translation of Erasmus.

Taverner's independent revision of MB is more important
for its New Testament than for its Old. Taverner was something of a Greek scholar, and his New Testament renderings, though they have no influence on the subsequent history of the English text, are of some interest. But he appears to have had no Hebrew knowledge whatever: the Old
Testament revision is very slight, and the changes are almost wholly stylistic. Taverner's stylistic habits are the
very opposite of Coverdale's: he tends to compress and sim-
plify where possible, with results that are sometimes quite
effective.

GenB is the most important of all the pre-A.V. renderings. It is, in the Old Testament, a thorough revision of the
GB text after the original Hebrew, and in the New Testament a revision of Tyndale after Beza. Whittingham, Gilby, Sampson, and the others whose names we do not know,
were better scholars than any who had yet come to the
work of translation; their Hebrew knowledge seems to have
been quite as competent as that shown by the combined
resources of the A.V. translators. They were in many respects fortunate in working at Geneva, the great center of
Protestant Bible scholarship. They were obviously in touch
with all the latest developments in Hebrew and biblical
studies on the Continent. There can be no doubt that, in
spite of their instructions, the A.V. translators respected
the GenB text (of the Old Testament, at least) considerably

more than that of BB. In innumerable instances A.V. rejects the BB text to adopt that of GenB.

The GenB translators seem to have been in fairly close association with the French scholars who were working at Geneva on a revision of the version of Olivetan. There must have been mutual consultation between those who brought out this French Geneva Bible in 1558 and the translators of the English Geneva Bible of 1560. Textual similarities between the two are thus more likely to derive from common methods and sources than from any dependence of GenB on the French. Though essentially a revision of GB, GenB has gone back, in the Old Testament, to the Hebrew text and made numerous and important changes. They seem to have made some use of Pagninus, but it is difficult to ascertain to what extent, for readings which appear at first sight to be adopted from Pagninus may have come independently from the Hebrew. There is much more revision in the text of the Prophets than in that of the historical portions of the Old Testament.

The Hebrew scholarship of the GenB translators is attested by more than one kind of evidence. The most important is the clear fact that in many instances they restored the literal meaning of the Hebrew text which had been obscured, through ignorance or through following secondary sources, in all the earlier English versions. Second, there is the translators' declared intention of translating "according to the Ebrue and Greke" and their association with some of the most competent European Hebraists of the time. Third, there is an interesting piece of evidence in their spelling and accentuation of biblical names, which indicates clearly the Hebrew pronunciation—Babél, Izhák,

Iaakób, Abimélech, etc. (It was probably against this practice as well as against the practice of using the Latin forms that the second rule of the A.V. translators was directed.) Further, there is strong evidence for concluding that the GenB translators were the first of the English translators to make considerable use at first hand of the Hebrew commentary of David Kimchi. A large number of the A.V. renderings which agree with Kimchi against most other interpretations follow GenB.

GenB is the first English Bible to break up the Old Testament text into verses, a perhaps unfortunate practice which has persisted until the "Bible designed to be read as literature" of our own day. The Puritan habit of text-quoting must have been to some extent responsible for this desire to have each verse numbered for ease of reference. The profuse marginal notes were another feature of the translation displeasing to most modern eyes as it was to contemporary Anglicans.

In spite of the evident desire for literalness in the GenB translation, the translators were by no means devoid of a developed sense of style, and many of the GenB renderings combine strict verbal accuracy with stylistic effectiveness: there are fewer instances than we might expect of A.V. adopting GenB's meaning with rephrasing, and an overwhelming number of instances of A.V. agreeing with GenB. Where A.V. does change the phrasing of GenB it is often because the latter prefers literalness to a paraphrase, while A.V. reserves the literal rendering for the margin. Thus although the GenB translators "in many places reserued the Ebrewe phrases, notwithstanding that thei may seeme somewhat hard in their eares that are not wel practised and also delite in the swete sounding phrase of the holy Scripture,"[15] the result does not seem to have been so harsh as they feared.

BB is a revision of GB whose sources are rather difficult to determine because of the erratic, not to say sloppy, manner in which the revision was done. GenB, Castalio, and Leo Juda all seem to have been used, but with little consistency. Münster was used in spurts, especially in the Prophets, and is the source of the majority of the improvements in accuracy at least in Isaiah. In some instances we find BB preserving a reading from GB which is obviously corrupt and which had been superseded by any one of many intermediate versions, and in others we find quite a minor improvement being incorporated from GenB or some other source. One's view of the nature of the translation is likely to change with every new verse examined. One thing, however, is clear: the readings they adopt are arbitrary and often ignorant, and the text as a whole is considerably inferior to that of GenB. The parceling-up of the work among different translators[16] with little or no common discipline may be largely responsible for the uneven character of the work, but this will not explain the unevenness within the chapters of one book, and even within a single chapter. Parker did, it is true, lay down some general rules for the translators: they were to follow GB except "where yt varieth manifestlye from the Hebrue or Greke originall"; they were to use Pagninus and Münster; they were not to include any controversial notes; "unedifying" passages

[15] From the translators' preface.

[16] For a discussion of the identity of the translators, chief of whom was Parker himself, see *Records*, pp. 30–32.

were to be marked so that the reader might be warned to skip them; and any rendering in GB which might give offence "of Lightnes or obscenitie" was to be altered.[17] But the GB text was not corrected from the Hebrew; Pagninus and Münster were not used consistently or exclusively; and GenB, which was the "opposition" text, was followed at least as much as any other secondary source. The New Testament of BB shows more consistency and original scholarship.

Several editions of BB followed the first of 1568, and these show progressive revision in the Old Testament, after GenB and Münster. Thus the 1602 edition (which served as a basis for A.V. and is the one used in the collation below) is slightly nearer the A.V. text than that of 1568.

The principles which guided the A.V. revision of BB we have already noted. The resources of the translators, their personnel, their attitude, and their equipment we have also briefly discussed. It now remains to discover just what they did with the tools which they had at their disposal; what the relation of the text is to the earlier English texts, to the original tongues, and to the sources which influenced their work. The results of such an inquiry, as the earlier pages of this chapter have been designed to show, cannot be absolutely certain. It is impossible to pronounce dogmatically on questions of sources and influence. But, if we confine ourselves to relations between texts, something at least can be achieved. To prove similarity is not necessarily to prove direct influence, and the nature of a textual relationship does not in itself prove anything except that this relation-

---

[17] *Observacions Respected of the Translators*, printed in *Records*, p. 297, from the original in the Record Office.

ship exists. With these limitations in mind, we now proceed to our final task, an examination of the results provided by a collation of the Book of Isaiah in the English versions up to and including A.V., the Hebrew, the Vulgate, LXX, Targum, the commentary of David Kimchi, and other texts. This will at least show the relation of the A.V. text to what all the external evidence goes to show as the most likely sources.

Isa. 1:2. בנים גדלתי ורוממתי is rendered by A.V. "I haue nourished and brought vp children," in agreement with C, GB, GenB, and BB. Thus רוממתי is given the sense of "brought up" rather than "exalted," as it is also in Münster ("filios educavi et evexi"). LXX and Vulg., however, suggest the latter interpretation (υἱοὺς ἐγέννησα καὶ ὕψωσα; "filios enutrivi et exaltivi") with which Kimchi agrees (גדלתי אותם ורוממתים מכל עם . . . .). A.V. agrees with the earlier English versions against the majority of other renderings.

5. על־מה. A.V. agrees with the other English versions in rendering "why." (GenB and C: "Wherefore"; GB: "whereby"; BB: "why.") This agrees with LXX, Kimchi, Münst., and Targ., but not with Vulg., which reads "super quo." Heb. and Targ., however, might mean "super quo": the phrase is ambiguous.

13. לא־אוכל און ועצרה. A.V. misreads the punctuation, following LXX and Vulg. Münst. makes the same error but compromises with an explanatory phrase. Kim. makes the meaning clear, as does Targ. (The clause is, "I cannot [endure] iniquity together with the solemn assembly.") GenB alone understands the punctuation of this passage,

following the explanations of Kim. and Targ. A.V., while not accepting GenB, also rejects the confused readings of GB, BB, and C; it seems an original attempt to understand the Heb.

18. לכר־נא ונוכחה. A.V. renders with GenB, Münst., and Kim. against the other English versions.

2:6. מקדם is rendered "from the East" in A.V., with "more than the East" in marg. A.V. marg. agrees with Münst. and Kim. A.V. text is a modification of BB and agrees with no other of the English versions. LXX (ὡς τὸ ἀπ' ἀρχῆς) is similar to Vulg. ("ut olim") and agrees with Targ.; but A.V. rejects this reading wholly.

9. In differentiating אדם from איש, A.V. alone of the English sixteenth-century European versions adopts the alternative explanation given by Kim., which agrees with Targ. Neither Vulg., LXX, nor Münst. makes the distinction clear.

18. In translating יחלף transitively, A.V., following GenB, agrees with Kim. and Münst. against LXX, Targ., and Vulg. A.V. marg. gives intransitive rendering. This is quite a crux, as יחלף should probably read יחלפו, plural and intransitive: A.V. had to find a way of making sense of the singular יחלף without emending the Heb. The choice was between making an intransitive form transitive or a singular form plural. The other English versions give יחלף a passive sense ("shall be rooted out") except BB, which is ambiguous.

3:3. ונשוא פנים. A.V. agrees with all the other English versions in translating "honourable man" (except that the other English versions omit "man") but is alone in the marginal reading, "A man eminent in countenance," which

is a literal translation from the Heb. Vulg. has "honorabi-
lem vultu," but none of the English versions render פָּנִים
separately as "vultu" (except, of course, Douai, which
translates Vulg. consistently: it reads "the honourable of
countenance"). A.V. agrees completely with Kim., who
explains the phrase מִי שֶׁהוּא נִכְבָּד מֵרוֹב עָשְׁרוֹ וּגְדֻלָּתוֹ.

5. A.V. is alone among the English versions in translating ירהבו הנער as "the child shall behaue himself proudly."
The other English versions have "shall presume." A.V.
agrees with Kim.'s explanation of ירהבו as meaning יחזק
עליו ויעזו בו פניהם.

6. GenB, translating הַמַּכְשֵׁלָה as "fall" where A.V.
has "ruin," is closer to the sense of Kim. (who explains
דברים שאין בני אדם עמדים עליהם אלא אם כן המכשלה as
[נגף <] מַגְפִיתָא = מַגְבִיתָא) and of Targ. (נכשלים בהם.
"stumbling block"?). A.V. agrees with Vulg. and the majority of other renderings but is probably less accurate as a
rendering of the Hebrew.

12. מְאַשְּׁרֶיךָ is translated "they which lead thee" in
A.V. text, and "they which call thee blessed" in A.V.
marg. The other English versions have either "thy
leaders" (BB, GB, C) or "they that lead thee" (GenB).
Both interpretations—"they who call thee blessed" and
"they who lead thee"—are given by Kim. Targ. has
מְשַׁבְּחָךְ, "those who praise thee."

19. A.V. alone of the English versions translates
הַנְּטִפוֹת as "the chaines," with "sweetballes" in marg.
These two alternative renderings correspond to Kim.'s second and first explanations, respectively.

In the list of ornaments and wearing apparel in verses
19–23, where the terms are difficult and unusual and the

Vulg. and LXX texts diverge considerably in places from each other and from the Heb., A.V. alone of the English versions adopts consistently renderings which follow the interpretations of Kim. The number of obsolete Elizabethan terms used in the A.V. rendering of this passage makes this somewhat difficult to discover, but reference to *NED* soon proves the point.

4:4. אם as "when" rather than "if" is found in A.V. and GenB, agreeing with LXX and Kim. BB reads "after that"; GB and C, "what time." Vulg. has "si."

5. ועל־מקראה is translated in A.V. "and vpon her assemblies"; GenB reads "vpon the assemblies." BB, GB, and C render "congregation" for "assemblies"—plural in BB, singular in GB and C. Vulg. renders "et ubi invocatus est," and LXX diverges considerably from the Heb. in this verse. A.V. agrees with Kim.'s explanation, and the reference to Exodus, chapter 13, in A.V. marg. is also in Kim.

חפה in the same verse is translated "a defence" in A.V. and GenB against BB, GB, and C, all of which read "preserued." Vulg. reads "protectio," while LXX renders the whole phrase differently with a verb—σκεπασθήσεται, "it will be sheltered"—instead of a noun. Kim.'s explanation is consistent with A.V. A.V. marg. gives the literal meaning of the Heb., "a couering."

5:1. A.V. agrees with GenB against the other English versions in rendering בקרן בן שמן, "in a very fruitful hill" (with literal translation from the Heb. in marg.). This agrees exactly with Kim., who cites Targ. (בְּטוּר רָם בְּאַרְעָ שְׁמֵנָא, "in a high hill in a rich land") in support of his interpretation. A.V., GenB, and Kim. are alone in this rendering.

2. In translating וַיְעַזְּקֵהוּ "and he fenced it," A.V.
agrees with GenB ("and he hedged it") in putting the object after the verb. The other English versions read "This
he hedged."

שֹׂרֵק is rendered by A.V. and BB "the choicest vine."
GenB renders "the best plants"; GB and C: "goodly
grapes." Both "choicest" and "best" agree with Kim.'s
explanation of שרק as הגפן שמוציא ענבים טובים שאין בהם
חרצן. Vulg. reads "electam," while LXX has merely ἄμπε-
λον Σωρηκ (or σωρηχ).

A.V. renders בְּאֻשִׁים "wilde grapes" with GenB and
BB. C and GB read "thorns" with LXX and Vulg. Kim.
explains בָּאֻשִׁים as "bad grapes" (ענבים רעים).

5. The introduction of the phrase "go to" in A.V. seems
to be a stylistic change of the A.V. translators: there is
nothing corresponding in any other rendering. It is probably meant to render the force of the Heb. particle נָא.

אוֹדִיעָה־נָא would mean literally "let me tell you, I pray."

A.V. and GenB agree against BB, GB, and C in rendering
והיה לבער as "and it shall be eaten vp." BB, GB, and C
read "that it may perish." LXX differs from Heb., reading
καὶ ἔσται εἰς διαρπαγήν (i.e., plundered), while Vulg. has "et
erit in direptionem." A.V. agrees with Kim.'s explanation
of (כלומר למאכל לבער).

6. A.V. renders לֹא יִזָּמֵר as "it shall not be pruned,"
agreeing with LXX and Vulg. against the other English
versions, which render "twisted" (GB, C) or "digged"
(BB) (all three rendering יֵעָדֵר by "cut," reversing the
Heb. order). GenB reads "it shal not be cut." Both A.V.
and GenB are consistent with Kim., who explains יִזָּמֵר as
= יכרת and adds. כריתת הזמורה להרבות בפירות

7. וָיְקַו is rendered by A.V. and the other English versions as in the Heb., "*he* looked for . . . ." Vulg. and LXX have "*I* looked . . . ."

מִשְׂפָּח is rendered "oppression" in A.V. and GenB. GB and C render "wrong"; BB renders "oppression" but makes nonsense of the phrase by completely misunderstanding the punctuation ("oppression for righteousnesse"!). A.V., as marg. indicates, understands מִשְׂפָּח as = סַפַּחַת, "a scab," not מִשְׂפָּח, "bloodshed." This is Kim.'s explanation. GB and C agree with Vulg. "iniquitas" and LXX ἀνομίαν.

8. A.V. rendering of וְהוּשַׁבְתֶּם לְבַדְּכֶם as "that they may be placed alone" agrees with GenB ("that ye may be placed by your selues") and with GB ("y⁺ ye maye dwel [vpon the earth] alone") in rejecting the interrogative of LXX and Vulg. (which is retained by C and BB). This is in accordance with what is demanded by the Heb.; but GenB's "that *ye* may be placed" is closer to Heb. than A.V. "*they*." (R.V. renders "and ye be made to dwell alone. . . . .")

9. The elliptic בְּאָזְנַי יְהוָה צְבָאוֹת is rendered by A.V. "In mine eares *said* the Lord of hostes" with the marginal alternative "this *is in mine eares* saith *the Lord*," agreeing with the sense of all the older versions and of Kim. Gen B has the same reading as A.V. marg., and the other English versions phrase variously, all different from A.V.

אִם־לֹא is rendered "of a truth" by A.V. (with the literal meaning "if not" in marg.) and BB. GenB renders "and surely"; C and GB omit. A.V. reading is against LXX (ἐὰν γάρ) and Vulg. ("nisi") and in agreement with Kim.'s explanation of the phrase as לְשׁוֹן שְׁבוּעָה.

11. יין ידליקם is rendered "till wine enflame them" by A.V. with the alternative "pursue them" in marg. GenB and BB also read as a temporal clause, against LXX, Vulg., and the other English versions. Kim. explains it as a temporal clause (עד שידליקם היין . . . .): his phrase is identical with that of A.V. and GenB.

13. וכבודו מתי רעב is rendered by A.V. "and their honourable men *are* famished" (with the literal "their glory are men of famine" in marg.). All the other English versions read "their glory." Kim. explains clearly "וכבודו"ופירוש ואנשי כבודו . . . . מתי כמו אנשי . . . ., which is precisely A.V.'s rendering. Vulg. renders "et nobiles ejus interierunt fame"; LXX has nothing corresponding. Targ. reads וְיַקִּירְהוֹן מִיתוּ בְּכַפְנָא, "and their nobles will die of famine."

13. צחה צמא is rendered by both A.V. and GenB "dried vp with thirst" against all the other English versions, which have "marred for thirst." This agrees with Kim., who explains צחה as = יובש. Other versions give a similar general sense with various phrasings.

15. In differentiating אדם from איש, A.V. again agrees with Kim. and differs from the other English versions. Cf. note on 2:9.

17. A.V. and GenB agree in translating כדברם "after their manner"; BB has "as they were wont"; GB, "in ordre"; C translates the phrase adjectivally, "their apoynted foder." LXX diverges widely here (ὡς ταῦροι); Vulg. has "iuxta ordinem suum," the rendering of GB. A.V. and GenB agree with Kim.'s brief explanation ופירוש כדברם כמנהגם. Targ. reads the whole phrase differently, ויתפרנסון צדיקיא כמא דאמיר עליהון ("and the righteous shall feed as was said of them").

17. וחרבות מחים is rendered "and the waste places of the fat ones" with GenB ("the desolate places of the fat") against the other English versions, Vulg., and LXX. This is precisely Kim.'s explanation, חרבות השמנים.

21. A.V. renders as GenB ("Woe *vnto them that are* wise in their owne eyes, and prudent in their owne sight") the phrase הוי חכמים בעיניהם ונגד פניהם נבנים; the other versions have the same general sense with a different phrasing.

24. A.V. renders לשון אש as "the fire" (giving the literal "the tongue of fire" in marg.). So BB, GB, and C. GenB, following Kim.'s explanation (הלהבות שהיא כצורת הלשון) literally, translates "the flame of fyre."

24. A.V. and GenB, alone of the English versions, translate חשש by "chaffe"; the others read "stubble." LXX and Vulg. both diverge from the Heb. here. LXX transposes the order. Kim.'s explanation is consistent with A.V. and GenB alone (חשש הוא הקש הדק). Similarly (vs. 24) A.V. and GenB agree with Kim. in rendering מק as "rottennes," a unique rendering among the English and other versions. LXX reads χνοῦς and Vulg. "favilla."

25. כסוחה is rendered "torne" by A.V., BB, and GenB, BB however retaining the phrase "did lye" from GB, which reads "dyd lye lyke myre." C reads "shal lye like myre." LXX and Vulg. agree in reading ὡς κοπρία and "quasi stercus," which is a possible rendering of the Heb., taking כ as prefix with סוחה = "mire." Kim., however, explains כסוחה as = כרותה, "torn," and is thus the probable source of A.V. and GenB.

30. A.V., BB, and GenB agree in the general sense of their rendering of והנה חשך צר ואור חשך בעריפיה against

the rather confused renderings of GB and C. A.V. phrasing
is partly that of GenB, partly that of BB.

6:1. A.V. renders וארא as "I saw also," with BB and
GenB. "Also" is superfluous (LXX has simply ἴδον and
Vulg. "vidi"); evidently meant as a rendering of the Heb.
prefix, וֹ, it shows a misunderstanding of the Heb. idiom.

9. In the phrasing of the second half of this verse, A.V.
adopts BB's rendering with some slight alterations. GenB
is close to BB in phrasing; the other English versions differ
from all three.

13. בשלכת is rendered by A.V. "when they cast *their
leaues*." So GenB. BB "in the fall of theyr leaues"; GB
and C, "brynge forth theyr fruites." A.V. is against LXX
and Vulg. and in exact agreement with Kim.'s explanation,
בהשליך עליהם.

7:2. In rendering נחה ארם על אפרים "Syria is confederate
with Ephraim," A.V. has the exact sense of GenB ("Aram
is ioyned with Ephraim") with diction from BB ("that
Syria and Ephraim was confederate together"). A.V. has
exactly the sense of Kim.'s explanation.

3. תעלת הברכה העליונה is rendered by A.V. and GenB
"the conduit of the vpper poole." The other English versions read "the ouer poole."

6. A.V. renders ונבקענה אלינו "and let vs make a breach
therein for vs" beside GenB "make a breche therein for vs."
LXX reads καὶ ἀποστρέψομεν αὐτούς; Vulg., "et avellamus
eum." A.V. and GenB agree with Kim.'s explanation.

9. אם לא תאמינו כי לא תאמנו is rendered by A.V. "if yee
will not beleeue, surely yee shall not be established," with
the marginal alternative, "*Doe yee not beleeue? it is because ye*

are not stable." GenB, with BB, is very close to A.V. text: "If ye beleeue not, surely ye shal not be established." This is the general sense of LXX and Vulg. and of Kim.

11. A.V. agrees with GenB against all the other English versions in rendering העמק שאלה "aske it either in the depth." So Kim. explains. Vulg., reading שאולה for שאלה, translates "in profundum inferni," which is the sense of BB, GB, and C.[18]

14. In translating עלמה as "virgin" against the meaning of the Heb. and (naturally) against Kim., A.V. follows the traditional Christian rendering, common to all Christian versions from the Vulgate on. (עלמה is now recognized by all Hebrew scholars not to mean "virgin" but simply "young woman"; see, e.g., *International Critical Commentary* on Isaiah, I, 122–36.)

A.V. agrees with the other English versions in translating וקראת שמו "and [she] shall call his name. . . . ." The marginal reading, "*Thou*, O Virgin, *shalt call*," is in no other version, but it fits in with the sense of Kim.'s explanation.

15. A.V. translates לדעתו as a purpose clause, with GB, C, Vulg., and most other versions (including Tyndale). Both GenB and BB translate—more accurately—as a temporal clause, GenB "til he haue knowledge," BB, "untill he know." (The literal meaning would be "toward the time when he knoweth"; R.V., "when he knoweth.") This is an infrequent but not unique case of BB adopting a correct original reading from GenB, while A.V. rejects it.

17. את מלך אשור is rendered "*euen* the King of Assyria"

---

[18] Tyndale, who translates Isa. 7:10–15 in his *Epistles*, has "Axe . . . . from alowe beneth," reading שאולה with Vulg.

by A.V. GenB has "euen the King of Asshúr." The other
English versions have "through" for "even." Vulg. has
"cum rege Assyriorum"; LXX simply τὸν βασιλέα τῶν
'Ασσυρίων. Kim. explains וּמִי יהיה חעושה הרעה הגדולה
הזאת שיביא ה' עליך—את מלך אשור, to which interpretation
the readings of A.V. and GenB conform exactly.

19. A.V. translates בנחלי הבתות as "in the desolate
valleys." So GenB and BB. C and GB omit "desolate."
LXX reads ἐν ταῖς φάρεγξι τῆς χώρας and Vulg. "in torren-
tibus vallium." Kim. explains פירוש הבתות חרבות.

20. A.V. again agrees with GenB in rendering בתער
השכירה "with a rasor that is hired." BB reads "with the
raser that he shall hyre"; GB and C, "with the rasoure that
he shal pay them withall." LXX readings vary here, some
agreeing with A.V., others reading שׂכורה (μεμισθώμενῳ).
Vulg. has "in novacula conducta." Kim.'s note agrees
with A.V.

22. Again A.V. agrees with GenB in rendering מרוב
עשות חלב as "for the abundance of milke *that* they shall
giue." (So Kim.: . . . . מרוב שיעשו חלב.) BB reads "that
they geue" beside A.V. "that they shall giue."[19] Neither
LXX nor Vulg. renders the sense of עשות.

8:4. GenB is alone among the English and other versions
in giving an active sense to ישא, as the strict literal sense
demands. A.V., the other English versions, LXX, and
Vulg. translate passively ("The riches . . . . shalbe taken
away"). Kim. explains the use of a verb with an indefinite
subject as equivalent to a passive.

---

[19] An interesting case where GenB appears to have adopted Kim.'s interpretation and BB is influenced by GenB without (apparently) knowing the source of
GenB; hence the change in tense: Kim. has יעשו, not עושׂום.

9. רעו עמים וחתו is translated by A.V. "Associate your selues, O ye people, and yee shalbe broken in pieces." GenB has a similar sense: "Gather together in heapes, o ye people, and ye shall be broken in pieces." The other English versions make no distinction between the two verbs, BB reading "Breake down, O ye peoples, and ye shall be broken down," and GB and C reading "Go together ye people, and gather you." This is a rare case of BB agreeing with Kim. against A.V. and GenB. (רעו ענין שבר . . . . אמר כנגד העמים שנאספים עם מלך אשור שברו ואחר קן תהיו נשברים.) רעו is a crux which puzzles all translators. LXX reads γνῶτε ἔθνη καὶ ἡττᾶσθε, i.e., reading דעו "take knowledge." A.V. translators seem to take רעו as from רעה (the root of רָע) and hence their rendering "associate yourselves"; but the form is doubtful. Vulg., too, reads "congregamini," which would explain C and GB.

11. A.V. renders בחזקת יד "with a strong hand"; GenB, "in taking of *mine* hand"; BB "in a mightie prophesie"; GB and C "and toke me by the hand." LXX and Vulg. take the phrase with the next clause. Both GenB and A.V. are consistent with Kim.'s explanation.

12. The phrase לא תאמרון קשר לכל אשר יאמר העם הזה קשר is another crux. A.V. renders "Say ye not, A confederacie to all them to whom this people shall say, a confederacie," which is close to GenB "Say ye not, a Confederacie, to all them, to whom this people saith a Conspiracie." BB renders "Ye shall not speake *words of* conspiracie, in all things when this people shall say, conspiracie." GB has "rounde with none of them, whosoeuer saye: younder people are bounde together," and so C. LXX and Vulg. punctuate differently from A.V., getting a different sense.

14. In translating למקדש as "the holy place," in keeping with the earlier English versions, LXX, and Vulg., A.V. preserves an antithesis which is nevertheless obscure in the construction of the sentence: "And he shalbe for a sanctuary; but for a stone of stumbling and for a rock of offence to both the houses of Israel." A.V., like GenB and unlike the other English versions, emphasizes the antithesis by putting "but" between the clauses where the earlier translations have "and." This emphasis of an uncertain antithesis was probably encouraged by Kim.'s explanation, which stresses the distinction: אמר כי הקדוש ברוך הוא יהיה לשני בתי ישראל לאחד למקדש והם הבוטחים בו ורוצים במלכות בית דוד ולאחד לאבן נגף. It is, however, very doubtful whether this antithesis really exists: למקדש is difficult; perhaps it is a corruption of למוקש.

20. A.V. follows the earlier English versions in rendering שחר as "light" (marg. "morning"). Vulg. has "matutina lux." LXX, reading שׁחַד for שָׁחֹר, renders the phrase δῶρα δοῦναι. Kim. agrees with all versions except LXX in explaining שחר as אורה. A.V. renders the whole phrase in the same general sense as BB, GenB, and Kim. against GB and C (who have the sentence badly mixed up) and Vulg. A.V. and GenB renderings are identical.

21. In translating ועבר בה נקשה ורעב as "And they shall pass through it, hardly bestead and hungry," A.V. is nearer BB ("And they shall wander through this lande hardly bestead and hungry") than any other of the English versions. GenB reads "Then he that is afflicted and famished, shal go to and fro in it"; GB and C, "if he do not thys, he stombleth and suffreth hunger." GenB is more consistent with the Heb., reading עבר rightly as a singular, while

A.V., probably in order to make the sense fit in with what
has gone before (whereas actually this sentence appears to
begin a separate fragment) reads a plural verb. Vulg. has
"et transibit per eam, corruet et esuriet," while LXX,
translating καὶ ἥξει ἐφ' ὑμᾶς σκληρὰ λιμός, reads an obviously
corrupt Heb. text—ועבר בכם קשה רעב. Kim. is of no help.

22. ואפלה מנדח is translated by A.V. "and they shall be
driven to darknesse," again the only one of the English
versions to translate the singular verb as a plural. Vulg.
and LXX diverge widely from the Heb. here, especially
LXX. Kim has the same general sense as A.V., but he does
not suggest a plural verb.

23. In rendering כי לא מועף לאשר מוצק לה, A.V. is
closer to BB than to GenB, which has a rendering of its
own from the Heb. Vulg. and LXX have nothing corresponding to the Heb. text here; BB follows Münst., while
GenB has its original rendering. Neither A.V. nor GenB
adopts Kim. here.

Verse 1 of chapter 9 in A.V. is the last verse of chapter 8
in Heb., as in GB. The other English versions adopt, as
A.V., the Vulg. division.

9:5. In rendering verse 5 as consisting of two antithetical
clauses, A.V. and GenB agree with Kim. against Vulg. and
the other English versions. (LXX differs widely here.)

6. In rendering למרבה המשרה ולשלום אין קץ "Of the
increase of his gouernment and peace *there shall be* no end,"
A.V. agrees with the sense of GenB, "The increase of *his*
gouernment and peace shall haue none end," against all the
other English versions, which render "He shall make no
end. . . . ." The construction of LXX agrees with A.V. and

GenB against Vulg. Kim. explains (לרוב המשרה ולשלום
אין קץ) as A.V. and GenB.

7. A.V. agrees with all other versions, including LXX
and Kim., in rendering ונפל בישראל as a past tense. The
"vav conversive" here, however, seems quite clear, and
in many other cases of such a construction GenB and A.V.
have changed what was a past tense in the other versions to
a future. Perhaps Kim.'s note, which also renders ונפל
as a past, though adding future implications, was the de-
cisive factor.

10. A.V. rendering of ואת איביו יסכסך "and joyne his
enemies together" (marg. "*Heb. mingle.*") agrees with BB
and GenB. C and GB have a diffuse and confused translation. The sense of יסכסך is more likely to be "mix up,"
"become confused," as Kim. explains in rendering יבלבלו,
and as LXX and Vulg. suggest. It seems likely that A.V.
or GenB misunderstood Kim.'s explanation.

15. A.V. and GenB agree in rendering מאשרי העם הזה
as "the leaders of this people" (A.V. has the marginal
alternative "*they that call them blessed*"). BB reads "the
guides of this people"; GB and C, "they which enfourme
the people that they be in a right case." LXX and Vulg.
agree, with οἱ μακαρίζοντες τὸν λαὸν τοῦτον and "qui beatifi-
cant populum istum." Kim. explains as "those who lead
. . . .," as in A.V. and GenB.

A.V. is rather confused regarding the tenses of the verbs
in verses 16–18. The tenses here are difficult, presenting a
problem which the Hebrew scholarship of the translators
was unable to solve.

17. A.V. agrees with GenB and Kim. in its rendering of

ויתאבכו גאות עשן against LXX, Vulg., and the other English versions. BB's rendering is a paraphrase of GenB.

18. Similarly, in rendering כמאכלת אש, A.V., GenB, and Kim. agree in sense (though GenB uses the literal "meat" where A.V. has "fuell"; A.V. marg. has "meat") against all the other English versions and LXX. Vulg. is as A.V.

19. Both A.V. and GenB render ויגזר "And he shall snatch," agreeing with Kim. (ופי' ויגזר ויחטוף כי החוטף גוזר הדבר ממקומו) against LXX, Vulg., and all the other English versions.

10:2. A.V. and GenB agree against LXX and Vulg. in translating להטות מדין דלים. BB has the same general sense as A.V.; GB and C are quite astray, though nearer to Vulg. text.

4. בלתי כרע תחת אסיר is one of the most difficult cruxes in Isaiah. Neither LXX nor Vulg. translates the Heb. text, which may be corrupt. A.V. and GenB agree against other English versions, LXX, and Vulg. in rendering after Kim.'s explanation "Without mee they shall bowe vnder the prisoners" (A.V.), "Without me *euerie one* shal fall among them yᵗ are bounde" (GenB). Once again A.V. translates a singular verb as a plural for the sake of the sense, and GenB prefers to keep the literal singular meaning, eking it out with an implied universal subject, "every one."

10. ופסיליהם מירושלים ומשמרון is rendered by A.V. "and whose grauen images did excell them of Ierusalem and of Samaria," agreeing with the sense, though not precisely with the phrasing, of GenB and with Kim.'s straightforward interpretation (פירוש שהיו חזקים מירושלים ומשמרון). BB, GB, and C agree in a confused reading. LXX and Vulg. are different again.

13. A.V. renders עתודתיהם as "their treasures," agreeing
with BB, GenB, and B against C ("their prynces"), Vulg.
("principes eorum"), and LXX (καὶ τὴν ἰσχὺν αὐτῶν). Kim.
explains ופי׳ עתודותיהם אוצרותיהם.

18. A.V. and GenB agree in rendering וכרמלו "and of
his fruitful field"; BB, GB, and C have "and [of his]
fieldes." Vulg. reads "et carmeli ejus." Kim.'s explanation fits in with A.V. and GenB.

כמסס נסס is a textual crux. LXX, Vulg., and Targ.
have each a different reading. A.V., GenB, and GB agree in
taking נסס from נס, "a banner." A.V. reads "and they
shall be as when a standard bearer fainteth," agreeing in
sense though not in exact phrasing with BB, GenB, and
GB. The quite different meaning of "flight" is contained
in different forms in Vulg., LXX, and C. Kim.'s interpretation agrees with that of A.V.: so Münst.

22. כליון חרוץ שוטף צדקה is another crux. A.V. agrees
with GenB in translating "the consumption decreed shall
ouerflow with righteousnesse"; BB renders "the decreed
consumption ouerfloweth with righteousnesse." GB and C,
"Perfecte is the iudgment of hym that floweth in ryghteous-
nesse." Kim. explains כליון as = גמור, but A.V. "consumption" suggests Vulg., which renders the phrase "con-
summatio abbreviata inundabit justitiam." LXX diverges.
כלה ונחרצה in verse 23 is rendered by the various versions
in accordance with their renderings of verse 22.

29. גבה מלון לנו, a difficult and probably corrupt phrase,
is translated by A.V. "they haue taken vp their lodging
at Geba"; GenB reads "they lodged in the lodging at
Gebá"; GB and C, "Geba shall be theyr restynge place."

If לָנוּ is really "for us," Vulg. alone has rendered it correctly; but it seems more likely that (if מָלוֹן לָנוּ is not a complete corruption) לָנוּ is from the verb לוּן, "to spend the night." So Kim. explains, and his rendering is that adopted by A.V. and GenB. GB and C seem to be trying to make sense of the passage by rendering לָנוּ as לָהֶם (or "nostra" as "eorum").

30. צַהֲלִי קוֹלֵךְ is rendered by A.V., BB, and GenB "lift vp thy voice." GB preserves the extraordinarily corrupt rendering of C, who translates the whole phrase, "The voyce of the noyse of thy horses (o doughter Gallim) shalbe heard vnto Lais"—one of many pieces of conclusive evidence of Coverdale's ignorance of Hebrew. Vulg. renders "Hinni voce tua." Kim. explains צַהֲלִי קוֹלֵךְ as הָרִימִי קוֹלֵךְ כַּשׁוֹפָר, which is the meaning of A.V., BB, and GenB.

A.V. renders הַקְשִׁיבִי לַיְשָׁה "cause it to bee heard vnto Laish"; GenB, "cause Laish to heare"; both renderings may be interpretations of Kim.'s note הָרִימִי קוֹלֵךְ כַּשׁוֹפָר כְּדִי שִׁישְׁמַע אַנְשֵׁי לִישׁ BB renders "giue eare to Laisa"; GB and C, "shalbe herde vnto Lays." LXX, ἐπακούσεται Λαισα (ἐν σα in some texts); Vulg., "attende Laisa."

31. הֵעִיזוּ is rendered "gather themselves to flee" by A.V.; GB renders "haue gathered them selues together." BB, GB, and C read "are manly." Vulg. and LXX diverge widely from Heb. Kim. explains as "gather."

11:3. וַהֲרִיחוֹ "and shal make him of quicke vnderstanding" (A.V.) agrees with the sense of GenB, BB, and Kim. against LXX, Vulg., and the other English versions.

6. A.V. translates וּמְרִיא as "and the fatling"; GenB "and the fat beast." None of the other versions has the sense of "fat" (LXX ταῦρος, Vulg., "ovis"). Kim. explains וּמְרִיא

thus: יש מפרשים שהוא ממיני הבקר הגדולים—probably the source of the idea behind "fat" in this context.

9. כמים לים מכסים. A.V. and GenB agree with Kim in the sense of their rendering of this phrase, against the other versions.

14. A.V.'s rendering of אדום ומואב משלוח ידם "they shall lay their hands vpon Edom and Moab" is not a literal translation of Heb. (such as GenB endeavors to give, without making very much sense), nor does it correspond to the rendering of the other versions, except LXX. But it agrees completely with Kim's explanation: שישלחו בהם ישראל ידיהם.

15. והחרים is rendered by A.V. "and . . . . shall vtterly destroy," with GenB against all the other versions, but in agreement with Kim. BB, GB, and C read "shall cleaue"; and Vulg. and LXX agree in yet another rendering (καὶ ἐρημώσει "et desolabit").

12:5. מודעת זאת is rendered by A.V. and GenB "this is knowen"; BB, GB, and C, "as it is known." Tyndale, who translates Isa. 12:1–6 among his *Epistles*, has "that is knowen." LXX and Vulg. render imperatively, ἀναγγεί-λατε ταῦτα "annunciate hoc"; so Targ. Kim. explains in a future sense: וזאת הגאות תהיה מודעת בכל הארץ.

13:3. A.V. translates למקדשי "my sanctified ones" beside GenB's "them, that I haue sanctified" and BB's "my sanctified." GB and C render "my debites." LXX has ἡγιασμένοι εἰσίν and Vulg., "sanctificatis meis." Targ. has למזמני ("those whom I have appointed for the purpose") and Kim. explains למקדשי as מדי ופרס.

4. מפקד צבא מלחמה is rendered by A.V. "mustereth the hoste of the battell" in agreement with the sense of

GenB's "nombreth the hoste of the battel" and Kim.'s explanation . . . . והוא היה מפקדם כלומר מונה אותם. Münst.
differs from Vulg. "praecepit militiae belli" and renders in
the general sense of Kim. and A.V., "numerat exercitum
pro proelio." BB adopts the sense of "mustering" or "numbering," rendering "mustereth his armie to battle." GB
and C render "was the captayne of the whole armye."

8. A.V. renders יאחזון "shall take hold of *them*"; GenB
has "shal take *them*," while BB, GB, and C read "shall
come upon them." LXX reads αὐτοὺς ἕξουσιν while Vulg.
lacks the pronoun (reading "tenebunt") which is supplied
by Münst., who reads "apprehendent (eos)." Kim. cites
Targ. יחדינינון ("will seize them") in support of his interpretation, which agrees with A.V. and GenB.

10. וכסיליהם is rendered by A.V. "and the constellations
thereof," while all the other English versions read "plan-
ets." Vulg. reads "et splendor earum" and LXX, καὶ ὁ Ὠρίων.
Kim. explains כסיל thus: כסיל הוא כוכב גדול נקרא בערבי
סוהל והכבבים המתחברים אליו נקראים על שמו כסילים.
which would account for A.V. Targ. has ונפיליהון (נפלא
= the constellation of Orion).

10. לא יגיה אורו is rendered by A.V. and GenB "shall
not cause her light to shine," against all the other English versions, which read "shall not shine with his [BB
'her'] light." Neither LXX, Vulg., nor Targ. has the
causative sense, but Kim.'s explanation would account for
A.V. and GenB. Münst. also adopts Kim.'s reading: "non
faciet fulgere lumen suum," but has not influenced BB.

18. וקשתות נערים תרטשנה is rendered by A.V. "*Their*
bowes also shall dash the yong men to pieces" beside GenB's
"With bowes also shal they destroie the children" and

"With bowes shall they destroy the yong men" of GB and
BB. C diverges widely, with "Then shall yonge men's
bowes be knapped asunder." A.V. alone agrees clearly with
Kim.'s unique explanation that the young men were shot
instead of arrows out of bows, to be dashed in pieces against
the rocks.

21–22. In its rendering of צִיִּים, אֹחִים, בְּנוֹת יַעֲנָה, שְׂעִירִים
and אִיִּים, A.V. follows Kim. wherever the other texts conflict, as does GenB except for צִיִּים and אֹחִים, where GenB
transliterates the Hebrew word. These terms are all obscure, and there is a great variety of renderings. LXX
and Vulg. disagree in every case. Münst. as a rule follows Kim. In the translation of אֹחִים, however, neither
A.V. nor Münst. follows Kim., and the reason seems to be
that in his interpretation of אֹחִים Kim. uses a לע"ז (vernacular word), פוּרוֹן, the Provençal "furon" a ferret; a
word which, as the translators of the sixteenth and seventeenth centuries took it to be Hebrew, must have puzzled
them completely. A.V. renders not "ferrets" but "doleful
creatures." This is an interesting piece of *negative* evidence
of A.V.'s use of Kim.

22. A.V. is alone in rendering בְּאַלְמְנוֹתָיו "in their desolate houses" (marg. "palaces"). The other English versions
all read "palaces." LXX has simply ἐκεῖ, and Vulg. reads
"in aedibus ejus." Kim. refers to Targ. בְּבִרְנְיָתְהוֹן as =
בְּאַרְמְנוֹתָיו and is therefore not A.V.'s source here. Münst.
renders "in magnificis aedibus ejus."

14:4. A.V. rendering of מַדְהֵבָה as "the golden city"
(marg. "exactnesse of gold") agrees against the other versions with Kim., who explains מַדְהֵבָה as זָהָב and adds
וְהוּא תֹאַר לְבָבֶל שֶׁהָיְתָה בְעֻלַּת זָהָב. LXX differs widely,

rendering ὁ ἐπισπουδαστής, and Vulg. renders "tributum," followed by C. BB and GB follow Münst.'s "aurum tribu-tum," rendering "the golden tribute." GenB: "and the golde thirstie."

9. In the translation of רפאים there is a clear-cut division between LXX, Vulg., and Targ. ("giants" or "mighty ones") and Kim., Münst., and A.V. ("the dead"). A.V. and GenB follow the latter group, and the other English versions the former. This division is frequent.

12. The rendering הילל בן שחר as "O Lucifer sonne of the morning" (A.V.), which is similar in all the English versions (BB, GB, C: "O Lucifer thou faire morning child"; GenB as A.V.) is regarded by many modern scholars as the source of the fall of Satan myth. Lucifer, however, is the name of the morning star, not of a person or devil. Both Kim. and Targ. explain as a comparison—כי היית כוכב נוגהא בין כוכביא (Kim.); בחייך כמו כוכב השמים (Targ.) Kim. adds: כוכב המגיה אורו הרבה ובה וכב . . . . השחר והוא נקרא הלל.

18. In rendering בביתו "in his owne house" agreeing with LXX, Vulg., and the other English versions), A.V. does not adopt Kim.'s rendering בקברו, which Münst. adopts in translating "in domo sui (sepulchri)" and which is also the rendering of Targ. (בבית עלמיה). Obviously a word like בית would be too simple to send the A.V. trans-lators to the commentators. They translated the Heb. lit-erally when they found it clear and sensible.

22. בין ונכד A.V. renders "son and nephew,"[20] agreeing with the sense of GenB and BB. GB and C render "and

---

[20] "Nephew," of course, meant "grandson" in Elizabethan English.

generacion," while LXX has σπέρμα and Vulg. "germen et nepotem." Kim. and Targ. agree with A.V. (נין הוא הבן ונכד בן הבן Kim; בר ובר בר Targ.) and Münst., who renders "filium et nepotem."

31. ואין בודד במועדיו is rendered by A.V. "and none shall be alone in his appointed times," agreeing in sense though not in exact phrasing with BB and GenB, against GB and C, which are closer to Vulg. The rendering of A.V., GenB, and BB corresponds to Kim.'s explanation.

15:1. In rendering נדמה "and brought to silence," A.V. agrees with GenB and with the more obvious meaning of Heb. A.V. is alone among the English and other versions in its marginal alternative "cut off," which corresponds exactly to Kim.'s explanation ופירוש נדמה נכרת. Targ. has ואינון דמיכין ("and they shall lie asleep," i.e., die), which is compatible with either of the two interpretations.

3. ירד בבכי is translated by A.V. "weeping abundantly," though A.V. marg. gives the literal meaning of the Heb., which is also the rendering of GenB. The sense of "abundantly" is not in any other of the versions; but it is in Kim.'s explanation וזה דרך הפלגה מרוב הבכי . . . . . (Where Kim.'s explanation is plausible but does not follow the literal Hebrew, A.V. sometimes, as here, accepts it while keeping the literal translation in the marg., or, especially when the literal meaning makes equally good sense, relegates Kim.'s rendering to the marg. while retaining the more literal translation in the text.)

5. In rendering בריחה עד צוער עגלת שלשיה, A.V. again agrees with GenB and Kim. against LXX, Vulg., and the other English versions.

16:4. A.V. and GenB alone of the English versions render "extortioner" against LXX and Vulg. and in agreement with Kim.'s explanation.

6. לא כן בדיו is rendered by A.V. "his lies shall not be so" with GenB. BB and GB render "and vayne are his lies"; C renders בדיו as "strength," with Vulg. LXX reads οὐχ οὕτως ἡ μαντεία. Kim. explains לא אמת כזביו, which appears to be the source of the translation "lies." Münst. retains the Vulg. reading. This therefore is one of the cases where A.V. = Kim. against Münst. but in agreement with GenB.

9. A.V. renders כי על קיצך ועל קצירך הידד נפל "for the shouting for thy Summer fruites, and for thy haruest, is fallen" (marg. "the alarme is fallen vpon" etc.). The Heb. phrase is difficult and ambiguous. GenB agrees with A.V. marg.; GB and BB agree with Münst. and Kim. in reading "for the cry of thine enemies is fallen vpon thy sommer fruites." Kim. explains clearly בזמן הקציר באו להם האויבים: והידד הוא לשון קריאה שצועקים השוללים כשיבאו על עיר פתאום. This is a case of Kim. = Münst. = GB = BB against A.V., though the A.V. rendering does not exclude Kim.'s interpretation.

Enough of the collation has perhaps been presented to make the reader aware of the general nature of the situation. A collation of the rest of Isaiah, of the kind shown in Appendix II, reinforces the conclusions which emerge from the above pages and suggests no further points of importance. A.V. is more dependent on GenB than on BB, though BB is behind a great deal of the A.V. text; BB itself adopts and rejects improvements introduced by GenB in about equal proportions. A.V. and GenB make equal use of the Hebrew text, and both make considerable use of Kimchi. In most cases where A.V. follows Kimchi, there is evidence for concluding that the influence comes through GenB. But there are cases where A.V. follows Kimchi against GenB, as well as some where GenB agrees with Kimchi against A.V. There are also a few cases where A.V. and BB follow Kimchi against GenB, but in each of these cases investigation shows Kimchi's rendering to have been adopted by Münster, whom both BB and GB certainly used. This would also explain the rare cases of A.V. and GB agreeing with Kimchi against GenB and BB. There are a very few cases of BB and GB agreeing with Kimchi against A.V. and GenB. In no case does A.V. prefer either LXX or Vulg. to the Hebrew text; and even where the Hebrew text is doubtful, A.V. will go with GenB to Kimchi for an interpretation before going to LXX or Vulg. Where the Hebrew text is obscure and Kimchi gives no help, GenB will hazard a literal interpretation even though the sense remain vague; A.V. might in such a case accept help from LXX or Vulg., and the former before the latter, except where the former's text diverges widely from the Hebrew. A.V. will not adopt a Targ. rendering where it differs from the other sources.

Thus A.V. is a critical revision of GenB and BB with reference to the original Hebrew text and with the help of Kimchi's commentary. There is a great majority of cases where A.V. and GenB agree with Kimchi against LXX, Vulg., and Targ. A.V. diverges from GenB generally for reasons of style and idiom; much more rarely for reasons of accuracy. Whatever other sixteenth-century sources A.V. may have used, the nature of its relation to the other English versions, to LXX, to Vulg., and to Kim. is clear. It is not always clear at what stage Kim.'s influence made itself felt, for it came in in three ways at least—through Münster, through GenB, and directly.

As a translation of the massoretic text of the O.T. as available to the translators in the rabbinical Bibles and the polyglots, A.V. is, on the whole, as accurate a rendering as the combined Christian scholarship of Europe would at that time have been able to produce. Further, it is a translation which, largely on account of its use of Kimchi, and more fundamentally because of the Jewish sources of so much Hebrew scholarship in Europe from Reuchlin to the beginning of the seventeenth century, preserves a surprising number of traditional Jewish renderings. Indeed, any translation of the Hebrew text was bound to be in some degree dependent on Jewish sources, because it was the Jews who determined the massoretic text and who constituted themselves its guardians. No pre-massoretic texts were allowed to survive, and the differences within the massoretic texts themselves were negligible compared to the variant readings which the translators would have had to cope with if all the existing Hebrew texts had not descended from the same comparatively late recension.

A translation of the O.T. which regards the Hebrew text as the original and all other translations as secondary sources whose variations from the Hebrew are suspect is based on a view which is essentially sound. But where all the available Hebrew texts belong to the same recension, and some of the other translations were made from the Hebrew text prior to that recension, there is obviously a chance that on occasions the secondary sources might be more accurate than the primary source. For example, the

text of LXX was made from the Hebrew text over a thousand years before the date of the earliest existing copy of the
Hebrew text, and the earliest manuscripts of LXX are many
hundreds of years earlier than the earliest existing Hebrew
manuscripts. Thus, though the original Hebrew antedates
by a vast period of time the Greek version made from it, the
LXX text as we have it is a translation of a Hebrew text
very much earlier than that represented by any existing
Hebrew manuscript. Further, the Hebrew text behind LXX
is not only earlier than that of any existing Hebrew manuscript; it is also two or three hundred years earlier than the
fixing of the massoretic text by Jewish scholars some time
in the first two centuries of the Christian Era. The same is
true, though to a less degree, of the Vulgate, which em-
bodies part of the Old Latin translation which in turn was
made from the Greek; so the Vulgate, too, may on occasion
transmit pre-massoretic readings which might represent the
original Hebrew text.

The A.V. translators were quite unaware of this point,
and even the Douai translators and those who maintained
the superiority of the Vulgate over the Hebrew text did not
appreciate the facts which gave a slight element of ration-
ality to their argument. But it is an aspect of which the
modern textual critic has become increasingly aware, and
any comprehensive scholarly attempt to translate the Old
Testament once again would be bound to endeavor to get
behind the massoretic text, where possible, through an examination of other renderings made from the pre-massoretic
Hebrew. This is especially true in the case of cruxes where
the Hebrew text makes little or no sense, and both LXX
and Vulg. differ widely. GenB tried in such cases to inter-

pret the Hebrew as literally as possible without making complete nonsense; A.V. tended to be less literal and to smooth the phrase out, but always with the literal rendering in the margin; both acted on the assumption that the Hebrew text as they knew it was correct and that any variation in LXX or Vulg. represented a corruption: whereas in particular cases the very opposite may have been true. Yet as between the Douai position and the A.V. position, there is no doubt that the A.V. translators chose rightly. Their instinct in rendering from the original was sound, though they had none of the modern apparatus for reconstructing the original with the help of secondary versions. A.V. translates the massoretic text as it is rather than the original Hebrew as it might have been.

Thus we find that on occasions the eclecticism of GB, which made equal use of the Hebrew, Greek, and Latin traditions, preserves a reading more likely to be that of the original Hebrew text than that of the massoretic text and A.V. GB's practice of putting in smaller type words that were in the Greek and Latin but not in the Hebrew often brought its text nearer to the probable sense of the original.[21] It was not, however, a very conscious or critical procedure in the sense that it would be if adopted by modern scholars.

There is a great deal more to be said about the text of A.V. A collation of the kind included in this chapter and in Appendix II might be carried through other books of the Old Testament, with interesting results. A careful examina-

[21] See G. B. Gray, "English Versions and the Text of the Old Testament," in *Mansfield College Essays* (London, 1909), pp. 109 ff. Gray cites many interesting examples.

tion might be made of the relation of the rhythm of the English to that of the Hebrew—or what was conceived to be the rhythm of the Hebrew by the A.V. translators—and some conclusion reached concerning the degree to which the style of A.V. is based on a deliberate imitation of the rhythm of the original. A comparison of the work of the different groups of translators with a view to finding any differences in sources or method might also be profitable. The present writer is aware that the foregoing pages are but a preliminary to a more extended study, and this work is presented as prolegomena merely.

APPENDIX I

SPECIMEN OF TYNDALE'S TRANSLATION OF PARTS OF ISAIAH IN HIS *EPISTLES TAKEN OUT OF THE OLD TESTAMENT* WITH AN INDICATION OF THE AMOUNT OF TYNDALE'S LANGUAGE RETAINED IN A.V.[1]

51:1–8

Herken vnto *me ye that folowe ryghteousnes* and *seke the lorde. Look* vnto *the rocke ye were* cut oute / *and to the* caue and pit *ye* were *digged* oute. *Look* vnto *Abraham youre father and* vnto *Sara that bare you:* how *I called him* onlye / *and blessed him and* multiplied him. *For the lorde* hath compassion on *Sion* and hath compassion on all that is decayed therein / *and will make hir wilderness* as paradise *and hir deserte* as *the garden of the lorde. Ioye and gladnes shalbe founde therein /* with *thankesgeuynge and the voyce of* prayse. *Herken* vnto *me my people /* & turne youre eares to me my folke. Ther shall a lawe go oute *from me /* and my *iudgement* will I stablishe to be a *light* vnto nacions. *My ryghteousnes is nye /* and *my salvacyon* shall go oute / *and myne armes shall iudge* nacions / and ylondes shall loke for *me* & shall tarye after *myne arme. Lyfte vp youre eyes to* heauen *and* beholde *the erth beneth.* For heauen *shall vanyshe awaye* as *smoke / and the erthe shall* weare awaye as a vesture / *and* the inhabiters therof shall peryshe awaye after the same *maner / but my salvacion shall* endure *euer / &* my *ryghteousnes shall not* perishe. *Herken* vnto *me ye that knowe righteousnes* and so let the people that haue *my lawe* in their hertes. *Feare not the* rebukes *of man nether* faynte for *their* blasphemyes. *For* wormes *shall eate them* as *a garment / and* mothes *shall* deuoure *them* as it were *woll. But my ryghteousnes shall* contynew *euer / and my saluacyon from generacion to generacion.*

[1] Words italicized remain in A.V.

11:1–5

There shall come a rodde oute of the stocke *of Jesse / and a braunche shall* sprynge *oute of his* rote. *And on him shall* lyght *the spirite of the lorde: the spirite of wysdome and* of *vnderstondynge / the spirite of councell and* of strength *the spirite of knowledge and* of reuerence / *and it shall make him* sauer *of the feare of the lorde. And he shall not iudge after the syght of his eyes: nether* shall rebuke *after the hearynge of his eares. But he shall iudge the* causes *of the poore with ryghteousnes / & shall* rebuke *with equitie for the* vmble *of the erthe. And he shall smyte the erth with the rodde of his mouth / & with the breth of his lyppes shall sleye the wycked. And ryghteousnes shalbe the gyrdle of his loynes / and faythfullness the gyrdle of his raynes.*

APPENDIX II

A SPECIMEN OF THE COLLATION ON WHICH THE CONCLUSIONS DISCUSSED IN CHAPTER IV ARE BASED

ISA. 40:1

Heb.	נחמו נחמו עמי
LXX	παρακαλεῖτε παρακαλεῖτε τὸν λαόν μου
Targ.	נבייא אתנביאו תנחומין על עמי אמר אלהכון
Vulg.	Consolamini consolamini popule meus
Münst.	Consolamini (o Prophetae) consolamini populum meum
Kim.	כל אלה הנחמות עתידה לימות המשיח והכפל לחזק
A.V.	Comfort ye, comfort ye my people
GenB	Comfort ye, comfort ye my people
BB	Comfort my people (o ye prophetes)
GB	Be of good chere my people
C	Be of good chere my people

ISA. 40:2

Heb.	דברו על לב ירושלים
LXX	λαλήσατε εἰς τὴν καρδίαν Ιερουσαλημ
Targ.	מלילו על לבא דירושלים
Vulg.	Loquimini ad cor Hierusalem
Münst.	as Vulg.
Kim.	No relevant note
A.V.	Speake ye comfortably to Ierusalem (marg. *to the heart*)

GenB   Speake comfortably to Ierusalém
BB   Comfort Hierusalem
GB   Conforte Ierusalem
C   Conforte Ierusalem

ISA. 40:6

Heb.   קול אמר קרא
LXX   φωνὴ λέγοντος Βοήσον
Targ.   קל דאמר
Vulg.   Vox dicentis. Clama.
Münst. Vox dicebat, clama.
Kim.   קול אומר קרא כאלו קול קורא .או פירושו קול נבואה
        קורא לנביא קרא.
A.V.   The voyce sayd: Cry
GenB   A voyce said, Crye
BB   The same voyce spake, Nowe crye
GB   The same voyce spake: Now crye
C   The same voyce spake: Now crie.

ISA. 40:9

Heb.   מבשרת ציון
LXX   ὁ εὐαγγελιζόμενος Σιων
Targ.   נביא די מבשרין לציון
Vulg.   tu qui euangelizas Sion
Münst. tu Zion annunciatrix
Kim.   ופרוש מבשרת ציון את ציון
        המבשרת, וכן מבשרת ירושלים.
A.V.   O Zion, that bringest good tydings (marg. O thou that
        tellest good tidings to Zion)

GenB	O Zión, thou that bryngest good tidings
BB	O Sion thou that bryngest good tydynges
GB	(O Sion) thou that bryngest good tydynges
C	(o Sion) thou that bringest good tidings

ISA. 40:17

Heb.	מאפס
LXX	εἰς οὐθὲν
Targ.	גמירא
Vulg.	quasi nihilum
Münst.	minus quam nihilum
Kim.	מאפס, פחות מאפס
A.V.	lesse than nothing
GenB	lesse than nothing
BB	lesse than nothing
GB	yee vayne vanite
C	yee vayne vanite

ISA. 40:21

Heb.	הלוא הבינותם מוסדות הארץ.
LXX	οὐκ ἔγνωτε τὰ θεμέλια τῆς γῆς;
Targ.	הלא תסתכלון למדכל קדם מן דברא יסודי ארעא
Vulg.	Numquid non intellexistis fundamenta terrae?
Münst.	An non intelligentiam didicistis ex fundamentis terrae?
Kim.	כלו' אם יש לכם דעת להבין תוכלו להבין ממוסדות הארץ.
A.V.	haue ye not vnderstood from the foundations of the earth?
GenB	haue ye not vnderstand it by the fundacion of the earth?

BB   haue ye not ben enfourmed of this by the foundation of
      the earth?

GB   Haue ye not bene enfourmed of thys, sence the foun-
      dacyon of the earth was layde.

C   Haue ye not bene enfourmed of this, sence the foun-
      dacion of the earth was layde:

ISA. 40:31

Heb   יחליפו

LXX   ἀλλάξουσιν

Targ.   ויוספון חיל

Vulg.   mutabunt

Münst.   mutabant

Kim.   יחליפו כמו העץ אם יכרת ועוד יחליף והוא ענין
         התחדשות הדבר בתמורת הדבר שחלף ועבר.

A.V.   shall renew (marg. *Heb. change*)

GenB   shal renue

BB   shall be increased

GB   shal be encreased

C   shal be encreased

INDEX

Abélard, Peter, 81, 99

Ælohim-triune, Displayed by His Workes, 157

Aggeus and Abdias Prophetes . . . . , 151–52

Aggeus the Prophete Declared . . . . , 151–52

Agobard, archbishop of Lyons, 93

Agricola, Rudolf, 85, 128

Alcuin, 93

Aldhelm, bishop of Sherborne, 79

Aleander, Jerome, 84

Aleman, Herman el; *see* Herman el Aleman

Aleman, Jochanan, 127

Allen, Cardinal William, 58–61

Ambrose, St., 154

Amolo, archbishop of Lyons, 95

Anatoli, Jacob (Jacob ben Abba Mari ben Simson), 99

"Andraeas quidam," 113

Andrewes, Lancelot, dean of Westminster, 66, 162, 163

scholarship of, 160

Andrewes, Roger, 163

Annotationes in quinque ex minoribus prophetis . . . . , 153

Antwerp Polyglot, 138, 147–48, 165

Aquinas, St. Thomas, 114, 154

Argyropoulos, John, 84, 85

Arnold of Villanova, 102

Arragel, Moses, 126

Athanasius, St., 154

Augenspiegel, 136

Augustine, St., 61, 91

Nicholas Gibbens' references to, 154

Reuchlin's attitude toward, 133

Authorized Version of the Bible, 11, 26, 30, 50, 51, 53, 62, 65–74, 78, 91, 92, 140, 149, 151, 155, 157, 165, 211

compared with text of Geneva Bible, 174

conclusions concerning sources and nature of the translation, 207–10

Hugh Broughton's attack on, 154

methods of the translators, 167–73, 209–10

relation to Bishops' Bible, 182

relation to Geneva Bible, 178–79, 180

relation of renderings in Isaiah to other texts and possible sources, 183–206

relation to Tyndale's Bible, 149

scholarship of the translators, 152, 153, 159, 160–66

sources of, 171–73, 209–10

state of Hebrew scholarship in England at time of inception, 148–66

stylistic influence of Coverdale on, 176

translators of, 160–65

translators' use of Kimchi, 153, 158

Bacon, Roger, 81, 102, 103, 106, 119, knowledge of Hebrew of, 108–13

Badius, Conrad, 49

Baldric, bishop of Utrecht, 80

Bancroft, Richard, bishop of London (1597) and archbishop of Canterbury (1604), 64, 65, 66, 67, 167

Barker, Robert, 69

Barlaamo, di Seminara, bishop of Gerace, 82

Barlow, William, dean of Chester, 64

Barthlet, Thomas, 30

Basil, St., 154

219